THE OCCULT FAMILY PHYSICIAN

BOTANIC GUIDE TO HEALTH

First Edition 1894
Antonette Matteson

New Edition 2020
Edited by Tarl Warwick

COPYRIGHT AND DISCLAIMER

FOREWORD

The method of medicine professed in this fine physic may seem primitive to the modern reader but compared to works from a century prior will appear not only tolerably adequate for basic illness but almost enlightened when compared to prior ages. The botanic period begins where the mercury injections and trepanning of the former period ends; a period of dark age style medicine which lasted well past the enlightenment and continued for some decades thereafter in surgical circles.

Matteson expands on the basic concept of botanic medicine here; in earlier works, the recipes involved lobelia and often not much else- and while that species is here considered a sort of sub-cure all, the *Materia Medica* contained in this text is actually fairly elaborate. While it does not, strictly, compare with thousand-page lists of herbal remedies, this book pairs two main sections (the herbal recipes, and the list of species of use and their categories) with other arcane material of a more strictly spiritual bent. For example, Matteson spends ten pages towards the end of this work expounding upon the concept of mediums and spiritism; a topic very much hotly debated in the late 1800s, which would not technically subside for a few decades after this work was completed.

I have done my best in editing this present work, to modernize some of the terms used. However some are, while archaic technically speaking, nonetheless known by enough of those interested in these topics, for me to retain them for continuity; for example, to be "costive" is to be constipated, and a "windy" stomach is a gassy one.

Matteson should perhaps here be praised most for the dietary content; the statements she makes are largely accepted even today with regards to food intake, although it ought to perhaps be noted that we now know that merely combining red meat with vegetables does not alter the "putrefaction" of the stomach. If we have one criticism to offer it might involve the short segment on "onanism" (masturbation) which is almost humorous since it claims that "self pollution" causes insanity and various other issues, even when it involves a female self stimulating; it might be worth noting that most contemporary works pretend as though females, unless plagued by lunacy or given over to "criminal proclivities" never committed such "sins."

It is worth noting that I have removed the (useless) testimonials from this edition since they are not related at all to the rest of the subject material.

This edition of "Occult Family Physician" has been carefully edited for format and content. Care has been taken to retain all original intent and meaning.

THE OCCULT FAMILY PHYSICIAN

DEDICATION

To the hands that produce our wealth, to the hearts that defend our homes, to the intelligence of you

THE WORKING CLASSES

The muscle and manhood of America, I dedicate this edition of our "Guide to Health." Your health is your patrimonial estate, which, like any other patrimony, may be recklessly squandered or carefully cultivated, in the one case it will yield you vigor of spirit, energy of will, capacity for enjoyment, and all that pride of independence which conscious strength can alone bestow; in the other, its produce will be feebleness of body, lassitude of mind, incapacity for work, dependence, humiliation and destitution. The object of this Guide, is to show you somewhat of the intrinsic value of your patrimonial estate, that you may the better know how to manage it, preserve it whole, and hand it down clear of all mortgage, to its next inheritors.

Your humble servant,
The Author.
MRS. A. MATTESON.

THE OCCULT FAMILY PHYSICIAN

PREFACE

We live in an age of utility, and stern reality, when things are valued according to their merit, and although great names have much to do with book making, as well as book selling, nevertheless, without the merit of utility, the greatest books and the greatest names have but an ephemeral existence We claim no credit for great learning, all that we shall seek to do, is to assist in awakening man and woman to a sense of the duties and obligations of life; we will endeavor to convince them that a knowledge of disease and its remedies is not incompatible with plain common sense, we aim to teach the means by which it is to be done. We have only to say we mean it to do good, and have a settled faith, founded upon twenty years practical experience, that it will do so.

To time, the great umpire and judge between men and systems, we submit our views, content to abide its decision, be it either for or against, and thus say, if our labors shall be found of no advantage, let them pass to be remembered only as an effort to do what there was no capacity to accomplish, and even then we shall be at peace, conscious that our failure
was a misfortune, not a fault.

THE AUTHOR.

THE OCCULT FAMILY PHYSICIAN

SALUTATORY

A CORRECT THEORY AND A SOUND PHILOSOPHY COMBINED, FORM THE BASE OF EVERY SCIENCE

In presenting this Work to the Public, the Author does so with the greatest confidence, feeling assured that her readers will appreciate her endeavors to alleviate the sum of human misery.

Nothing in this "Guide" is recommended on theory, but from the practical experience of intelligences from the spheres beyond. The use of poisons are avoided, and the sheet anchor of the Medical Profession "Mercury" is altogether repudiated. The means recommended are sanitary, assisting nature to overcome disease by administering those remedies which act in harmony with the eternal laws of nature: remedies from the vegetable world. We are told that all schools of Medicine, are apt to be one sided; we, from the other side of life, are more apt to be otherwise, for we reject only those agencies, that are not in harmony with the animal economy, ignoring nothing in nature's wonderful *Materia Medica*; not so with the old school of Medicine, who have formed a compact to put down all other schools and methods of practice. Why? because we differ from them, in that we include in nature's methods, the grander forces of the Spirit, Magnetic, Clairvoyance, Psychoma or Hypnotism, Electricity, Water cure, and also the power of sunlight, etc., which are beyond question, in advance of the old stereotyped process.

They are alone, rating all others as quacks, whose vibrations rebound upon themselves. As the experience for the last three hundred years, clearly shows that the mineral practice has left in its tracks, records horrible to contemplate, and yet this same class, under the hypocritical pretense, that the peoples lives should be protected from quacks, apply to our legislature for laws to protect the poor people. We know that the small and crippled minds are ever trying to force the people to run in their own paltry ruts. How many lives they destroyed by forbidding the use of cold water or pure air during fevers, heaven only knows. For hundreds of years they have jeered, reviled and persecuted the noblest souls; such men as Harvey, Jenner, Preissnitz, Mesmer, Thompson and many others, and years after they adopted their methods; but still continue the use of several hundred poisons; still continue their barbarous treatment of Moxas and hot irons.

The old system does not understand Chemical affinity, is ignorant and nervous; mental and muscular processes cannot explain respiration, pulsation and the wonderful polarities of system, and has not yet learned the basic principles of health or disease. During our experience for the last twenty years, we are positive that ninety nine hundredths of all the quackery has been under the shelter of diplomas. I can positively state that during that time I have never lost a case, except where the vitality of the patient had been exhausted prior to my having diagnosed the case. In saying these things, I do not ignore the fact that the old school has men of great learning, and skill, to whom the world is indebted, and from whom all systems have learned regarding the coarser departments of force. But a grander system, more sure and reliable, and more searching, is raising upon the world, it ascends into the heavens and scours the earth for power not only to heal, but to ennoble mankind.

INTRODUCTION

"Loss of Health is in every instance an infringement
of one or more of Nature's laws,"

Before entering immediately upon the subject
before us, we herewith append a brief sketch of our life as a
trance and healing medium. Having been born in Baden,
Germany, in the year 1847, I removed with my parents at
the age of five years to America and settled in Erie County
New York, where I have since resided, when at an early age
I found myself subordinate to the control of certain occult
influences, or that subtle and unseen force through which
intelligence communicates with mortals, after a length of
time I became convinced of the existence of intelligent
spirit, personality, without a material organism, the same
intelligent force proved to me the material body is
subordinate to its behests and uses, disclosing in trance and
on the purely intellectual plane, both its presence and
independence, it touches the visual organs, and
Clairvoyance, or Spirit Vision beholds and proclaims what
the material eye does not and cannot see: A force enters or
seems to possess, a portion of the gray matter and cells of
the Brain, and will dictate messages, diagnose cases,
irrespective of distance, and prescribe the necessary
remedies for the cure (if curable) of such cases.

During the twenty years of my mediumistic
experience, many hundreds, in fact I may say thousands of
remarkable cures have been made through the aid of my
spirit guides, or, as some of our scientific brethren term it,
psychic or soul force, or intelligence: name it what you will,
the fact remains the same. But skeptical science, although at
work upon the trance condition, with its varied and
multiplied manifestations, has not yet risen to this spiritual
altitude, ever ready to denounce and persecute those whom
they cannot and will not understand. For where my patients,

have been given to understand by the attending Physician, that their cases were incurable, and that they must die, have been restored to health, in many cases were to all outward appearances, hopeless; but by the aid of that unseen intelligence have been apparently snatched from the grave. Often have these so-called scientific or professional men formed combinations to break down my work, and as often have they failed, the more intelligent, honorable, high minded and honest in scientific ranks, frankly confess its source to be supernal, though the numbers are yet few.

Inasmuch then, as the various stages of development is an acknowledged science by such men as, Crooks, Flammarion, Gollner, Weber, Boutterof, Buchanan, Mapes and scores of others, it is not creditable for the small minds to condemn or ignore it, or pronounce judgment without a thorough investigation. It is not our purpose to write a work on Spiritual Philosophy, but we will explain to the best of our ability, for the benefit of those who do not understand the spiritual philosophy, what a spirit is. Ages ago it has been shown that within this gross physical body of ours there is a spiritual body, St. Paul even affirmed. That spirit is ethereal matter, capable under certain degrees of development, of that psychic or soul force, which, in those mediums who are more thoroughly developed, readily unite and vibrate with that of spirits. It is rare that spirits find a medium with just the quality of psychic force that will vibrate in harmony with their own, and where there is a want of that perfect harmony, there you will find error, and mistakes naturally follow, and the medium often denounced as a fraud by ignorant and hasty people. In most cases where Mediums are thoroughly developed a familiar spirit gives the messages as the earthly telegrapher does for the one who desires to send it, but even when the familiar may have good control, when the vitality of the Medium has been exhausted beyond a natural limit, the thought vibrations as expressed by the spirit, come very indistinct, and ofttimes not the fault of the control, but the medium.

Death in no way changes the mental characteristics of the Ego or Spirit. Is it at all strange that mistakes are made, when we consider what nice conditions are requisite for them to communicate at all? Mental or spiritual telegraphy is far more subtle and far more difficult than our most perfect methods of communicating, and as it is very hard to find another who can give our thoughts or diagnose cases correctly, we need not wonder that spirits, who have lost their physical organs of speech, and have silently to impress their thoughts, so often fail to give entire satisfaction. I have said that the spiritual body within is the counterpart of our outer one; consequently it has spiritual organs.

It is the influences by which we are governed and surrounded, that causes a quickening influence of the magnetism of either some mortal or spirit, the spirit organ of vision, perceives the higher vibrations of the same, either which gives physical sight, or there is a more attenuated spirit ether. In either case the Medium perceives spirits and spiritual things, as readily as remote physical objects. This is direct or objective clairvoyance, there are few who possess this power. A more common force is the subjective, this latter is induced by a mortal or spirit hypnotizer, or control, as it is termed, who by will-force photographs the object seen by the clairvoyant upon his *sensorium* or mind. Short of spiritual manifestations by disembodied spirits, clairvoyance is one of the best scientific proofs of immortality we have.

It is as I have already stated, a mental function without, or independent of, a material organ, and materialism has never been able to nullify its force. Clairaudience has the same relation to the organs of hearing that clairvoyance has to sight. It is the opening or quickening of the spiritual ear by the same process; by it, the still, small voice of ministering angels become audible. Angel whispers become something more than a poetic fancy. The sound of a voice that is still to ordinary mortals, becomes to the spirit ear of the medium as audible as the voice of many waters, or as sonorous as that of a mortal orator in most emphatic utterances. Clairvoyance and Clairaudience, as well as all other conditions of development, may be induced by close and persistent study, or any method, that will secure concentration, introspection, and lifts the individual out of self and away from the memory-sphere and consciousness of outer surroundings, has the desired effect. The development of psychometric sensitiveness will often lead to the desired result of clairvoyant perception. In fact all the phases of mediumship are possibilities inherent in the spiritual constitution of embodied man and woman, are more or less active and capable of development by exercise in every human being, and may be classed under the general head of intuition, spirit perception, or a development of the sixth sense. Since I have already exceeded the limited space allotted for the subject of spirit control, etc., I would state that it is not our purpose to advance any new theory, but a correct theory, based upon sound philosophy, which is the base of all science. Our object is to give our quota to strengthening the bulwarks of Medical Botany, and we wish it to be so in truth, and trust that the day is not far distant that it will be taught in our public schools, so that the people may gain sufficient knowledge to enable them to remove all diseases that flesh is heir to, and that man may know himself and leave not a single outlet but that of old age. For such is our confidence in the benevolence of the Creator, that within the vegetable kingdom maybe found remedies for all the maladies of mankind.

The practice of medicine has its foundation in nature, and disease a natural consequence of progressive life, thousands of years must and did pass, before men thought of employing minerals as medicine, and the use for the last three hundred years has demonstrated their injuriousness; and had their been nothing by which disease could have been removed but minerals, the race would well nigh become extinct. Do you imagine there was no foundation for those traditions which come dimly down from the past or remote ages, as shells found now on the mountain tops inform us where the seas have been? What was the old Colchian Magic, but the minute study of nature in her lowliest works? What was the fable of Medea, but a proof of the powers that may be extracted from the germ of the leaf? The most gifted of all the Priestcrafts, the mysterious Sisterhoods of Cuth, concerning whose incantations, learning vainly bewilders itself amid the maze of legends, sought in the meanist herbs what, perhaps, the Babylonian Sages explored in vain amid the loftiest stars. To the old Circeean Promontory, came the wise from the farthest east to search for plants and simples, which your Pharmacists of to day, would fling from them as weeds I with all their boasted learning.

We are indebted to Egypt, that universal school of the ancient world, for the origin of medical science. Their knowledge was famous even in the days of Moses, and her physicians are celebrated in his history. The ailment and ablutions recorded in his books, so congenial to the health of an eastern clime, enforced on the observations of the Israelites, have been ascribed to his knowledge of the Egyptian science of medicine by those who have denied to him the prerogative of having acted under inspiration. Many books on medicine were written by the Egyptians. The name of Esculapias (the meaning in Greek is "Merciful Healer,") was given him on account of the great skill in healing disease. It will be impossible to go through the whole history of medicine in the space allotted us; but we will give the reader a birds-eye view of its progress from the early ages down to the present time. Chiron the learned sage, brought medicine from Egypt to Greece. Esculapius, the scholar of Chiron, flourished before the Trojan war. The secrets of his art he communicated to his children, and they were retained in his family until they burst forth with peculiar splendor, and shone out to the possession of the

world, in the writings and character of the great
Hippocrates, who was born in the island of Cos. He is called
the "father of medicine."

It was he who caused tablets to be hung the temples
describing the name of diseases, and the mode of their cure.
His noble mind soon rectified the defects in the system of
his ancestors, and he found out and applied the remedy
equal to its vast importance, he silently effected a revolution
which changed the face of medicine, and caused it to rank
with the sublimest part of human science. From what is
related of him in history, there was but one sentiment in his
soul, the act of doing good. Celsus was next, he was born in
Rome. He followed in the same path as Hippocrates; he
wrote eight books on medical science. He died much
beloved, and was held in estimation by the Emperors of
Rome. Galen was born at Pergamos; he closely followed his
great leader Hippocrates, but. like all other reformers, he
had to pass through the fire of persecution; his skill aroused
the jealousy of the Roman Physicians, who persecuted him,
and he left Rome and went back to Pergamos.

He was afterwards sent for by the Emperor to see
his two sons, who were smitten with a plague, and he cured
them. After this all hostilities ceased, he died at a good ripe
age, in the year A. D. 200. His fame was great; he wrote
many volumes on philosophy and medicine. A pleasing
melancholy pervades the soul as we trace the memorials of
these devoted and magnanimous men, benefactors of the
human race. They seem to redeem the very character of man
from all the vile aspersions that have been cast upon it; they
shine as splendid beacons on the solitude of time, to point
out to the traveler, on his journey through life, the road to
glory, and the haven of immortality and peace. After Celsus
and Galen medical science stood stationary. In the agitation
and decline of the Roman Empire, all learning was arrested
in its progress; and when it fell, the arts and sciences
perished in the shock. The few fragments that remained

were concealed among the Priests, and Monks, and secular clergy; but a dreary and dark desolation spread over the universe of mind. The knowledge of a few simples answered all the wants of the people. In those scenes of broil and battle, when nothing was to be seen or heard but the alarm of war, and garments rolled in blood, there was no time to die of disease! No! it was on the bloody field of martial strife that death reaped the harvest of his millions. All the finer feelings and causes of disease were absorbed and swallowed up in the vortex of war. Thus through the long and dreary night of a thousand years, a morbid melancholy and mortal death sat brooding, like an incubus on the nations of Europe; but "man cannot be enslaved for ever." At length superstition broke her chains, science aroused her giant form, and shook off the slumber of ages. The spirit rebounded with the crash of its long depression, and took her place on the sublime elevation of freedom and range of thought. Religious liberty, civil liberty, the diffusion of science, the equity laws, and the amelioration of the condition of the poor, all proclaim her bright and rapid progress to the uncreated splendor of eternal day.

After the revival of learning the works of the ancients were held in great repute. In the early part of the sixteenth century the far famed Paracelcus advanced his chemical system to the world- He professed to have found the elixir of life in "Mercury" as a medicine; but he died at the age of forty eight. Such, then is the man to whom we are indebted for the introduction of the mineral practice, which has continued up to the present day, entailing misery on the human race to an amount beyond all computation. Dr. Harvey discovered the circulation of the blood in the middle of the seventeenth century. The great Sydenham, the first of the moderns, was the father of medical science in its present robes of modern fashion. His pathology was simple and comprehensive; the oppressed and exhausted state of the system comprised his rationale of disease and mode of cure. The simplicity of his views caused others to follow in his footsteps.

"To add to the science of medicine," said Sydenham, "two facts must be kept in view: 1st, to give a full and complete description of disease,- 2nd, to discover a fixed and perfect remedy, or mode of cure."

By thus reasoning, we perceive that even the great Sydenham, intuitively understood that there are two educations, one of the mind, the other of the soul, or psychic. The illumination and knowledge, given through the soul, cannot be taught as men study the various external sciences, but must be evolved from the higher impulses of the heart, and depths of our inner consciousness. Thus by the aid of my guides, am I enabled to offer to the public, the true essence of that, which nature's God ordained should be for his use as a medicine, viz: "the vegetable kingdom," for this is the medicine of nature.

FAMILY BOTANIC GUIDE

PRESERVATION OF HEALTH

A state of health consists of the different organs performing, in an easy and regular manner, all their proper offices. This state on which our happiness depends is the legitimate result of a correct mode of living. Those who transgress nature's laws may as well expect to breathe without air, or live under water, without incurring a penalty in the shape of disease commensurate with their breach of law. Ask of the person who has not been free from pain for a series of years, what they consider as the greatest earthly blessing; and their answer is health, and when deprived of this, all nature wears a gloomy aspect; the glistening sunbeams, the opening flowers, the rippling streams, the green clad trees, or the soul cheering notes of the feathered songsters, have no charm for him.

The loss of health admonish him that he must close his eyes on all things earthly. Then it is that he looks back on a misspent life with sorrow. The result of a violation of the physical laws of our nature is to produce misery and disease according to the extent of those violations. Thousands there are rolling in wealth, who would give all they possess, to be able to enjoy sound health the balance of their lives. If health be so valuable that the miser would pour out his gold, and the epicure forego his sumptuous fare in order to regain it when lost, is it not worth preserving? Is it not the height of injustice to charge upon Him, or providence, as some of those who profess to know more about the mysterious dealings of Divinity than they do of the physical and psychical laws by which we are governed ? These laws are unchangeable, by which all matter, whether animate or inanimate, are governed. In order, therefore, to preserve health, proper regard must be paid to food, drink, clothing, exercise, pure air, and the cold water bath. A few simple rules should always be observable. Eat three times a day, and that moderately, and regularly, and of such food as is easily digested. Masticate your food well, which is the first process of digestion. The most wholesome food is unbolted wheat, bread, potatoes, corn-meal, oat-meal, rice, tapioca, and all kinds of ripe fruit, and in general a vegetable diet; meat should be eaten sparingly, particularly in hot weather, and the best drink being cold water The real object for eating should be kept in view, viz.: to supply the body with a proper amount of nutriment, according to the amount of active exercise taken, as well as the powers of the digestive apparatus; and not to eat to gratify a depraved appetite merely.

VENTILATION

We are all aware of the necessity of breathing, and the agreeable freshness and reviving influence of a pure morning air, must convince us that breathing a pure atmosphere is conducive to health; yet we carefully exclude the air from our dwellings, as if its approach were noxious; in order to guard ourselves from the external air, we often retard that renewal of the atmosphere which is necessary to prevent its becoming stagnant and unfit to support life. Few persons are aware how very necessary a thorough ventilation is to the preservation of health. We can preserve life without food for a considerable length of time; but keep us without air for a very few minutes and we cease to exist. It is not enough that we have air- we must have fresh air; for the principle by which life is supported is taken from the air during the act of breathing. One-fourth of the atmosphere is capable of supporting life. The remainder serves to dilute the pure vital air, and render it more fit to be respired. A full grown man takes into his lungs nearly a pint of air each time he breathes, and when at rest he makes about eighteen respirations in a minute, consequently 1,080 in an hour, or 25,020 in twenty-four hours. By each respiration one pint of air is sent into the lungs, in one minute about eighteen pints, and in one hour upwards of two hogsheads, in twenty-four hours about fifty-seven hogsheads, and as the air enters into the lungs it is exposed to the action of the blood, which changes its purer part (Oxygen gas), into mixed air (carbonic acid gas), which is not only unfit to support animal life, but is absolutely destructive to it. One hundred and fifty grains, by weight, of this poisonous ingredient are added to the air of a bed-room in one hour by a single sleeper- more than one thousand during the night. Unless there be a sufficient quantity of air to dilute this, or unless ventilation provide for a gradual removal of foul air, while fresh comes to take its place, health must be seriously undermined. There are more cases of consumption brought on by a continuous breathing of the impure air of close confined rooms and factories than from any other cause.

It will bring on consumption in the soundest constitution. The oxygen of the air we breathe regulates our appetite, and the chyle undergoes its last vital change in the lungs, and that change depends on the perfect performance of respiration and a sufficient supply of pure air. When in any way obstructed, disease is the result, and the body wastes away. An admirable provision of nature is here visible, to prevent the now poisonous air from being inhaled a second time. While in the lungs the air receives so much heat as to make it specifically lighter than the pure atmosphere; consequently, it rises above our heads as it is thrown off from the lungs. It is only necessary to observe the countenances of those who inhabit close rooms and houses- the pale hue of their skins, their sunken eyes, and languid movements- to be sensible of the bad effects of shutting out the pure air. Flowers in water, and living plants in pots, should not be permitted, as they greatly injure the purity of the air of our bedrooms, by giving off large quantities of carbonic acid gas similar to that thrown off from the body. Ventilation therefore, resolves itself into the securing a constant supply of fresh air, to vitalize and invigorate the system, all else being equal.

SYSTEM

To our medical opponents we would say we never intended to be personal unless we were ourselves personally attacked, nor do we for one moment entertain the least animosity against any one, for we have a far higher and nobler end in view, viz.; to convince rather than to condemn, and, if possible, to enlist them in our ranks, thus assisting us to alleviate the sum of human misery, and we confidently hope the day is not far distant when our system will be investigated by the higher and more spiritual classes of society, and like the coming together of the positive and negative element, some bright ray of light may be elicited. Truth will stand erect amid all opposition. We would at any time prefer an open enemy to a doubting friend. We do not trifle with others, neither do we intend that others shall trifle with us. We come through our medium to explain the nature and qualities of those productions that nature has so benevolently provided for us, and to show that by a simple process that disease may be cured and man restored to health through that unseen intelligence, which has so often made itself manifest in all ages. Those means are placed within reach of all, and it is the imperative duty of all to be fully acquainted with the provision of nature. In fact, man should know himself. All wisdom centers there. Unfortunately, that is a knowledge that men appear the least inclined to pursue; they are content to know everything but that which most especially relates to their own interests. The medical profession would wrap all in mystery. Monopoly delights in mystery, and then forsooth, it is dignified by the appellation Science, and the world is kept in awe, or ignorance, lest the impositions practiced upon them should be divulged. Unlike most other affairs of this changing world, the science of medical botany has a sure and certain basis, with unalterable truth for its foundation, on which a structure is raised on the laws of nature alone. Secure upon such a foundation, we may smile at the puny attempts of man to overthrow it, and may bid defiance to every power arrayed against it. "Truth crushed to earth will rise again."

GENERAL DIRECTIONS IN CURING OR PREVENTING DISEASE

1. Be careful to always keep the determining powers to the surface, by keeping the inward heat above the outward, or the fountain above the stream, and all will be safe.

2. It must be remembered that heat is life, and cold death; that fever is the friend and cold the enemy; always help the friend by opposing the enemy, in order to restore health.

3. That the organization and construction of the human frame is, in all men, essentially the same, being formed of the four elements. Earth and water constitute the solids of the body which is made active by heat and air. Heat stimulates in a peculiar manner, and gives life and motion, other things being in harmony with the whole organism.

4. A perfect state of health arises from a due balance or temperature of the elements; when disturbed the system is more or less disordered, and all disorders are caused by obstructed perspiration, which may be produced by a variety of means; that medicine, therefore, must be administered that is best calculated to remove obstructions and promote perspiration.

5. Canker is caused by cold, and there is always more or less of it in all cases of disease; continue the use of such articles calculated to remove it, as long as there is any appearance of disorder, and when the disease is removed use such tonics as will restore the digestive powers, keeping

the bowels mildly open.

6. Always use the prevention, which is better than the cure, on the first appearance of disorder; use such simple remedies before it becomes seated.

7. In case of fever, increase the internal heat by giving such medicines that will open the pores of the skin, so as to overpower the cold, when the natural heat will be equally distributed over the whole body, and a balance restored, or what is called the turn of the fever.

8. In giving medicine to children, give about one-half, or more, or less, according to age, of the quantity directed for a grown person, and be particular to offer drink often, especially to children who are unable to ask for it.

9. Never stop relax of the bowels too suddenly; give mild astringents, with mild stimulants. In dysentery, which is a relaxation of the larger bowels, it is better to inject into the bowels such astringents recommended under that head.

10. In all cases of burns, scalds, or frozen limbs, where the skin is off, guard against canker; apply poultice of cracker and slippery elm, made with raspberry leaf tea. And for fresh wounds or cuts use freely of the Tincture of Myrrh, by saturating a cloth, and to the parts apply.

11. Never make use of a purge where there is canker of the stomach or bowels; use such remedies under the head of canker or anti-septic and anti-canker remedies. Avoid such medicines as mercury, arsenic, antimony, calomel, preparations of copper or lead, and also niter and opium. They are poisons, and an enemy to health.

12. Beware of bleeding and blistering, cupping and salivation, as they are productive of much harm. They waste the strength of the patient, without doing much good. Never

eat meat that is tainted or in anyway diseased; for one ounce in the stomach is worse than the effluvia from a whole carcass.

13. Remember that regularity in diet is very important to preserve health; always make it a point to get up from the table when you are able to eat a little more. This is important to those who have weak, digestive organs.

14. Ardent spirits is slow poison; it is taken into the stomach to stimulate, but the effect is soon over, and much use of it destroys the tone of the stomach, injures the digestive powers, and often the cause of disease By a strict observance of the foregoing directions you may save much pain and expense, and enjoy good health and long life, which is the prayer of the author.

MATERIA MEDICA

STIMULANTS

Pure healthy stimulants are those substances which act in harmony with the laws of nature, and, while they stimulate, do not effect the brain to injure it, nor increase the pulsation beyond its natural standard. When taken, they have a pungent taste, and, when swallowed, impart to the stomach a genial sensation of warmth, which, under favorable circumstances, produces perspiration. Thus, healthy stimulants carry the requisite proportion of blood to every part, or, in other words, restore an equal balance in the circulation, and may be employed safely in fevers and every state of congestion. They exert a healthy action in the system, without irritating the parts they come in contact with; arousing the dormant energy of the nervous system without deranging the animal economy. Food is sufficient stimulant in a healthy system, keeping life's wheels in motion, but when, from causes over which we have no control, the food fails to impress the stomach in a healthy manner, it is necessary to resort to a stimulating medicine. Stimulants are indispensable in the treatment of disease. When about five out of every eight pounds of food taken into the system pass out of it again by the skin, leaving only three pounds to pass off by the bowels, lungs, and kidney's, thus we see at once when the skin is inactive, or the circulation feeble, the blood will be charged with impurities, and unless stimulants are administered to keep up a determination of blood to the service of the body, to let out the impurities, disease is sure to creep in; or if the blood recedes from the surface, leaving the skin pale, cold, and contracted, stimulants are necessary to bring the blood to the surface, or death will be the result. In contending for the use of stimulants, we recommend not the use of acrid, or narcotic, or poisonous stimulants, but those that act tn harmony with the animal economy and the laws of nature.

For we know whereof we speak, when we say, that from this side of life we know that nature has been more than bountiful to man if he did but realize it, for the vegetable kingdom is full of such substances necessary for the cure of all diseases that man is heir to, without resorting to such substances as phosphorus, tartar emetic, or alcohol, and many other poisonous ingredients used extensively by the medical profession.

CAYENNE

Capsicum Baccatum, or Bird Pepper

Capsicum is the botanical name of a large genus or family of plants which grow in various countries, as Africa and in North and South America and in other warm countries, We use only the bird pepper, as it retains its heat longer in the system than any other, and is the best stimulant known. It has a pungent taste, which continues for a considerable length of time. When taken into the stomach it produces a pleasant sensation of warmth, which soon diffuses itself throughout the whole system, equalizing the circulation. Hence it is useful in inflammations and diseases which depend upon a morbid increase of blood in any particular part of the body. It is very useful in apoplexy, by placing the feet in hot water and mustard, and at the same time give a teaspoonful of cayenne pepper in a little water. This treatment has caused a reaction, taken the pressure of blood from the brain, and by this means saved the patient. Some may ask, will it not produce an inflammatory action? We say decidedly not, for there is nothing that will so soon equalize the circulation, and restore the patient. We have used it in every stage of inflammation, and never without beneficial results. The natives of all tropical climates make free use of the bird pepper, as one of the ingredients of their dishes, and do not find it injurious. In many parts of this country the natives steep the pods and, by adding the juice of some sour fruit, with sugar, drink the tea hot in fevers, and for colds, sore throat, and when exhausted by fatigue. The Indians make an excellent gargle by keeping the pods in hot water, and adding sugar, use it for sore throat, and relaxed state of the uvula, as well as hoarseness. Bleeding of the lungs is easily checked by the use of cayenne and the vapor bath; by this means circulation is promoted in every part of the body, and, consequently, the pressure upon the lungs diminished, thus affording an opportunity for a coagulum to form around the ruptured vessel. In advocating the use of capsicum, we do not wish it to be understood that it will cure everything, nor do we recommend it to be taken regularly, whether a stimulant is required or not. Medicines ought to be taken only in sickness. Capsicum is an invaluable remedy in the botanic practice.

MOTHER OF THYME

Terpyllum- A wild plant, very pretty and fragrant. It grows in little tufts by the wayside; leaves, very small and oval; two at each joint, smooth, and of a bright green color. The flowers are of a pale red, in little tufts at the top of the stalks; the plant has a fragrant smell, and an aromatic and agreeable taste. For all nervous diseases it is a very valuable remedy. An infusion of the fresh plant may be used, or a decoction of the dry herb. If used persistently will cure nervous disorders. The infusion drank before going to bed will prevent nightmare.

VIRGINIA SNAKE ROOT

Stim. Diapho. Tonic and Diuretic

A valuable medicine in typhus fevers, to keep the skin moist. It is a good medicine for pains in the back and kidneys; a teaspoonful of the powder in a cupful of boiling water three times per day.

THE OCCULT FAMILY PHYSICIAN

LOBELIA INFLATA

Stimulant, emetic, expectorant, and relaxant

This herb is a most valuable anti-poison. Much has been said and written as to the properties of lobelia; and instead of being a poison, practical experience- which is far better than theory- has proved that it is one of the most valuable herbs in the botanic practice. If medical men would divert themselves of theory, and give heed to facts, they would have discovered in the following analysis of its chemical properties truth from error: Lobelia, resin, chlorophyll, gum, lobelic acid, fixed oil, salts of lime and potassa, oxide of iron, and woody fiber. Many Indians who were troubled with shortness of breath, asthmatic affections, hooping cough, and in fact many diseases of the chest and lungs, have used this herb with striking success. I am satisfied that it is as kind and destitute of all hazard as boneset or any other herb, though it may be more efficient. It is already beginning to be appreciated by the medical world.

It tends to remove obstructions from every part of the system, and is felt even to the ends of the toes; it cleanses the stomach, and exercises a beneficial influence over every part of the body; it is very diffusible, however, and requires to be used with ginger or some other stimulant. There is no medicine that is half so effective as lobelia in removing the tough, hard, and ropy phlegm from asthmatic and consumptive persons. It is an indispensable medicine in fevers, bilious, and long standing chronic complaints. It is useful in poultices to assist suppuration. The medicinal virtues of this herb are so multifarious that a large treatise might well be written on its curative powers. Suffice it, however, to say that it is a general corrector of the whole system, innocent in its nature, and moving with the general spirits. In healthy systems it will be silent and harmless. It is fully as well calculated to remove the cause of disease as food is to remove hunger, as it clears obstructions in the circulation, not regarding the name of the disease. In asthmatic attacks, take a tablespoonful of the acid tincture; in croup for children, one half the quantity. For deafness, take one drachm each: Tincture of lobelia, tincture gum myrrh, oil of sassafras, tincture of laudanum, olive oil, mix, and apply lint wet with the liniment in the ear, night and morning, then syringe out with warm water and soap.

PRICKLY ASH. (BARK AND SEED)

Stim. Diaph. and Anti-Scorbutic

It warms and invigorates the stomach; is very useful in cold hands and feet (depending on a sluggish circulation); is very useful in paralysis; and very useful in gleet. It is also very good for fever, ague, lethargy, and makes an excellent bitters. Dose, half a wine glass two or three times a day

CLOVES

Stim. Arom. Carmi.

The clove is a native of the East Indies, and some parts of Africa, and is a powerful aromatic: The oil will relieve tooth-ache. They are warm, cordial and strengthening; they expel wind, and are a good remedy for the colic. Dose of powder. 2 to 3 grains. Infusion 1 to 2 ounces. Tincture, 20 to 80 minims.

GINGER

Stim. Car. and Tonic.

Ginger has a pungent and aromatic taste; its aromatic and anti-spasmodic properties render it extremely valuable. It is very useful in cold, flatulent colic, and in laxity and debility of the intestines; persons subject to flatulence or a windy digestion, have been known to receive great benefit from the use of ginger tea; gouty persons have for years been known to gain relief from the use of ginger, mixed in any liquid, taken an hour before eating. It is one of the best stimulants for the stomach and bowels. Combined with purgatives, it corrects their griping tendency. Ginger promotes the circulation through the smaller blood vessels. It is useful in torpid and phlegmatic habits where the stomach is subject to a slimy condition, and the bowels distended with flatulence.

ANGELICA

Stim. Carm. and Tonic.

The stalks, leaves and seeds possess the above named properties, which are strongest in the seed. It has a pungent taste, and an agreeable aromatic odor. The whole plant has the same virtues. It is cordial and tonic. It has been used by many against pestilential and contagious diseases. The root is also very valuable; the best comes from the south of Europe. A syrup made from the herb and stalks is good for pleurisy, shortness of breath, and diseases of the lungs, more particularly by adding one half tincture of lobelia. It is also good in stranguary, or stoppage of urine, and removes obstructions of the liver and spleen. The juice dropped into the eye removes dimness of sight, and into the ears deafness. Dose, of the powdered root, from 10 to 20 grains; distilled water, 1 ounce; flu. extract, from 5 to 15 grains; infusion, a half wine glass; tincture, a drachm; spirits, from a half a drachm to 3 drachms.

ANISEEDS

Stimulant and Carminative.

Aniseeds are the product of a small plant growing on the islands in the Mediterranean sea; they possess stimulating and carminative properties, useful in indigestion, flatulence and colic. The essential oil is extensively used in cough mixtures. Dose of powdered seed, 10 to 30 grains; infusion, a wine glassful; compound spirit, 1 to 4 drachms; essential oil, 5 to 20 drops on sugar.

MINT: PEPPERMINT.

Menth Piperata. Stom. Stim. and Sudorific.

It is a garden plant, much like the wild mint. The whole plant is used fresh or dried. It is good for flatulence, allays nausea and vomiting, and will often cure colic almost instantaneously, and drank freely, is good against the gravel. Peppermint water is generally made by rubbing down the oil with a little lump sugar, and a few drops of spirits of wine, and then filtering. The oil is a powerful carminative and stimulant, which render it useful in flatulence attending indigestion and diarrhea. The dose of the oil is from 1 to 3 or 4 drops. It may be taken in water or any other vehicle. It has the same virtues that most of the mint family, only more powerful.

PENNY ROYAL

Stim. Diap. and Carmi.

The *mentha pulegium* of botanists. It flowers in August and September. It is a well known plant. The herb is warm, pungent, and aromatic. The infusion is warming to the stomach; relieves spasms, hysterics, or colics; it makes a cooling drink for children in fevers. It is a favorite female herb, removing all obstructions peculiar to females arising from obstructed perspiration. It should never be boiled, as the volatile essences escape; taken in decoction, it is good for pains in the head, and it clears the eyesight.

SPEARMINT

Feb. Diu. Stim. Arom.

This is the *mentha viridis* of botanists. It is valuable for its aromatic and other properties which reside in its volatile oil, of a pungent and peculiar odor. The whole plant is used fresh or dry, and is excellent to allay nausea or vomiting. It is beneficial in pains of the stomach and bowels, and to expel wind.

CALAMINT, OR MOUNTAIN MINT

Stimulant, Stomachic and Diuretic.

It is good for pains in the head; it is also beneficial for gravel complaints, combined with rosemary and wood bettany; is good for water on the brain; it is a good female herb.

WATER MINT

Stimulant, Aromatic, Carmenative, Feb.

This herb is also used as a remedy for colic, pains in the stomach and bowels, and it promotes menstruation. A single dose will frequently cure colic. It removes obstructions and strengthens the system. Its virtues ought to be better known and more used. It has prevented more doctors bills among the poorer classes as it has prevented disease from taking a hold of the system, which means a great deal, since medical men have learned the art of making large figures.

DIURETICS

Diuretics are those medicines which increase

secretion of urine and thus stimulate the kidneys to a vigorous action. From many causes the kidneys become inactive, and consequently do not secrete from the blood that quantity of urine which is necessary to keep the blood in a state of purity; and when the kidneys do not separate the urine from the blood, it is carried through the circulation, producing various diseases of the skin, also stone stranguary, gravel and dropsy; in fact, it is nature's bleeding point, and it should be borne in mind by every botanist and by the heads of families, that the body cannot be in a healthy state while the kidneys are in a torpid condition.

CUBEBS

Aromatic and Diuretic

Cubebs are good for scalding of urine, gleets, gonorrhea and all relaxations of the mucus glands of the secretive parts. It is an excellent remedy for flour albus, or whites, and combined with a little sweet niter and copaiba will cure gonorrhea.

BURDOCK SEEDS

Diuretic, Nervine and Tonic.

A strong decoction of the seeds is excellent in inflammation of the kidneys and bladder. It is a good nervine, and is a useful remedy for convulsions, fits and spasmodic affections.

BURNT SAXIFRAGE

Few remedies will excel this for gravel in the kidneys, and stone in the bladder. It affects a gradual dissolution of the stone and gravel.

HEMLOCK BARK

Diuretic and Astringent.

This is an excellent remedy for pains in the back and kidneys; it is also useful to stop relaxes of the bowels, and makes a good wash for old sores. The oil of hemlock is a superior remedy in gastric irritation of the stomach, and allays vomiting in cholera, etc. The dose is from five to ten drops in sweetened water every ten or twenty minutes until relief is afforded.

WOOD SAGE

Diuretic and Tonic.

This herb will remove obstructions from the kidneys and liver; it is also a good poultice, with equal parts of chickweed, pounded, for all kinds of indolent ulcers and boils, and is excellent for relax of bowels.

DANDELION

Diuretic, Tonic, Alterative, Diaphoretic.

No plant is better known the world over than the dandelion. Its medicinal virtues are many. The leaves and root are bitter, and contain a bitter milky juice. It is of an opening and cleansing quality and therefore very effectual for obstructions of the liver, gall and spleen, and the diseases that arise from them, as the jaundice and hypochondriasis; it opens the urinary passages in young and old, hence it has been called by the people of some countries, piss-a-bed, it will cleanse inward ulcers in the urinary passage, and by its drying and temperate qualities heal them; for which purpose the decoction of the roots or leaves in white wine, is very effectual. It promotes rest and sleep to bodies distempered by the heat of ague, fits, etc.

The dandelion therefore is a most useful herb, and ought to be more extensively known, on account of its valuable medicinal virtues. It is as valuable as sarsaparilla, and is often given in dyspepsia, dropsy, cutaneous eruptions, and other disorders. A decoction is made of the fresh root sliced, one ounce to a pint of water, boiled down to a half pint, and strain, adding two drachms of cream of tartar; take a wine glass full two or three times per day. The extract may be used with the same result, dose of the extract is from ten grains, to half drachm. The French use the leaves in salad, and the Germans roast the root for coffee, for which it makes a very good substitute, being similar in flavor and much more wholesome, it enters largely into our pills and other preparations.

BUCHU LEAVES

Diuretic and Aromatic.

An infusion of the leaves is good for increasing the secretion of of urine and removing obstructions in the bladder. Old people especially will find great benefit by taking the following preparation: Pour one pint of water upon one ounce of leaves and simmer gently for one hour, strain, and take a wine glass full three times per day.

PARSLEY PERT

Diuretic.

This is a well known remedy for the gravel; it is a good diuretic, and exercises great control over the kidneys and bladder. A tea of this plant may be taken alone, or combined with others.

UVA URSI

This is a powerful remedy in lumbago and has no equal in chronic inflammation of the kidneys and bladder. It is a specific in the ulceration of those organs. A tea may be made by boiling the leaves, one ounce to the pint of water, simmer gently for one hour, strain, and take a wine glass full three or four times per day.

WILD CARROT (seeds and tops)

A very useful diuretic and useful in gravel and stone and other disease of the urinary organs.

TANSY

Diuretic, Tonic and Stimulant.

This is a good medicine for stranguary, pains in the back and loins, useful in painful menstruation, and is a valuable herb for female weakness; and seldom fails to cure palpitation of the heart in a few days. The flowers dried and powdered are a cure for worms.

STAR THISTLE

Calcitrapa- The star thistle has narrow leaves lying on the ground, indented at the edges, soft, or a little woolly, green, from which rise weak stalks parted into many branches, all lying on the ground, a pretty bush, set with divided leaves on top, where stand small whitish green heads, with sharp white thorns, which are very sharp, out of which rise flowers which are yellowish with reddish purple threads, that resemble the flowers of the thistle. The seeds are winged with down. The root oblong, growing in clearings and commons, and flowering in July and August. The seed and herb is a good remedy for stone in the bladder.

The root in powder drank in wine, will cure fistula if taken fasting in the morning. It opens obstructions, and is good for the gravel.

ST. JOHN'S WORT

It grows a foot and a half high. The stalks are round, thick, firm, upright, and at the top divided into several branches. The leaves are narrow, short and obtuse at the end, and if held up against the light, they appear full of small round holes. Large and bright yellow flowers abundantly grow at the tops of the branches, full of yellow threads, which, when rubbed upon the hand, stain it red, like blood. The seed is black and smells like resin. It grows in meadows, woods and copses. A decoction of the flowers, is a powerful diuretic, promoting the flow of urine. It is also good for gravel, and inflammation of the ureters. It is also useful in intermittent fevers, dysentery, hemorrhages, chest complaints and jaundice. For wounds, the tops gathered fresh and bruised are used. Boiled in wine it is excellent for inward wounds and hurts. It is a good wound herb, made into an ointment. It soon closes cuts, wounds, etc. The decoction of the plant and flowers and especially of the seed, with the juice of knotgrass, relieves vomiting, spitting of blood, and obstructions of the urine. Two drachms of the powdered herb drank in a little broth, expels choler and congealed blood from the stomach. A warm decoction of the leaves and seeds taken before fits of ague, relieves, and, eventually drives them away. The decoction of the seed, frequently and continuously taken, will cure sciatica, falling sickness, and palsy. It will also cure St. Vitus dance. The blossom will remove film from the eye, simmered in sweet oil.

SHEPHERD'S PURSE

It is a very common plant, with long rather broad leaves, which spread upon the ground, a round stalk nine or ten inches high, it is very astringent and glutinous. It is also used in diarrhea, looseness of the bowels, and bloody urine. It makes a good ointment for wounds, cuts, etc.

MOUSE EAR

Pilosella: This is a small herb possessing great virtues. Mouse ear is a low herb creeping upon the ground by small strings, like the strawberry plant, by which it shoots forth small roots, and many short leaves, set in a round form together, very hairy, from among the leaves spring up two or three small hoary stalks about a span high, with a few smaller leaves thereon; at the tops, one flower only appears, consisting of many pale yellow leaves, broad at the point, and a little dented in three or four rows, very like a dandelion flower, and reddish underneath the edges. It grows in loose sandy soil and dry places, and flowers in July and August, and remains green most of the winter. The decoction drank is good for jaundice, even of a chronic character, and it is a special remedy in stone in the bladder, and the tormenting pains thereof and griping pains in the bowels. It also restrains inward bleeding, and is a specific for wounds both inward and outward, The green herb bruised, and bound on a cut or wound, quickly heals it. The distilled water makes a wash for wounds and sores.

MOTHER-WORT

Cardiaca.

It is one of the most useful herbs to relieve obstructed menstruation; it may be made into a syrup. which when taken, will allay inward tremors, faintings, etc. It is also useful in chronic head-ache, hysteric complaints, and especially for curing palpitation of the heart, arising from hysteric causes. In fact, there is no better herb to strengthen and gladden the heart of the female; hence its name, mother-wort. It is also very useful to regulate the menstrual flow where there is excess. We also use it in connection with prickly ash, for quickening and regulating the circulation. It is one of the principal ingredients in our female syrup for preventing painful menstruation. There is no better herb than mother-wort for cleansing the womb and removing obstructions in the female at the time of life known as the change of life. A wineglass full of the decoction should be taken three times per day.

KIDNEY-WORT

Diuretic, Deobstruent, Hepetic and Balsamic.

Kidney-wort has many thick, flat and round leaves growing from the root, each having a long footstalk fastened underneath, about the middle of it. It is of a pale green color, and rather hollow on the upper side like a saucer; from which rise one or more smooth, hollow stalks, half a foot high, with two or three small leaves thereon, rather long, and divided at the edges; the tops are divided into long branches, bearing a number of flowers, round a long spike one above another, which are hollow like a little bell, of a whitish green color, after which come small heads, containing small brownish seeds. The root is round and smooth, grayish without, and white within. It may be frequently found growing among the rocks and stony places at the bottom of old trees, and on those that are decayed. It flowers in June in this latitude. Its medicinal virtues are greatly extolled by some medical writers. Some claim the juice and the extract will cure epilepsy. The juice allays inflammation of the liver and stomach and strengthens the bowels. The juice of the herb outwardly applied restrains erysipelas. It heals pimples, sores, etc., and taken inwardly it relieves inflamed kidneys, and combined with other diuretics will cure gravel and stone. Made into an ointment, it is good for the piles, sciatica and swelled testicles; the ointment or the juice alone is good for scrofula sores, chilblains and stops the bleeding of green wounds.

PELLITORY OF THE WALL

Diuretic and Nervine.

This is a powerful diuretic and is also a good nervine. It is excellent in dropsy, gravel, lumbago and diseases of the bladder. It is also good for water in the head and convulsive fits.

QUEEN OF THE MEADOW

Diuretic, Aromatic and Astringent.

This is a most valuable medicine for all obstructions of the urinary organs. Bad cases of gravel and dropsy have yielded to this plant alone, where the conditions have been such that it was not necessary to administer a compound remedy. The dose is a teaspoonful of powder in a cupful of water three or four times per day, as the case may require.

BROOM TOPS

Diuretic and Anti-Scorbutic.

Is useful in retention of urine, and is a good remedy for water on the brain, combined with smartweed and queen of the meadow in equal parts. It effectually cures gravel and stone in the bladder.

CROWFOOT, OR BUTTERCUP

The common crowfoot is so well known it needs no description. They grow very common everywhere, especially in fields, and by the roadside. This fiery and hot-spirited herb is not fit to be given inwardly but an ointment of the leaves or flowers will raise a blister, and may be applied to the nape of the neck to draw rheum from the

THE OCCULT FAMILY PHYSICIAN

eyes. The herb being bruised and mixed with a little mustard will raise a blister as perfectly as cantharides, and with far less danger.

CUCUMBER

This makes a good wash for hot humors of the eyes. The usual course is to bruise the cucumbers and distill the water from them. It is also good for ulcers in the bladder, taken internally: The seed is good to provoke urine and cleanse the urinary passages.

PAREIRA BRAVA

Tonic, Aperient and Diuretic.

This plant is a native of South America and has been extensively used by the people of that section for diseases of the urinary passages, such as chronic inflammation of the bladder, in allaying irritability of that organ, and correcting the disposition to profuse mucous secretions; and is used generally for the same affection by most physicians. In Brazil it is used in the cure of the bite of poisonous serpents, an infusion of the root being taken internally, while the bruised leaves of the plant are applied to the wound. The dose of the fluid extract is from half to a fluid drachm.

BUTTERNUT BARK

For habitual costiveness use the inner bark of the butternut.

SMARTWEED OR WATER PEPPER

Emmenagogue, Diuretic and Anodyne.

Smartweed, also called water pepper, possesses

great medicinal virtues. It is of a cooling nature, and effectually cures putrid ulcers, kills worms, and cleanses putrefied parts. The juice is good for cold swellings, softens and removes congealed blood or bruises, etc. The leaves bruised cure the felon, inflammations at the beginning, and to heal green wounds. The smaller species of smartweed effectually cures obstructions of the urine, in gravel and stone; and in jaundice and dropsy it has wrought great cures. It has been used extensively by the women of this country for promoting the menses. Always steep in cold water. Never boil it. It is also very useful for sores in cattle and will drive away the fly in the hottest time in summer. It may be found in watery places, ditches and such like places, which are for the most part dry in summer.

KNOTGRASS

Polygonon: A common wild plant growing in fields pathways and on long railroad tracks. The stalks of knotgrass vary in height, round jointed and of a dusky-green color. The plant lies on the ground, leaves small and oval, and not indented. The flowers are small and white, with a slight red tinge, and make their appearance in August and September. It is an excellent astringent, will stay bleeding of the mouth, mixed with common red wine, and bleeding of the nose, if applied to the temples or squirted up the nostrils. If taken in decoction it is cooling to the blood. It also restrains profuse menstruation and bloody flux. It is very useful in that most distressing complaint, stranguary, provoking urine and easing pains in the bladder, and it is an expellant of stone and gravel in the bladder. The decoction will destroy worms. A decoction, of the whole plant is a first-rate astringent, applicable to all bleedings, and especially to the bleeding piles. The juice made into an ointment is a splendid remedy for inflammations, breakings out, hot swellings, gangrene, canker and green wounds. The juice is good for sores in the ears.

JUNIPER BERRIES

Stim. Diu. Diap. and Stomac.

Juniper is a native of Europe, but is cultivated in this country. It is a trailing shrub, seldom more than two or three feet high, spreading in all directions. The common juniper flowers in May, but does not ripen its fruit till late in the following year. The berries grown in this country are not considered equal in strength to the European berries. The berries of the juniper when taken, impart to the urine the smell of violets, and often producing irritation when taken in large doses, but is considered to be a safe and reliable remedy for diseases of the urinary organs, more particularly when combined with other diuretics. The berries are a good diuretic, and for pains in the back and kidneys, far better than common gin, which is so much used for those complaints. They also promote the monthly terms of woman. The oil is the most essential, taking from ten to fifteen drops on sugar three times per day. On weak stomachs the oil will not settle.

WATER LILY

Of these there are two kinds, viz: the white and the yellow. The white lily grows plentifully in most of our inland lakes and needs little description. The yellow kind is little different from the former, save only that it has fewer leaves on the flowers, greater and more shining seed and a whitish root both within and without. The fresh root is the part chiefly used, given in strong decoction. The leaves and flowers are cold and moist, but the roots and seeds are cold and dry. The leaves cool inflammations and the heat of ague, and so do the flowers, either in syrup or conserve. The roots are more effectual to restrain all fluxes in man or woman, and is an effectual remedy in scalding of urine, boiled with wine and water and drank freely two or three times per day.

MANDRAKE (*podophyllum*)

We have found this root invaluable in many cases of chronic disease, such as venereal, scrofulous, bilious and dropsy, and in incontinence of urine will invariably give immediate relief. It makes one of the best medicines for purging the liver of impurities, causing a reaction where the liver has become torpid. The following compound will be found useful in the diseases aforesaid, viz: Extract of mandrake, one-half-ounce; cayenne pepper, one fourth ounce; mix with a little mucilage and roll to the common-sized pill. Dose, from two to four every night, or sufficient to regulate the bowels.

KNAPWEED

It has many long and dark green leaves, dented about the edges, sometimes a little torn on both sides, and rather hairy, among which arises a long round stalk, four or five feet high, divided into many branches; at the tops stand great scaly green heads, enclosing a number of dark purplish red thrums or threads, which, after they are withered, come black seeds wrapped in down, resembling thistle-seed, but smaller. The root is white, hard and woody. It is found in fields and meadows and flowers in July and August. It is a good remedy for bloody flux, bleeding at the nose and inward bleeding. It is also good in catarrh affections, restraining distillations of thin and sharp humors from the head upon the stomach and lungs. It is used also for cuts and sores, as it soon dries them up and heals them gently. It may be made into an ointment for outward application.

PIMPERNEL

Common Pimpernel has several weak, square stalks

lying on the ground, having two small and almost round leaves at every joint, one against another, very like chickweed, but without foot stalks; for the leaves compass the stalk. The flowers stand singly on tender foot stalks. They consist of five small round-pointed leaves of a scarlet color, with threads in the middle. The distilled water is used for cleansing the skin from any roughness or discoloring thereof, being boiled in wine and given to drink.

It is a good remedy against pestilential fevers, if used in connection with the spirit bath, and allowing the patient to sweat freely, and use the same twice at least. It cures stings and bites of bees, wasps and even mad dogs; used inwardly and applied outwardly. It removes obstructions of the liver and kidneys, provokes urine and expels gravel and relieves inward pains and ulcers. The decoction, or distilled water, is effectual to be applied to all fresh wounds and to old ulcers. A little honey mixed with the juice and dropped into the eyes removes clouded mists, or thick films which grow over them. It is a good remedy in the first stage of consumption, boiled with milk and mutton suet.

TONICS

Medicines which increase the tone of the muscular fiber; they consist of vegetable bitters. These remedies act by their influence on the digestive organs, and hence on the whole system. The use of a bitter principle is exemplified in the case of animals which feed on them, for it has been found that if restricted to a food which has not a sufficiency of a bitter principle, they soon become weak and die. The wisdom of nature is manifest in the fact that the majority of plants in the vegetable kingdom contain this bitter principle so essential to animal existence.

CENTUARY

Anti-Bilious and Tonic.

It is a most pleasant bitter, creates an appetite, is very beneficial in jaundice and chronic liver complaints. It may be used alone or combined with others, for indigestion.

GOLDEN SEAL

Tonic Sax.

This is a pure and excellent tonic, and one of the best for canker or ringworm, by taking a level teaspoonful twice a day in a teaspoonful of hot water; small children one-half quantity. It also keeps the bowels moderately open, without acting as a purgative or reducing the strength of the patient; it is an excellent medicine for dyspepsia, combined with white poplar bark in equal quantities; also for loss of appetite and affections of the liver; audit also makes a good wash for sore and inflamed eves.

BUCK BEAN, OR BOG BEAN

It is a very useful remedy in all cutaneous diseases arising from obstructions of the liver and spleen.

UNICORN ROOT

Ton. Exp. and Stomachic.

It is good for loss of appetite, pains in the breast and sides; it is excellent in female weakness and nervous disorders. We use it in connection with our female remedies.

WHITE POPLAR BARK

Tonic and Diuretic.

This is an excellent remedy for debility, indigestion, faintness at the stomach, head and impure state of the blood. It possesses superior diuretic properties and is very useful in gleet, stranguary obstructed urine. It is a good remedy for old people and for those who have been brought low by disease. It is the most renovating medicine that can be employed; it is an excellent medicine for loss of appetite, and combined with buchu leaves and juniper berries, makes one of the very best compounds as a general restorative. Take two ounces each of the above mentioned articles, bruise the berries and boil gently for two hours in three pints of water; strain and sweeten, and take a wineglass full three times per day.

PERUVIAN BARK

Ton. Ast. and Febrifuge.

It is excellent in weak stomachs, and for gently correcting an overflow of urine. Persons who are unable to retain their urine will find this bark very efficacious. It is often recommended by the faculty to be taken in port wine, though we consider it far preferable to be taken alone, more particularly when the stomach is in a weakened condition. It is also a valuable remedy in intermittent fevers. An infusion may be made by simmering two ounces of the bark in three pints of water down to one quart, the dose is half-wineglass full three or four times per day.

SWEET FLAG

It is an aromatic stimulant and tonic, and very useful in weakness of the digestive organs, loss of appetite and general weakness. Combined with peruvian bark, it has been of great service in the low stages of malignant fevers. The roots powdered and infused, or decocted, has cured the colic, flatulence and ague. The dose of the root is from 20 to 40 grains; of the infusion 1 to 2 ounces and the tincture 1 to drachms.

GENTIAN ROOT

This is an excellent tonic for general debility; it also possesses superior anti-septic properties as well as febrific. It is a good remedy to add to purgative medicines to prevent their debilitating effects. All purgatives should be so compounded. The best way to prepare a concentrated infusion is to pour boiling hot water upon 4 ounces of gentian with 2 ounces of dried orange peel, a sufficiency of water should be used to exhaust the strength in the root and peel, and then boil in a porcelain pot, until there is left half pint of the concentrated infusion to every ounce of gentian used. Then to each half-pint add half-ounce of alcohol. The effect of the alcohol is to coagulate it from a quantity of jelly-looking substance, which must be separated by straining. This is one of the best strengtheners of the human system. The dose is one teaspoonful in an ounce of water.

COLUMBA ROOT

This is a mild tonic and good for weak stomachs. It may be taken alone or combined with others; We use it in affections of the liver and spleen. It is very useful in jaundice, more particularly when combined with gentian and barberry bark. Simmer one ounce of the above in three pints of water for two hours; strain and sweeten; dose, one-half wineglass three times a day.

BITTER ROOT (Indian Physic)

It is called also Wandering Milk Weed. The root is

very bitter and a sovereign corrector of the bile. It removes constipation, causing the bowels to move in a natural way. A strong infusion, with hot water, if drank freely, will operate as a cathartic, sometimes as an emetic. It is sure to throw off fever in its first stage, and should be used in all cases of constipation. It is used by us in connection with other herbs.

ALTERATIVES

These are medicines which are called by many blood sweetners, or in other words purify the blood by changing the morbid action of the secretions. They are beneficial in eruptions of the skin; but it must also be remembered that they are beneficial only in proportion to the stimulating effect they produce upon the various organs of the body, so as to invigorate and give tone to the various organs which separate, or, in other words, secrete the impurities from the blood, as perspiration, urine, bile, etc. What is it but the healthy action of all the organs whose office it is to separate and remove the waste matter, which it is constantly receiving? If persons would prevent the many diseases which afflict the human body, more particularly diseases of the skin- they must see that the digestive organs are in proper tune, for there in the stomach is the center of sympathy, where your food is prepared to build good or bad blood. And it is a positive necessity that the skin should be kept clean, so that the waste matter shall not be taken up, or reabsorbed, and passed again into the blood, which will again be impregnated with impurities that ought to have passed off through their natural channels, so that too much stress cannot be put upon the necessity of the use of the cold water bath, friction by rubbing, and outdoor exercise, with plenty of vegetables and a very limited amount of fresh meat.

SASSAFRAS

Anti-scor., Alter., Stim. and Aperient.

The bark of the Sassafras is very useful in rheumatism and all eruptive diseases; aged people will find this a very useful remedy for all aches and pains consequent upon the loss of vitality with declining years. It has a sweet aromatic taste, and an odor like that of fennel, owing to the presence of a volatile oil, in which its virtues chiefly reside, though it contains fatty matter, resin, gum, albumen, wax, etc. It makes a very nutritious beverage; and has been found to recruit strength, when exhausted, more rapidly than either cocoa or chocolate, sit lighter on the stomach than either animal or vegetable jellies. It is a first rate sweetener of the blood.

SCABIOUS

There are several kinds of Scabious, but those we describe are the most familiar. Common field scabious have many hairy, soft, whitish green leaves, some of which are very small, and rough on the edges, others have hairy green leaves deeply and finely divided and branched a little; they are naked and bare of leaves for a good space, but on the tops stand round heads of flowers, of a pale bluish color. The flowers the size of a small walnut, and composed of many little ones. The root is large, white and thick, growing deep in the ground. There is a field Scabious differing in nothing from the former, but in being smaller. The corn Scabious differs little from the first, but it is larger in all respects, and the flowers more inclined to purple, the root is a surface creeper. The first grows usually in meadows. The second in dry fields, but not so plentifully as the former. The third in standing corn or wheat, or fallow fields, and flowers in July and August. Scabious is used for the cure of coughs, shortness of breath, and other diseases of the chest

and lungs, and is a good expectorant. It has been used very extensively
for the cure of asthma and pleurisy, and inward abscesses, ulcers, etc. The decoction purifies the blood, and makes a good wash externally for old sores and cutaneous eruptions. The green herb bruised and applied to any carbuncle or sore, is found by certain experience to dissolve and break it in a few hours. The decoction will cure pains and stitches in the side, and will take away scabs and cure itch. The juice made into an ointment with fresh lard, is effectual for the same purpose. The dried root given in powder, promotes sweat, and is useful in fevers, and by curative properties tends to heal all inward wounds. A syrup made of the juice with honey has the same effect. The juice of Scabious, with the powder of borax and samphire, cleanses the skin of the face, or other parts of the body from freckles, pimples, etc. The head washed with the warm decoction, cleanses it from scurf, sores, dandruff and itch.

SCURVY GRASS

Anti-scorbutic and Diuretic.

This plant possesses anti-scorbutic and diuretic properties. It has superior powers as a blood cleanser. The juice or decoction taken in the spring every morning fasting, will answer this purpose. It removes obstructions in the liver and spleen, and restores the body to a more lively color. It makes a good wash for the mouth and gums in scurvy. It may be mixed with orange juice which makes it more agreeable.

NETTLE

It is common everywhere, and needs no description. It is a valuable plant, and not appreciated as it should be. The young shoots in spring, form a wholesome vegetable, boiled like other green table vegetables, and eaten. It is a good blood remedy, and removes the phlegmatic superfluity left in the body by winter. Cancer has often yielded to the juice of nettles, by taking the juice inwardly, and mixing a little oil of laudanum with the juice and rubbing the parts outwardly. The use of limbs, lost by rheumatism have been restored by the same preparation. Excessive corpulence may be reduced by taking a few of the seeds once a day for a few weeks. For Goiter take a few seeds night and morning, powdered; it makes a good gargle for it, as well as a poultice of the leaves. Nettle is anti-asthmatic; the juice of the roots or leaves made into an electuary with honey and sugar opens the bronchial tubes of the lungs, the stoppage of which causes wheezing, shortness of breath, etc. It stimulates expectoration of phlegm very freely. For retention of urine, and for gravel and stone. The flowers and seed should be made into a conserve. The decoction of the plant kills worms in children. The seeds serve to fatten fowls, and a good stimulant for horses.

FLUELLEN

This herb is also a good remedy in connection with others of its class, for canker, secondary symptoms and an excellent remedy for the regulation of the menstrual flow in woman. It is very effectual both to heal as well as close green wounds, to cleanse and heal foul ulcers, sores, etc. It makes a good ointment, made with lard, for cuts, bruises, etc.

ARCHANGEL

Alt. Anti-Bil. Bal.

There are two kinds of this herb, growing often near each other; they are very much alike, but very different in taste. One is a bitter, the other of a balsamic taste. They may be used together, as the one removes canker, the other is a corrector of the bile. So that you may use your own judgment whether it will answer your case or not. Nature is bountiful in her gifts to choose from.

CLIVERS

Anti-Scor. and Diu.

It is known by so many names the world over; the common clivers has rough square, green stalks; it is a creeper, or climber, and will stick to anything it touches. It grows in damp places, among bushes and old clearings, and flowers in July and August. It exercises great control over diseases of the skin. A strong decoction is very useful in bloody flux, and it will also, if continued persistently to be taken, prevent a person from making too much fat. An ointment made from the herb is good to relieve hard swellings or kernels in the throat. Its diuretic properties are appropriate to remove speedily the slimy matter and obstructions from the kidneys and bladder. Always make the infusion in cold water, if the herb is green.

WOOD SANICLE

A very pretty plant growing in shady places. It has large round leaves, standing upon long, brownish stalks, every one deeply cut, or divided into five or six parts; some are cut like the leaf of crow's foot, or butter cup, and finely dented at the edges, smooth and of a dark, shining color, inclining to red at the rim, from which rise up small, round green stalks, without any joint or leaf except at the top, where it branches into flowers, having a leaf divided into three or four parts at that joint with the flowers, which are small and white, starting out of small round greenish yellow heads in a tuft, in which afterwards are the seeds, which are small round burrs, almost like the leaves of clivers, and will adhere to anything they touch. It has a fibrous root. This herb has no equal in the cure of scrofula, tumors, green wounds, or inward bleeding, there is no better herb to be found that can give such instant help when the disease falls upon the lungs or throat. It will cure malignant ulcers in the throat and mouth by gargling with the decoction of the leaves and roots made in water, sweetened with honey. For scurvy we recommend it to be combined with sarsaparilla, sassafras and dock root, for which it is almost a specific taken in that form.

MEADOW FERN

Aromatic, Alt.

Meadow fern burrs, made into the form of an ointment, with fresh lard, is an excellent remedy for the itch, or any external poison, and bad humors or sores. It is also good for salt rheum, more particularly if a decoction is taken at the same time prepared from the leaves, buds, or burrs.

GUIACUM, OR LIGNUM VITAE TREE

The wood and gum are both used for the cure of chronic, cutaneous and syphilitic diseases, as well as rheumatism, in connection with the compound, decoction of sarsaparilla. It is recommended alone as being very useful in rheumatism, but we would recommend it to be combined with other articles.

BURDOCK ROOT

Anti-Scor. and Diu.

Burdock root has been successfully used in many chronic diseases, as scurvy, rheumatism and other impurities in the blood. It is a good diuretic, and used in connection with green broom, has cured bad cases of dropsy where other powerful medicines have been ineffectually used; as a blood purifier, it ranks as one of the best. A very useful medicine may be prepared from the following ingredients, viz: Burdock root, two ounces; yellow dock root, 2 ounces; slippery elm bark, 1 ounce; mezeroon root, 1 ounce; licorice juice, 1 ounce. Simmer gently in three pints of water down to 2 pints; when cold, strain, and add one quarter ounce of iodide potass. A wineglass full may be taken three times per day. This preparation is one of the best blood purifiers we know of. We have cured many bad cases of scurvy by the aid of this preparation, and the use of the vapor bath to assist nature to perform a cure, keeping the bowels regular with our stomach pill, the formula of which will be given under that head, or may be had of the author.

PRINCESS PINE

Alt, Diu.

It is an excellent remedy for scrofula. It is also very useful in cancers, tumors and diseases of the urinary organs. Princess Pine and the roots of the Wild Lettuce dried out and powdered together are excellent to cure all bad humors. Take a teaspoonful of the powder in a glass of hot water and bathe the affected parts with it. It is also very useful to restore weak nerves.

SELF-HEAL

Prunella Vulgaris.

Self-heal is a small, low creeping herb, having small roundish-pointed leaves of a dark green color, without dents on the edges, from which rise square, hairy stalks a foot high, which spread into branches with small leaves set thereon, up to the tops. Flowers small, and of a bluish purple, they stand in a kind of short spikes or heads. It is found in the woods and fields and flowers in June and July. The herb, as its name implies, is a special remedy for green wounds and ulcers; it even cleanses and heals them. It is also used as a syrup for inward sores or wounds, more particularly when combined with sanicle and other wound herbs. The Germans have a proverb which is verified in this, that he needs neither physician nor surgeon who has self-heal and sanicle to cure himself.

SARSAPARILLA (Similax.)

Alt Deo. and Dem.

Sarsaparilla is very useful in skin diseases. It possesses the power of improving the general state of the system, and restoring the vigor to the constitution when broken down, and is a general corrector of all the secretions of the body. There are 11 kinds of sarsaparilla, differing very widely in quality. The kind with a reddish brown bark is much stronger and better than any of the others. A very large quantity of the commonest kind is sold at the present day, in consequence of its low price; but those who regard it their chief professional duty to restore their patients to health as speedily as possible will shun the use of worthless ingredients in their medicines, which should not only be of the best kind, but also fresh, so that you may gain the full strength of the herb root or bark, etc.

SUDORIFICS

Are medicines which produce perspiration. When this effect is produced in a great degree, so that sweat is collected in drops on the surface of the skin, the medicines or means employed are designated sudorifics.

YARROW

There is scarcely another herb in the whole botanic practice that has done so much good as yarrow. It has prevented more doctor's bills, which is saying a good deal, since medical men have learned the art of making large figures- than all they have written on medical science. The whole plant is used, and it is so common it needs no description. It is one of the very best remedies for a cold, taken in the form of a tea, with ginger. It is also a good remedy for whites, in women, and combined with poplar bark and gold seal in equal parts, is very useful in piles. The juice is a specific to stay hemorrhage in the bowels. It is good also for bloody flux and profuse menstruation. An ointment made of it cures green wounds and sores. It arrests the falling off of the hair by washing the head with a decoction of it. It will also relieve those who can not retain their water. The leaves make a good tobacco, mixed with rosemary and currant leaves. The leaves chewed will ease the tooth-ache.

ROSEMARY

Ton., Ast , Diaphoretic.

Rosemary is comforting to the stomach and brain; the oil mixed with spirits of wine forms what is called the oil of rosemary. A tea made from the leaves is good for pains in the head. It makes a good wash combined with yarrow leaves and southern-wood. The following ingredients make one of the most valuable preparations for preserving the hair: we know, viz: Two ounces rosemary leaves, three ounces southern wood and one ounce of yarrow leaves; simmer the whole in three pints of water, gently, down to one quart; when cool, strain through a cloth; then add four ounces of compound spirits of ammonia, and four ounces of olive oil. Apply with a sponge at bedtime.

HYSSOP

Exp. Diap. Sud.

Is a good remedy for coughs and colds and it also makes a good drink in typhus, and low fevers, keeping the pores of the skin gently open.

FEATHERFEW

Ner. Stom. Stim.

Is serviceable in female obstructions and hysteria. It makes a good drink for mothers before and after confinement.

PLEURISY ROOT

Sudorific, Diuretic, Laxative, Tonic and Anti-Spasmodic.

Pleurisy root is a sovereign remedy for pleurisy, or inflammation, difficulty of breathing, tightness of the chest asthma and catarrh affections of the lungs. It is employed with advantage in fevers of all kinds, whether high or low or sinking typhus, keeping the skin generally moist. It makes a good remedy and is a specific in measles, being far superior to saffron.

CHAMOMILE

Diap. Tonic.

They are very useful in weak stomachs, and if taken freely will remove a slight cold; they make a good fomentation in cases of inflammation; they form a good assistant while taking an emetic, and will cure the itch by washing the parts effected.

PURGATIVES

Purgatives are agents which quicken the perisaltic motion- first, by stimulating the muscular fibers of the intestines, and the contents of the bowels are quickly discharged; second, by stimulating the exalent vessels terminating in the inner coat of the intestines and the mouth of the excretory ducts of the mucous glands; and, also, by stimulating the liver, pancreas, etc., so as to produce a more copious flow of their secretions into the intestines.

RHUBARB (India, Turkey or China)

Turkey is the best. India ranks next and China about on a par with that grown in our own country, called Turkey rhubarb. Rhubarb operates first by evacuating the intestinal canal, and then gently astringing or restoring the tone of it. It must be regulated according to circumstances.

JALAP

A-bil. Cath.

The jalap root comes from South America and is said to take its name from a city in Mexico. It is a stimulant cathartic, acting briskly on the bowels, especially the larger bowels, and although occasionally griping severely, yet safe and efficacious. It is a good purgative in the torpid state of the intestines in low spirits, melancholy and slimy state of the bowels, to which children are often troubled with. The dose is from ten grains to half drachm, given in the form of powder, pills, or bolus, fasting, with a little cream tartar and ginger.

ALOES

Stim. Cath.

The juice of the aloe resolves itself into a very little resin, is used as a stimulating cathartic, acting chiefly on the lower bowels; it is a tonic when taken in small doses. There are three kinds, the socotrine, or cape, being the best, as it is the mildest in its effects. For indigestion, lowness of spirits and jaundice aloes are serviceable, as they stimulate action on the rectum, as well as on the uterus, therefore must not be prescribed in piles, nor in pregnancy. Pills are the best form for taking it, combined with other purgatives, to prevent after constipation. As they act on the colon and rectum, they expel seat worms. Dose from three to ten grains if taken alone.

SENNA LEAVES

This is a most certain and effective purge and mild in its action upon the bowels. It should always be infused and combined with ginger to prevent griping; one ounce steeped in half-pint of hot water, with a teaspoonful of ginger powdered; strain, and take a cupful going to bed. This is far superior to salts.

MOUNTAIN FLAX

This is a mild purgative, and very useful for children. It is also very useful for dropsy of the bowels, rheumatic pains and catarrhal affections. It has also given relief in bilious disorders. It is very good for habitual costiveness taken in infusion.

EXTRACT OF BUTTERNUT

It is a very gentle and mild, but effective purgative; it has the good property of not binding after it has operated. It makes a good medicine for worms in children. The green shell of the nut bruised forms a good blister; when applied it should be covered with a wet bandage and kept moist; the blister will rise in about three hours, and is superior to that produced by Spanish flies. It is a very good anti-bilious remedy, for which it is greatly celebrated.

ALDER TREE (common)

Deob. and Refri.

The common alder tree is well known. Its stem is treelike and full of branches; the bark rough and dark brown color. Its flowers white and berries are black. It grows in moist places, and flowers in May and the seed is ripe in July. A decoction of the leaves is good for burns and inflammation, and especially for inflammation of the breast. The juice of the bark or berries make a good purge, and in small doses prove an efficacious deobstruant, promoting the fluid secretions. The leaves put under the bare feet, galled with traveling, greatly refresh them.

ASTRINGENTS

Medicines which render the solids more dense and firm by contracting the fibers. They lessen excessive discharges by contracting the parts they come in contact, lessen morbid sensibility or excitability; hence they tend indirectly to restore the health impaired by these causes. Employed in the form of a poultice, they have a tendency to dry and shrivel up the skin, and for that reason should not be employed as poultices where it is necessary to promote suppuration and hasten the discharge of matter. Astringents and gelatinous substances employed to nourish the sick should not be taken into the stomach at the same time, as the tannin of the astringents combines with the gelatin and forms a solid indigestible mass. Vegetable astringents may be properly termed detergent, or cleansing medicines, for they have the effect to cleanse as well as contract the inner or mucous coat of the stomach and bowels; hence the great value and importance of this class of remedies. For effectually removing the morbic substance which collects on the tongue and roof of the mouth in fevers, some astringent tea may be used; and it is by a similar way that astringent medicines act on the mucous membrane of the stomach and bowels, removing its morbid and vitiated secretions, and enabling it to perform its functions in a natural and healthy manner. The word canker is freely used by some persons, but is not generally understood. Canker signifies anything that corrupts, corrodes, or destroys, therefore the anti-canker medicines are the astringents. It is always well to take, such as bayberry tea, before taking an emetic, in order to detach the vitiated matter from the mucous coat of the stomach previous to vomiting. Astringents are useful in hemorrhage of the stomach, lungs and bowels, and are indispensable in diarrhea and dysentery, but should be used in connection with some stimulant, such as ginger or cayenne. In many diseases they are specially beneficial, as will be shown in their proper place.

BISTORT

Is one of the most powerful astringents in nature. It is good for all bleeding, whether internally or externally; it is useful in diabetes in conjunction with tonics. The decoction is good as an injection in flour albus, or whites, and gleet. It makes a good wash for running sores.

BAYBERRY (Bark or Root)

Is decidedly the best cleansing medicine ever discovered. It makes a good wash for old sores, as well as a good gargle for putrid sore throats. When taken inwardly it produces a stimulating effect upon the mouth, and leaves it clean and moist; it cleanses the inner coat of the stomach; is a valuable medicine in diarrhea and dysentery, and a sovereign remedy in scrofulous ulceration, used in the form of a poultice. The wax, which is found upon the berries, makes a valuable ointment for all eruptions of the skin. It is the principle ingredient in the celebrated composition powder, so well known the world over.

WITCH HAZEL

A tea made of the leaves may be taken freely with advantage. "It is the best thing for bleeding of the stomach," and also in complaints of the bowels I have used it with good effect.

SQUAW VINE

Indian name, Cocash. The roots and tops are used. I have given it in what is known as canker rash and effected a cure. It is good also for rheumatism, or for nervous affection, and made with hot water and spirit is very useful for cold hands and feet.

QUINCE TREE

Cydonia Vulgaris: Is so well known it requires no description, the fruit of which imparts a pleasant flavor to pastry. A syrup made of quinces is a pleasant addition to beverages during sickness. The juice of the quince made into a syrup with sugar is excellent to stop vomiting, and to strengthen the stomach. The green fruit is astringent and restrains flux and diarrhea. The syrup made of the juice is still more so. The mucilage is used externally as an emollient and sheathing application to cracked lips and nipples. Bandolene, used by hairdressers as a cement for dressing the hair in braids, is merely this mucilage evaporated. It also appears to have narcotic properties, for a strong decoction sweetened with honey destroys flies. If a little vinegar be added it promotes the appetite; some spices being added, it revives fainting spirits and removes obstructions from the liver. If you would add a purge, add honey instead of sugar; and if more laxative, rhubarb; and if more forcible to bind, use the unripe quinces.

PRIVET

Legistrum Vulgare: A wild shrub, growing five or six feet high, The flowers are small and white. The fruit is a black berry. The tops are used, and are best when the flowers are in bud. A strong infusion in water, with the addition of a little honey and wine, make an excellent wash for the mouth, and throat when sore and inflamed, and when the gums are apt to bleed. It also makes a good wash for all sores.

SUMAC

It has been very effectually used by me for the cure of dysentery: The bark is used; also the leaves and berries, when ripe; sweetened, it makes a pleasant drink in fever. It is an excellent gargle for sore throats, especially after mercurial salivation; it is also good for stranguary, or obstructed urine.

MARSH ROSEMARY

This is good for canker and sore mouth, and should be used in connection with Bayberry; a larger proportion of Bayberry than Rosemary should be used in such cases.

HEMLOCK

The common Hemlock requires no description; the inner bark is used; an infusion of the bark in hot water is a good medicine for canker and diseases arising from it, and combined with Lily Root and Bayberry Bark is a sovereign remedy for obstructions of the urinary passages, and for rheumatism, caused by uric acid forming in the blood.

BLACKBERRY, ROOT AND LEAVES

A mild astringent and very useful for looseness of the bowels, more particularly in children and those of a weakly habit.

GUM CATECHU

This is the most powerful astringent in nature. It is useful in all cases of bowel complaints, not attended with inflammation. It is used extensively for cholera in connection with stimulants and carminitives, prepared in the form of a tincture, and which will be given its proper place.

TORMENTAL

Tormentilla Erecta: Sometimes called Septfoil. It has reddish, slender branches rising from the root, lying on the ground, not quite upright, with many short leaves closer to the stalks than Cinquefoil, (which this is very like), with the foot stalk compassing the branches in several places, but those that grows on the ground are set upon long foot-stalks, which leaves are like those of cinquefoil, but long and less dented about the edges; some divide into five and some into seven, on account of which it is called Septfoil; yet many have six and some eight, according to the fertility of the soil.

The flowers are small, of a beautiful shining yellow; they grow on slender footstalks, in shape and color like the crow-foot flowers, but more beautiful and less of them. The root is short and thick, brown without, and reddish within. It grows in woods and shady places. Tormental is most excellent to stay all kinds of fluxes of blood. A decoction of the root sweetened with molasses, and the patient given a vapor bath, is a good remedy for expelling venom, poison, fever, or other contagious diseases, such as small pox, measles, etc. Taken inwardly, it is a sovereign remedy for flux of the stomach, spleen or bowels; and the juice wonderfully opens obstructions of the liver and lungs, and thereby arrests the yellow jaundice. It is also good for tooth-ache, combined with alum, by mixing equal parts and filling the cavity. A plaster made of the root and vinegar is good for those who cannot retain their urine. It should be externally applied to the back against the kidneys. The powder of the root mixed with ointments and plasters, that are applied to sores and wounds, increases their power to heal. The leaves and root bruised, and mixed with vinegar, is good for scrofulous sores on the neck, or behind the ears, etc. A strong decoction makes a good wash for inflamed eyes. It is, in fact, one of the most powerful, yet mild astringents operating, without producing any stimulant effect, and well calculated to check all diarrhea where the general excitement is considerable. For this purpose it must be combined with some simple tonic, such as Poplar Bark. It is also beneficial in cases of weak bowels liable to frequent relaxations, although they may be of short duration. In case of kidney troubles, combine with Tag Alder. I could relate many wonderful cures performed by the aid of this root, which have resisted the treatment of the physicians and their remedies, and ofttimes given up as incurable.

The most frightful ulcers of the legs have yielded to its use, which were considered incurable, as well as the most scorbutic ulcers, fluxes, etc. Persons troubled with ague will find a strong decoction of the root sweetened with honey one of the best remedies. The decoction is made by boiling two ounces of the bruised root in thirty ounces of water till it is reduced one-third, and strained. Dose, half wineglass full two or three times per day.

FOR CANKER

Take of Bayberry Bark, White Pond Lily Root, and

the inner bark of the Hemlock two ounces, or equal parts of each, pounded and well mixed together, and simmer in three pints of water down to one quart, sweeten, and take a wineglass full three times a day. If the above cannot be had, take as a substitute Sumac, (bark, or berries), red raspberry or witch hazel leaves, or marsh rosemary; either of the articles described, are all good for canker, and may be used together or separate. When the violence of the disease requires a course of medicine, add one ounce of American Valerian to the above mentioned compound: continue for several weeks, add one ounce of licorice root to one quart of the mixture.

VERMIFUGES

These are remedies which destroy or expel worms.

WORMWOOD

This is a wild plant growing by the way-sides and clearings. It has a strong smell and is intensely bitter. It is a good tonic, and useful in some stages of indigestion and low spirits. Its powers in expelling worms have long been known. It will frequently bring away the small seat worms in large quantities. An infusion may be made of the plant, and an ounce to an ounce and a half given two or three times a day. It makes a good fomentation in all kinds of swellings. Salt of wormwood is pure carbonate of potass obtained from the ashes of this and other plants. In small doses, say 8 or 10 grains, dissolved in a little rose-water, and taken twice a day, is very useful in indigestion and bilious complaints, attended with acidity of the stomach.

PINK ROOT

Spigelia Marilandica.

This root is a native of the southern states, and is

one of the most powerful athelmentics to be found in nature's laboratory for the expulsion of lumbrici worms from the alimentary canal. It was first introduced by the Cherokee Indians among the whites as a vermifuge. The following is the manner of preparing it: One ounce of Pink Root, simmer gently in one quart of water for two hours; Dose, half to a wineglass full every two hours, with a dose of senna and ginger every third hour until it operates. Infused in wine, it has proved very useful in intermittent fevers.

WORMSEED

Vermifuge and Aromatic.

This herb grows wild and is considered a specific for worms. Eight or ten drops of the oil may be given twice a day, or it may be given in powder, from half to a teaspoonful two or three times a day in molasses or syrup.

MALE FERN (Root)

This is a good remedy for destroying the tape-worm, and is a safe vermifuge. If taken two or three times per day, in teaspoonful doses, and a brisk purge of senna and ginger in the morning before breakfast and followed for several mornings, it will generally have the desired effect of removing the tape-worm without any danger. Let the food be light while taking this class of medicines

KOUSSO BRAYERA

Vermifuge.

This is considered by many as a specific for tape-worm, and has been used with great success in ridding the system of that terrible destroyer of health, ever since its introduction into this country from the east. It seldom fails to effect a cure in a few days if taken in the following manner: Dose, for the first morning, a cupful of senna tea with a little ginger, as hot as can be drank, fasting; second morning, half-ounce of powdered Rousso, infused in a half-pint of boiling water, with a tablespoonful of lemon juice added, and sweetened with sugar; let it be drank during the hour before breakfast; third morning, same as the first. It is seldom the dose requires repeating, but have never known the second to fail to effect a cure.

NERVINES

Nervines are medicines which have the effect of composing or tranquilizing the nerves without impairing or deadening sensibility.

SKULLCAP (Scutellaria)

This is a valuable nervine, and one so often used for nervous excitability; it is often used with good results in palsy of the limbs, more particularly when used in connection with some mild tonic. We have used it with good effect in delirium tremens, fits and convulsions. In any of the above complaints pour one pint of boiling water on one ounce of the powder and let it settle. Take a wineglass full three times a day.

LADIES' SLIPPER

Nervine.

Valerian is a good nervine, and as it possesses no narcotic properties, it may be used freely without apprehension of danger in all nervous diseases, such as nervous head-ache, epilepsy, delirium tremens, restlessness and low fevers; having the effect to quiet the nerves, allay pain and promote sleep. Dose, same as skullcap.

THE OCCULT FAMILY PHYSICIAN

MAPLE BARK

Tonic and Nervine.

The bark of the maple in decoction strengthens the nervous system, and is also a good remedy for strengthening the liver and spleen, and will ease pains in the sides and chest.

ASFOETIDA

Exp. Ner. Stim. and Anti-Spas.

This is the resin extracted from the root of the shrub which grows in this country, as well as some parts of Europe. It has a very strong, unpleasant odor, but it is a very good nerve tonic; it is also useful for a weak state of the stomach, and in hysteria, colic and spasmodic asthma. The better way to take it is in pill form, using the pure gum, after eating.

EMMENAGOGUES

This class of medicines promote menstruation, when arrested by causes over which we have no control.

PENNYROYAL

This is a favorite female herb; will generally remove obstructions peculiar to females, arising from obstructed perspiration. It should never be boiled, always infused, as the volatile essences escape by boiling.

MOTHER WORT

It is one of the most useful herbs to relieve

obstructed menstruation; it is useful in chronic head-ache, hysteria and nervousness.

TANSY

This also is considered a very useful herb in combination with Mother Wort for green sickness, or chlorisis, and imperfect menstruation.

SAVINE

Juniperus Sabina: It grows two or three feet high. Its leaves are numerous and firmly planted. The flowers are very small, of a yellowish color, producing a blackish purple berry. It is a native of the southern states and many parts of Europe, but may be cultivated in gardens. It has powerful cathartic, emmenagogue and stimulant properties, acting especially on the uterus of the female. Those who use it for the purpose of abortion run some risk of their lives; in many cases it has ruined the constitution, through ignorance of knowing how to use it, by taking large doses for that purpose. It is a powerful irritant and sometimes proves fatal. Yet it indicates a more powerful determination to the uterus than most other plants of its nature, but taken as an emmenagogue, in small doses of half-drachm to a drachm, in dry powder, twice a day, will be found very beneficial in amenorrhoea. Fresh savine leaves bruised, quarter of a pound; hog's lard, one pound; yellow wax, quarter of a pound. Boil the leaves in the lard till they become crisp, then filter, with expression; add the wax and melt them together. This is a valuable ointment for drawing purposes.

COTTON BARK OF ROOT

The bark of the root is used extensively by the people of the south for the purpose of relieving suppressed menstruation, as well as a more forcing medicine where it is needed, but in chlorisis it should never be used, as it would do more harm than good; it is a very active drug, given in fluid extract for the above-mentioned purposes.

SOUTHERN WOOD

This herb also enjoys some reputation as an emmenagogue, combined with ground pine, or Mother Wort; it is a very useful herb to relieve the violent pains felt in the hips, sides, loins, back and thighs, as well as the sensation of bearing down or forcing.

EXPECTORANTS, DEMULCENTS, EMOLLIENTS AND PECTORAL

These are medicines which promote the expulsion of mucous from the trachea or windpipe, or any accumulation of morbid matter, which may have fastened upon the passages to the lungs, they have a soothing and softening effect, emetics may be classed under this head. Demulcents and Emollients, are those substances which envelope, or surround, and guard acrid matter, and cover the surfaces that are too sensible to external impressions. They are useful in diarrhea and dysentery, and in the form of poultices; they are also beneficial in Coughs, irritation of the lungs, or inflammation of the urinary passages.

LOBELIA INFLATA

Lobelia is a powerful expectorant, but as we have already given a description of this herb prior, it will be all sufficient.

ELECAMPANE ROOT

Inula Helenium: It is a large downy perennial plant, it grows wild in some places, it grows four or five feet high, and the stalk is round, thick and reddish. The flower large and yellow. The leaves large, rough and pointed. Flowers on the top of branches, something like a double sunflower. The fresh roots are used for windy stomach, stitches or pain in the side caused by the spleen; and will relieve coughs, shortness of breath, and wheezing in the lungs. The dried root powdered and mixed with honey or sugar, will serve the same purpose. And if infused in hot water, and mixed with honey, it will cure the hooping cough. The decoction, or the juice in honey, is good for those who spit blood. Boiled in vinegar, beaten and mixed together with fresh lard, is an excellent remedy for the itch. The virtue is in the root of this plant.

HOREHOUND

Expectorant and Tonic

There are two kinds of Horehound, white and black; the white is the one we here recommend. It is an old remedy, but nevertheless a good one. It promotes expectoration; is good in hoarseness, coughs, and pulmonary diseases. As a decoction it is useful in female weakness, removing obstructions, etc. The dose is a handful of leaves to sufficient boiling water, cover up close, let it stand for half-hour, strain and sweeten with molasses or honey, a wine-glassful may be taken three or four times a day. In coughs, add a teaspoonful of vinegar to the dose.

MOUSE EAR

Expectorant, nervine and anti-spasmodic.

This is a good remedy for croup in children, as well as whooping cough, by adding a few drops of the tincture of lobelia to the dose. It is also useful in dry tickling coughs and affections of the lungs, more particularly if combined with others in this class.

SKUNK CABBAGE

Expectorant, nervine and anti-spasmodic.

This is a good remedy in asthma, coughs, and catarrhal affections of the lungs. It is also good in fevers combined with pleurisy root and a small quantity of lobelia, a teaspoonful may be taken two or three times per day, or oftener if the case demands it.

COMFREY ROOT

Expectorant and Demulcent.

The root of *sympthytum officinalis,* is the kind we recommend, and bears a white flower, long and hollow, it relieves spitting of blood, and bloody urine. A syrup made from the root will not fail to cure inward hurts, bruises, wounds, and ulcers of the lungs, and loosens tough phlegm. It will relieve a cold in the head, cures bloody flux, whites in females, and check profuse menstruation. It makes a splendid poultice, in knitting broken bones. It also makes a good remedy for sore nipples. It is good in moist ulcers, gangrene and mortification, the syrup is prepared as follows: Take three ounces of green comfrey root, clean and sliced, one ounce white pond lily, one horehound, one cudweed, one wound wort, and two ounces ginger root; boil the whole gently in two quarts of water for one hour, then pour it hot on two nutmegs powdered fine, a level teaspoonful of cayenne, and one pound of loaf sugar, strain, and bottle for use. The dose is half a wine-glassful three or four times per day, or less, where the case requires it.

POLYBODY ROOT

This is a perennial herb of the fern tribe, it is a small herb consisting of nothing but roots and leaves, bearing neither stalk, flower or seed. The root only is used; it is a safe and gentle purge, used as a decoction it promotes the flow of urine. It is also good in jaundice, dropsy and will remove phlegm copiously combined with mallows, it removes hardness of the spleen, stitches in the side and colic. The fresh roots beaten into powder and mixed with honey, and applied to the nose, will cure Polypus.

ALL-HEAL, OR WOUND WORT

This is a very useful herb. It grows in wet ground, has five or six pairs of winged leaves. The flowers are yellow and stand in clusters around the stalk at the joints, and bear light yellow fiat seeds, bitter in taste. The root is perennial, long, thick and a hot, biting taste. As its name implies, it is a good wound herb; the leaves being bruised, and applied to a fresh wound, will stop the bleeding and cure the wound. It relieves gout, cramps, and pains in the joints, vertigo, falling sickness, and made into an ointment cures the itch.

ALMONDS

Sweet Almonds are emollient and demulcent, and an emulsion of them is useful in bronchial diseases, in tickling coughs, hoarseness, dysentery and affections of the urinary organs.

LIVERWORT

Lichen Vulgaris: There are many species of this plant. The common Liverwort grows close and spreads much upon the ground in moist and shady places, with many small and green leaves, or rather sticking flat to one another, very unevenly cut in on the edges and crumpled, from among which arise small slender stalks an inch or two high at most, bearing small star-like flowers at the top; the roots are very fine and small. It is a good herb for most diseases of the liver. It is to be given in strong decoction and is very effectual in yellow jaundice. It is good also for diseased kidneys and whites, and somewhat useful in the first stages of consumption. It stays the spreading of ringworm and other running sores and scabs, and is an excellent remedy to fortify the liver against disease and make it impregnable. It grows in damp places.

LUNGWORT

Lungwort derives its name from its supposed efficacy in diseases of the lungs. It is mucilaginous and rather astringent, and is regarded as emollient and pectoral. It is good, therefore, for coughs, wheezing and shortness of breath. An infusion is the best way of taking it. It is more effectual combined with other expectorants.

MAIDEN HAIR (Golden)

Its medicinal virtues are much the same as those of the White Maiden Hair; it makes an excellent wash for the hair, cleansing it, and promoting the growth. It grows in dry, shady places, and bears a small yellow flower or head. The Black Maiden Hair is a very useful diuretic and acts powerfully on the urine.

COLT'S FOOT

Tussilago, Farfara.

Colt's Foot shoots up a slender stalk with small yellowish flowers, the stalk being somewhat thick and hairy; these come before the leaves. The root is small and white, spreading much under ground. It grows in wet, sandy places, and flowers in May. It is a most valuable herb, and is not sufficiently appreciated. Its powerful expectorant qualities have rendered it celebrated as a remedy for coughs. It abounds with mucilage; it is slightly bitter and possesses tonic and demulcent properties. A decoction is made by boiling a handful of leaves in a quart of water till reduced to a pint, sweetened with rock candy, and acidified with a slice of lemon. A wineglass full to be taken three or four times per day. This is very useful in coughs and in all diseases of the lungs, shortness of breath, wheezing, etc. It thickens the expectoration when thin, and of course must allay inflammation. The syrup of Colt's Foot is one of the best known remedies for chronic bronchitis. Boiled in milk it is excellent for consumptive patients with distressing cough. It is a good remedy, combined with Wormwood, for calculous complaints; sweetened with honey, it is good for colds and asthma. The leaves of the Colt's Foot, combined with Eyebright, Buckbean, Betony, Rosemary, Thyme, Lavender and Chamomile Flowers make a first-class smoking tobacco. Persons troubled with asthma will find relief by using the above compound. Let the Colt's Foot preponderate.

MARSHMALLOWS

Dem. Emoll. and Pectoral.

Marshmallows are so common they need little description. The root is the most used. It has emollient and demulcent properties, which render it useful in inflammations and irritations of the alimentary canal and of the urinary and respiratory organs. The dry roots boiled in water give out half their weight of a gummy matter like starch. It is excellent given in decoction for calculous disorders. It also promotes urine and will bring away gravel and stone. It cures stranguary and is good in coughs. It is a gentle aperient, easing pains in the bowels. Boiled in milk it relieves diseases of the chest and lungs, if taken frequently. A poultice made of the leaves, boiled and bruised, with some barley flour and oil of roses, is a good remedy for hard tumors, inflammations and swellings, and against hardness of the liver or spleen, being applied to the parts.

The juice of the mallow boiled in sweet oil is good for roughness of the skin, scurf in the head, dandruff, or dry scabs in the head; if anointed with it or washed with the decoction it will preserve the hair from falling off. The roots are the most useful for coughs, shortness of breath, hoarseness. The Indians use the bruised mallows in bloody flux with wonderful effect. It seldom fails to effect a cure in from two to three days. About 5 ounces of the dried root to 2 or 3 ounces of raisins, freed from the seeds, put into 5 pints of water and boiled down to three pints and then strained, is a good form of administering it, combined with a little licorice juice.

SLIPPERY ELM

Dem. and Emoll.

The bark of the elm, so universally known, requires no description. There is no better remedy; taken as a gruel, for inflammation of the stomach, bowels, kidneys or bladder, it contains more gelatin than any of its class. It sheathes the part, or covers it from irritation. A gruel made with milk makes a nice supper for weak and consumptive patients. A tea made from the bark will ease tickling coughs. It makes one of the best poultices for boils, carbuncles and inflammations. It is also good for scalding urine, and to bathe the parts where broken out with sores.

ALDER TREE (Black)

Anti-Bilious and Herpetic

The alder is more like a shrub than a tree and seldom grows to a great size. The branches are smooth, slender and of a dark brown or purple color. The inner bark is yellow; when infused produces a saffron color. The leaves resemble those of the ordinary alder tree, or the female dogberry tree: The flowers are white, which produce small round berries, first green and blackish when ripe. A decoction of the inner bark is useful in bilious affections and the dropsy. The bark, compounded with acrimony and fennel, and taken every morning, is very effectual against jaundice and dropsy. A decoction of the dried bark removes obstructions in the liver and spleen, and removes the hardness of the former. The outward bark is astringent and is useful in fluxes. The outer bark boiled in vinegar kills lice and will cure the itch, and removes scabs. It also makes a good wash for the teeth, easing tooth-ache and fastening loose teeth. As a decoction, it is an excellent drink in the beginning of spring. On account of its purifying and exhilarating qualities it ought to be esteemed as a jewel.

ALKANET

Deob. Dis. Hep.

Alkanet is very serviceable in old ulcers, inflammation, burns and erysipelas. The best way is to make it in to an ointment, or make a vinegar of it. It is useful in yellow jaundice, spleen and gravel. Will cure the bite of venomous snakes when applied to the wound green. It stays fluxes and ring worms; when taken in decoction it will drive out the small pox and measles, and in ointment is excellent for green wounds, etc.

LEOPARD'S BANE

Its botanical name is Arnica Montana. It is a very common perennial plant in many parts of Europe, where it has long been medicinally used. The flowers are yellow; compound consisting entirely of tubular florets and are distinguished from other similar flowers, (with which they are often mixed, from ignorance or fraud,) by the common calyx, which is shorter than the florets, and consist entirely of lancet shaped scales, lying parallel and close to each other, of a green color, with purple points. These flowers have a slightly bitter taste, combined with a degree of acrimony, and when rubbed with the fingers have a somewhat aromatic smell. They contain a great deal of resin and a portion of essential oil. We very seldom use this herb internally, but as an external application it is beneficially used in the treatment of wounds and contusions.

MEADOW SAFFRON

Colchinus Antumnale: It is a perennial bulbous rooted plant growing in wet meadows, flowering in September. It is a native of many parts of this country. It is poisonous to animals of all classes, but their instinct causes them to avoid the foliage in the fields. It is very useful in humeral asthma and for the cure of gout and rheumatism, in both of which it is a specific.

MARIGOLD

Calendula Officinalis: They need no description they are so common. They strengthen the heart exceedingly and are very expulsive and little less effectual in bringing out the small pox and measles than saffron. The juice of the marigold leaves mixed with vinegar, and any hot swelling bathed with it, instantly gives relief. The flowers mixed with alcohol make a good liniment. The tincture is useful for curing warts. It may be used as a lotion by adding 10 drops of the tincture to 2 ounces of water. It is special service in severe cuts and lacerations; they are speedily relieved by it, and pain and bleeding arrested by its external application. It will heal wounds so completely, when properly applied, as to leave no scar; if there should be any, it is scarcely perceptible. It has a wonderful power to heal without producing suppuration, or the formation of matter; it contracts the mouth of the small arteries which may have been cut across longitudinally.

Where the cut cannot be closed it may be washed

with the lotion; it may be diluted as above, or be used in a pure state with perfect safety. It may be applied by cloths and bandages, as the case may require.

DISEASES

THEIR CAUSE AND CURE

INDIGESTION - Dyspepsia.

Indigestion is the most common disease with which civilized people are afflicted, and it assumes so many forms that it is beyond our power to describe it. The stomach being the center of sympathy, all the other organs suffer more or less from the disease. It mostly commences in a slow and gradual manner, giving the first warning by an uneasy sensation at the pit of the stomach, especially after eating, accompanied with costiveness or relax in the bowels, cold hands and feet, sometimes thirst, nausea, and vomiting. These are succeeded by a long train of symptoms, such as nervousness, flatulence, heartburn, tenderness at the region of the stomach, chilliness, rising of wind in the throat, distentions of the bowels, despondency, imperfect vision, and many other symptoms almost too numerous to enumerate.

The causes that produce these effects are various. The most frequent causes are intemperance in eating, want of proper and invigorating exercise, drinking to excess such drinks that inflame the mucus membrane of the stomach and brain, and last but not least, the taking strong powerful medicines prescribed by the family physician, such as Oculus Indicus berries, Nux-vomica, Tobacco, etc. We desire to say, that tobacco has such a baneful effect, and in fact, is a virulent poison to the dyspeptic, that even physicians seldom prescribe it now as a remedy. The use of tobacco injures the power of digestion, by causing the person using it to spit out that saliva which they ought to swallow, and hence produces flatulence, which they take it to prevent. Another cause, is neglecting to chew the food, thereby causing the stomach to have more than its share of the work of assimilation to perform. Too much animal food, particularly when taken late at night, is another prolific source of indigestion. Whatever the cause may be, you cannot expect to find a cure as long as the cause is suffered to remain. The amount of nutriment to be found in the various vegetable substances suitable for nourishing the body, are all sufficient for those who suffer from this distressing complaint. Grain, and other nutritious vegetables, yield us, not only in starch, sugar and gum, the carbon which protects our organs from the action of oxygen, and produces in the organism the heat which is essential to life, but also in the form of vegetable fibrin, albumen and caseine, our blood from which the other parts of our body are developed. These important products of vegetation are especially abundant in the seeds of the different kinds of grain, and of peas, beans, and lentils, and in the roots and juices of what are commonly called vegetables.

We perceive, therefore, that many of the vegetables used as aliment contain more nutriment than meat; besides they are sooner digested, and the sooner made into blood, and more nourishment to the body is the result. The following table, will show the amount of nutriment each article contains; and will be useful, to those who are compelled to live on a vegetable diet. One hundred pounds of brown bread contains... 80 lbs. of nutriment.

Do.	meat (average) 35
Do.	beans 85
Do.	potatoes 25
Do.	carrots 14
Do.	peas 84
Do.	oatmeal 91
Do.	rice 92
Do.	pearl barley 84
Do.	wheat 85

We have briefly pointed out the causes which produce this fashionable disease; to those not troubled with indigestion it will show a preventative which is better than cure. The treatment we recommend to be adopted to those suffering from indigestion will vary according to the symptoms, age of the patient, as well as the conditions of life. For recent cases in young people take the following:

Centaury 1 ounce.
Acrimony 1 ounce.
Columbia root 1 ounce.
Raspberry leaves 1 ounce.

Add three pints of water, simmer gently down to one quart, strain, then add a teaspoonful of Fluid Extract of Ginger, and a teaspoonful of Bi-carbonate of Soda. Take a wineglass full three times per day. Or where there is nervous debility in persons who are advanced in years, take the following:

Peruvian bark 1 ounce.
Juniper berries 1 ounce.
Gentian root 1 ounce.
Bitter root 1 ounce.
Queen of the Meadows 1 ounce.

Simmer as the last. Take a wineglass full three times a day, and regulate the bowels as much as possible with diet, exercise, and external friction, where there is flatulence, or acid stomach, take a half teaspoonful of Bi-Carbonate of Soda in a little water night and morning.

PLEURISY AND BRONCHITIS

Inflammation of the lining, or membrane of the lungs, called the "Pleura," and the air passages called the "Bronchi." These forms of inflammatory disease may be known by the pains which generally accompany them, either in one or both sides, sometimes extending throughout the chest, which increase upon coughing, or upon taking a long breath. The patient does not lie upon the side affected, but generally upon his back, as the easiest position to lie. The pain commences with a violent pricking about the short ribs, which extends itself toward the back bone and shoulder blade, when inflammation attacks the substance of the lungs. The matter expectorated is often mixed with blood. The pulse is quick and hard, the urine high colored, and accompanied with chills, fever, thirst and restlessness. The treatment to be adopted should be to relieve the pressure from the parts affected. First, give a vapor bath, and bathe the parts with chamomile and cayenne tea, and if the pain continues, prepare the following medicine: Blue Vervain, Elder Flowers, Pleurisy Root, Summer Savory, Licorice Root; of each one ounce, and add one-half teaspoonful each of Cayenne and Lobelia; simmer for half hour in three pints of water; strain, and sweeten with molasses. The dose is a wineglass full every hour, until the patient is in a sweat; then reduce the quantity to one-half until relieved; at the same time lay cloths over the parts affected, wet with the chamomile and cayenne tea; let it be as hot as can be borne without scalding, and lay a dry cloth outside, so that it may retain the heat longer. Continue the above treatment for a few hours, and we have no fear for the result.

INFLAMMATION OF THE BOWELS

Peritonitis and Enteritis.

This is one of the most dangerous forms of inflammatory disease, and requires prompt and efficient treatment. It is not necessary for us to specify the particular part of the bowels, but as the symptoms are seen and felt, the same treatment is requisite in all. It commences with chills, pain and hardness of the belly, which gradually increasing, becomes most intense, with hot skin, great thirst, vomiting, with short and heavy breathing. The tongue is red around the edges and covered with a dark brownish, coat of thick mucous in the center, bowels very costive, and the patient lies upon the back with knees drawn up towards the body. Immediately on discovering the attack, place a hot brick, with a cloth wet with vinegar wrapped around it, and a dry flannel outside, to the feet, with bottles of hot water to the sides and an injection of Marshmallow or Slippery Elm, made to the consistency of thin gruel, with a teaspoonful of powdered ginger added, and thrown into the bowels, warm; a large hot poultice must be prepared of oatmeal and mustard; twice as much oatmeal as mustard should be used; then placed between two cloths and placed over the whole abdomen, after which a medicine may be prepared and given as follows:

Wild Mint 1 ounce.
Queen of the Meadow 1 ounce.
St. John's Wort 1 ounce.
Slippery Elm Bark 1 ounce.
Sweet Flag Root 1 ounce.

Add two quarts of water and boil down to one quart. Take one ounce of myrrh powder, mix with two tablespoonfuls of warm water, then pour the quart of hot herb tea on to it, with a tablespoon full of ginger added, and give a wineglass full every half hour; as soon as possible renew your poultice as soon as it becomes cool. Sometimes the feces in the bowels becomes lodged in the lower part, so hard, that it is difficult to give the enema; in that case a small sperm candle, warmed at the end and smeared with sweet oil, should be passed up the seat as far as possible. Remember that the bowels must be relieved, for much depends upon this. Should the pains continue, apply hot fomentation of hops, and bear in mind that the only chance of success lies in relieving the parts of the pressure, and in getting a passage for the blood through the inflamed and congested vessels which line the whole of the bowels. It is a disease which in some instances proves fatal in a few hours; but rarely, unless there has been long previous excess or negligence. If the pains abate gradually; if natural stools are passed; if a universal sweat, attended with firm equal pulse and copious discharge of urine come on, a favorable termination may be expected. If, on the other hand, there is a sudden remission of pain, sinking of features, and distension of the belly, an unfavorable termination may be expected. All our aims should be directed to bring about the "favorable termination." This is all any physician can do; and he who devotes himself to the work is the most skillful in the profession of physic, whether a collegian or not. So, reader, see that you remove the feces from the bowels by injections, for on this depends the life of your patient; follow the treatment laid down here and we have no fear or the rest. I wish to further caution the patient; that after the disease is conquered, be careful not to make too free; rest for awhile, take light nourishing food, avoid fat meat, strong drinks and cold. Should there be a tendency to constipation after the disease has gone off, relieve the bowels with the injection, and use some mild tonic, such as Columbia Root, Gentian Root, Myrrh or White Poplar Bark; any of these will answer the purpose to assist to restore the stomach to its natural tone.

INFLAMMATION OF THE LUNGS (Pneumonia)

Inflammation of the lungs generally commences with cold chills, a hot and dry skin, hurried and laborious breathing, tightness of the chest, distressing cough, scanty and high-colored water and dull pain in the chest. The tongue is dry and of a dark color. The pain is sometimes peculiarly acute, and at other times heavy and dull, either on the left or right side, under the breast or collar bone, spine or shoulder blades. At other times there is little or no pain, when the real nature of the case may be known by the constant difficulty of breathing, painful cough and presence of fever. The most common causes of this disease, are exposure, violent exercise, etc. This disease seems to baffle the medical profession, for their success in treating it is certainly not flattering, It is lamentable to read the statistics of those who have died under this disease, many of whom might have been saved under a proper treatment. Look for one moment at the old system of treating this disease by the so-called regular physicians. The first thing they do, is to bleed copiously by the use of the lancet, as well as cupping, says Dr. Graham; also, apply 10 to 20 leaches over the chest, and after the fever subsides apply blisters, over the chest and between the shoulders. And he goes on further, and states that calomel and opium cannot be dispensed with. We ask any sensible person if this treatment in itself is not sufficient to kill an healthy person, and if the patient should rally, they then repeat the dose; hence the reason for such great mortality among those unfortunate enough to have been afflicted with pneumonia. There is no disease so thoroughly under control of the botanic practice as inflammation of the lungs. It is here that cayenne pepper works wonders, and have often cured this disease with nothing more than cayenne and raspberry leaves. But our plan is to give, as near as possible, a remedy useful to all alike, as well as simple. Take the following:

Slippery Elm Bark, Crushed 1 ounce.
Thyme 1 ounce.
Coltsfoot Flowers 1 ounce.
Hyssop 1 ounce.
Marsh Mallow 1 ounce.

Simmer in two quarts of water, down to three pints; strain, and add a teaspoonful of cayenne. Take a wineglass full every half hour. Apply hot bran poultices, or chamomile scalded with vinegar, or take two flannels, put two ounces of chamomile in each and heat them in the oven, changing every 10 minutes, till the violence of the symptoms abates. If the bowels are confined, give an injection of gum myrrh, Turkey rhubarb and ginger powder; half a teaspoonful of each article; pour half-pint of hot water on them; mix them well, and inject into the bowels. Apply hot stones or bottles to the feet; and, if possible, give a vapor bath. If this treatment is persevered in, we have no fear of the result.

INFLAMMATION OF THE KIDNEYS (Nephritis)

This affection commences with chills, a shooting or dull pain in the small of the back, and a benumbed sensation in the thigh of the side affected. There is a desire to make water, with great difficulty in passing it, and the urine is ofttimes red. If both the kidneys are affected the urine is entirely stopped, and the perspiration acquires a urinous smell. Fever and vomiting are not unusual. This disease may arise from injuries, strains in the back, or from colds, induced by wearing or sleeping in damp linen. Give a steam bath, take cayenne and prickly ash, equal parts, make a strong decoction, and lay cloths wrung out over the parts affected, as hot as can be borne, and then a dry flannel outside of that, then prepare the following tea:

Tansy 1 ounce.
Dandelion roots 1 ounce,
Uva Ursi 1 ounce.
Marsh Mallow roots 1 ounce.
Burdock seeds 1 ounce.

Add two quarts of water, boil down to one quart; strain, add a teaspoonful of ginger, and sweeten with molasses. Give a wineglass full every hour for the first four hours; then every two hours. Wash the patient down in tepid water, vinegar and cayenne, followed by friction over the parts affected. Let the food be light, and the drink linseed or slippery elm tea. Keep the bowels moderately open with senna and ginger. The result, a cure.

INFLAMMATION OF THE WOMB (Hystertia)

This disease is ushered in by fever, a feeling of cold, and severe pains across the small of the back and in the region of the womb; severe cold, or adhesion of the placenta to the womb. This form of disease requires very active treatment and considerable care, on account of the extremely sensitive nature of the part affected. Give a steam bath for several days, 20 minutes duration each time. To sit over a decoction of chamomile and poppy heads as warm as convenient, or to apply hot flannels steeped in the same to the lower part of the abdomen once or twice a day, will assist to ease the pain. The following medicine should also be taken:

Pellitory 1 ounce
Comfrey root 1 ounce
Buchu leaves 1 ounce
White Poplar Bark 1 ounce
Uva Ursi 1 ounce

Boil in two quarts of water, down to one quart. Strain; take a wineglass full three or four times per day.

INFLAMMATION OF THE BRAIN (Phrenitis)

The membranes of the brain may be the seat of the inflammation, or it may attack the substance of the brain itself. It generally commences with a sensation of fullness in the head and flushing in the face, severe head-ache, throbbing in the temples, redness in the eyes, dryness of skin, extreme thirst, intolerance of light and sound and violent delirium. The pain is dull or shooting, according as the substances of the brain or its membranes are affected, and in some cases occupies the whole of the head. The stomach and bowels are more or less disordered, and the liver often in a torpid state, as indicated by the whitish color of the stools. As the disease advances the delirium increases in violence, and the patient talks in a wild, incoherent strain. The breathing is slow and often laborious, imperfect vision, deafness, difficulty of swallowing and convulsions. Where the head is shaved, blistered, leeched, cupped, bled and dosed with poisons, as under the old system of treatment, the disease often proves fatal in five or six days. The disease may be produced by external injuries on the head, suppression of the menses, changes from heat to cold, checked perspiration, drunkenness, intemperance in eating, and protracted study. The unfavorable symptoms are weak pulse, cold and clammy skin, grinding of the teeth, bleeding from the bowels, red, yellow, or dark-colored urine. The treatment in this disease must be prompt and energetic. There is no time to lose, for unless we recall the blood from the head, or in other words, restore the equilibrium to the circulation, the inflammation may reach that stage that it would be impossible for medicine to have any effect. As soon as possible place the feet in hot water and mustard twice a day; hot bricks with cloths wet with vinegar must be applied to the feet, and an injection given every three hours, as directed for inflammation of the lungs. A cloth dipped in cold vinegar and water must be applied to the head, and the following medicine administered:

> Catsup 1 ounce.
> Rosemary 1 ounce.
> Red Sage 1 ounce.
> Marjoram 1 ounce.
> Wood Betany 1 ounce.
> Pennyroyal 1 ounce.

Add three pints of water, simmer down to a quart ; strain, and pour boiling hot upon one ounce of skullcap and a half-teaspoonful of cayenne pepper; let it settle, and give a wine-glassful every hour. Children half quantity, omit the pepper. You cannot give too much, as the medicines are in accord with the laws of nature.

THE OCCULT FAMILY PHYSICIAN

INFLAMMATION OF THE SPLEEN (Splenitis)

This like inflammation of the liver, comes on with intermittent sensations of heat and cold; thirst, fever, loss of strength, wakefulness, sickness, and vomiting of a green bilious matter, often with faintness and bleeding from the nostrils. There is a severe pain in the left side extending generally to the bowels, diaphragm, and left shoulder, and like the liver, the spleen often becomes enlarged and indurated or hardened. The treatment must be the same as that here recommended for the liver.

INFLAMMATION OF THE LIVER (hepatitis)

An inflammation of the liver is denoted by tension, soreness, and pain in the right side like that of pleurisy, with pain about the right shoulder, difficulty of lying on the left side, and a short dry cough. It is not so common in this section of the country, as in the southern states, and in fact, all warm climates. There are many it is true who suffer from disease of the liver, but in our experience it is of the chronic kind, and almost always connected with some other disease. As a rule, when not chronic we have been enabled to cure it in a few days, by prompt treatment, but it often terminates in abscesses, and what is called scirrhus, or hardness of the liver. Then it becomes chronic, for which treatment must be according. Our treatment is to resort to the injection, as recommended in inflammation of the bladder, lay on the stimulating poultice upon the part affected, and if the enema has not produced vomiting give an emetic; then give a vapor bath, (a pail of hot water, with a hot brick thrown into it, and placed under a cane-seated chair, is the poor man's bath.) Keep up the perspiration, foment the parts continually as the poultice gets cold, and gently rub in tincture of myrrh liniment alternately. As inflammation internally, is more difficult to reach, than when seated externally, your efforts to restore the circulation of the blood to its normal condition, must be persistent. For it is highly dangerous when abscess begin to form; the matter must be absorbed and carried through the system by the blood. It will be well to give our liver pills nightly. After the first night, if there appears any degree of constipation, as soon has the pain has subsided, make the following medicine.

> Bayberry bark 1 ounce.
> Liver wort 1 ounce.
> Dandelion root 1 ounce
> Yarrow 1 ounce.

Bruise and boil the bark in three pints of water down to a quart, add the herbs, and half an ounce of curative powder; see index. Mix well, let it settle, strain, add half ounce licorice juice, and when cold take half a wine-glassful from four to five times a day. If the liver has become hard, add to the medicine half an ounce of dandelion extract, and an ounce of horse radish root; a poultice of horse radish leaves should be applied over the part; salt meat should be carefully avoided, and the patient should take freely of stimulating vegetables, such as mustard and cress, water cress, etc., remember that strict adherence to the rules laid down will be necessary to overcome the difficulty, and nothing less.

INFLAMMATION OF THE STOMACH (Gastritis)

This disease is ushered in by a constant burning pain in the pit of the stomach, accompanied by fever, restlessness, depression of spirits, bowels very irregular in their action, and frequent retching after eating or drinking; the tongue is mostly red and inflamed. As the disease progresses other symptoms arise, such as difficulty of swallowing; hurried and oppressed breathing, great prostration of strength, cold clammy sweats, and delirium, sometimes fits will ensue. The welfare of the whole vital economy depends in a great measure upon the healthy condition of the stomach, first cleanse the stomach with an emetic of lobelia with a few grains of cayenne added, a teaspoonful of powdered lobelia to the half pint of boiling water, drink the clear. A fomentation of cayenne, prickly ash bark, and chamomile, half an ounce of each, with two quarts of boiling water on them, apply over the region of the stomach, with flannels wrung out of the liquor, as hot as can be borne. And as soon as the bowels are relieved, make a medicine as follows:

Marshmallows 2 ounces.
Raspberry leaves 1 ounce.
Ginger powder .5 ounce.
Sweet flag root 1 ounce.

Boil in three pints of water down to one quart, adding the ginger after the boiling, strain and sweeten with sugar, or molasses and take a wine-glassful every two hours.

QUINSY, OR INFLAMMATION OF THE THROAT
(Cynanche Tonsillaris)

Quinsy is prevalent in spring and fall, or when the weather is cold, with a heavy damp atmosphere. It generally commences with chills, succeeded by fever and pain in swallowing. As the complaint advances, swallowing becomes more difficult, the throat is often so much swollen that it renders the breathing difficult, and the patient is unable to speak. The mouth is dry and parched, and the tongue is covered with a white coating, and if the inflammation is not checked, ulcers form in the throat.

When the above symptoms make their appearance, give a vapor bath, and take the following: Sumac berries, Blood root, Raspberry leaves. Red sage. Cudweed, Slippery elm bark, simmer in two quarts of water down to one quart; then mix half ounce of gum myrrh, a tea-spoonful of rhubarb, and a tea-spoonful of ginger; mix with a little hot tea, then pour the clear hot liquor upon them; mix the whole well together, and take a wine-glassful four times a day, and be sure and use the gargle, which may be prepared as follows:

Cayenne pepper Half-an-ounce.
Salt 1 ounce.
Camphor half-a-drachm.

Pour a cup of boiling water on them, strain, add the same quantity of good cider vinegar, gargle the throat every two hours; apply a flannel round the throat, wet with the quinsy embrocation hot, every hour. Persistence in this treatment will cure the worst cases. Boil these ingredients in two quarts of water for twenty minutes, and pour the liquid upon one ounce of gum arabic, keeping it hot until the gum is dissolved. Take a wine-glassful warm with half a tea-spoonful of anti-spasmodic drops, three times a day, or oftener if required, until the pain is abated,

INFLAMMATION OF THE LEGS

Gatherings, Running Sores or Swellings.

For painful swellings, inflammation and running sores, the following is a good external remedial agent: Take the water you boil your potatoes in, and in one quart of it boil one ounce of foxglove leaves for ten minutes, then bathe the parts affected with the lotion warm for half an hour twice a day; if an open wound add one ounce of tincture of myrrh to the lotion, and keep a cloth wet on all such wounds, until cured.

INFLAMMATION OF THE EAR

This disease is mostly caused by a cold, or sometimes by an abscess formed in the ear. Delirium and convulsive disorders have been brought on by extreme pain in the ear. As soon as the disease is discovered, it should be treated as follows: A hot poultice of slippery elm, or marshmallow leaves should be applied between two cloths, or before applying the poultice, boil one ounce of rosemary leaves, strain, and while hot, pour into a long-necked bottle, and steam the side affected, for half hour, the patients at the same time having their feet in hot water and bran, and drink freely of ginger, or yarrow tea. The object should be to prevent suppuration or discharge, for there is danger when this takes place. Should it so happen, however, that the disease terminates in suppuration, follow out the treatment already recommended, and make a lotion as follows:

Bistort root 1 ounce.
Marshmallow root 1 ounce.

Boil in a pint and a half of water down to a pint; strain clear, bottle, and inject into the ear with equal parts of new milk, blood warm, five or six times a day. A small glass syringe will answer every purpose here. If the disease continues, the use of the steam bath once or twice a week, will assist to throw off the disease, a medicine may also be prepared as follows:

Skullcap powder 1 ounce.
Anti-spasmodic powder 1 ounce.
Ginger 1 ounce.

Pour three pints of boiling water on the powder; sweeten. Take a wine-glassful every two hours.

COMMON SORE THROAT

This is a common attendant upon colds, pain is experienced when attempting to swallow, and often attended with a slight cough, sometimes nausea. When such symptoms occur, put the feet in warm water, with a spoonful of mustard in the water, and take a handful, of either plantain or yarrow, pour a pint of boiling water on the herb, cover up close, let it stand for half an hour or more, strain a cupful, and drink as hot as possible, sweeten to taste, and add a little ginger which will improve the remedy. Do this going to bed, and your cold will have disappeared by the morning; if the throat is sore, rub with the quinsy liniment, or the common cayenne liniment, made by adding to half pint of cider vinegar a tea-spoonful of cayenne pepper, and a tablespoonful of common salt, shake and it is ready for use.

PUTRID SORE THROAT

Cynanche Maligna.

Malignant sore throat differs from the common quinsy in being attended with a dark crimson redness of the throat, spreading ulcerations of a dark foul appearance, greater general debility, and from the accompanying fever being of the typhus kind. It is generally contagious, and sometimes epidemic. It generally makes its appearance among those that are uncleanly, where the atmosphere is warm and damp, by the inhalation of putrefaction into the system, when the body is in a weak and relaxed condition. It is sometimes epidemic and will last for months, when it is most fatal on its first appearance, gradually becoming milder, till towards the end of the epidemic, it is attended with less danger. It gradually commences with fever, attended with nausea and vomiting, soreness and inflammation of the throat; the breath is very offensive; dark or ash colored spots appear upon the inflamed parts, which produce deep ulceration. Great prostration follows. In the worst cases, the sloughs corrode deeper and deeper, and spread throughout the whole alimentary tube, or canal, the symptoms of irritation continue to increase; incipient mortification supervenes; a severe purging comes on; and if not relieved at this stage, the patient expires. Cleanliness, a free ventilation of pure air, and fumigation with nitrous acid vapor, are indispensable, united with strong anti-septic gargles; The following treatment if persevered in, will generally effect a cure. Take a vapor bath and use the following medicine:

>Cudweed 1 ounce.
>Golden seal 1 ounce.
>Blackberry leaves 1 ounce.
>Prickly ash 1 ounce.
>Gum myrrh 1 ounce.
>Rhubarb .25 ounce.
>Cayenne 1 drachm.
>Iodide of potass 1 drachm.

Mix a little hot water with the myrrh and rhubarb; mix together; add two quarts of water and boil all the ingredients for a half hour; take a wine-glassful every three hours. Then make the following into a gargle: sumac berries and cranesbill root, of each half ounce, cayenne pepper quarter ounce, boil in one pint of water for ten minutes, strain, and when cool, add half an ounce tincture myrrh. Gargle with a table-spoonful every hour. If the bowels are sufficiently open, give a dose of bilious powder occasionally, and an emetic of lobelia and valerian once a week.

CONSUMPTION

Phthisis Pulmonalis.

This disease, which has baffled the most scientific, has often yielded to the botanic remedies. It is a disease which attacks the young and blooming, and the most lovely of our species, enters into our dwellings unseen and unlooked for, pursuing the noiseless tenor of its way, and, vampire like, drinks the vital stream, and then fans with its wings the never-dying hopes that perpetually flutter in the hectic breast. And what hopes have those who place themselves under the care of the medical profession, when nearly one and all declare that it is impossible to cure consumption? Many of their number, who stand high as an authority in physiology, make use of the following expressions: "Look at consumption. There is an affection you see day by day, cutting off individuals of every age, sex and rank; yet none has been more carefully studied upon the old plan, nor has proved a more fruitful source of dogma and disquisition. Eminent observers have described all its phenomena, even to the minutest details, but what is all this description but so much natural history? Will it throw any light on the treatment of the affection? Not a particle." Many medical writers of the old school say that "Tubercular phthisis consumption with ulcers- is an incurable disease," and Dickson, in his "Fallacies of the Faculty," says: "I do not know a single disease where two of the medical authorities agree; take consumption, as an example. Some writers assert that pulmonary consumption is only curable by mercury, while others ascribe the frequency of the disease to the use of mercury. Others, again, say that it is an inflammatory disease and should be treated by bleeding, and cooling medicines, and starving While others, equally as celebrated, claim it to be a disease of debility, and should be treated with tonics and stimulants and a generous diet. In fact, we could go on quoting the opinion of medical authors of the old school without number, each of whom differ widely as to the cause and cure of this one disease. Who can be surprised at the failure in the practice of medicine when such is the conflict of opinion among the profession on this one disease? Is it not heartrending to reflect that, with all our boasted knowledge, and all the faculties we possess- the improvement pf science and the colleges where men are trained exclusively to the healing art. thousands of our fellow mortals die annually from this disease alone? And though we confess it is a disease hard to cure, owing to the inability to gain access to the lungs, except through the circulation, it will be evident to every unbiased mind that we stand a far greater chance of success than the drug practitioners, seeing that we use no poisons but those remedies only that act in accordance with the laws of nature; and we could refer our readers to numbers of cases where we have been successful after the faculty have failed."

The causes that produce this malady are malformation of the chest, prominent and narrow chests, also various employments, such as millers, trimmers of grain, stone cutters, and those exposed to the fumes of metals or minerals, living in damp and unwholesome air, close application to study without taking proper exercise, excessive flow of menstrual flux, continuing to suckle children too long under a debilitated state, or coming from crowded assemblies into the cold air when the body is overheated. The symptoms it begins with are a short, dry cough, that at length becomes habitual; nothing is expectorated for some time except a frothy mucous; the breathing is somewhat impeded; upon the least bodily exertion oppression at the chest is experienced; the body becomes gradually leaner, with great languor; dejection of spirits and loss of appetite prevail. As the disease advances the cough is more troublesome towards night, and this not being arrested at once, in time forms small tubercles, and these increase in size until they are as large and in shape of a small bird's egg; they often exist in clusters and then run into each other and form hard yellow masses; these at length soften and change into cream color, inflame and break; and they then open into the bronchial tubes and are discharged by expectorating; they often form open ulcers, from which issue large quantities of matter, and sometimes blood; a pain is felt under the sternum bone, which prevents the patient from lying only on one side without a fit of coughing; there is also flushing of the face, the hands and feet are affected with a burning heat, and respiration is difficult. In the evening there is an increase of the symptoms and by degrees the fever assumes the hectic form, evidently of the remittent kind, and is increased twice a day, first about noon, and second about 5 or 6 o'clock, when it increases till about midnight. The urine is now of a brownish red color, the mouth is unusually moist and the thirst considerable; the tongue appears clean, but having rather a red appearance; the bowels are generally costive till towards the latter end, and then much relaxed; night sweats break out, and induce great debility. In the last stage of this disease the emaciation is so great that the patient has the appearance of a walking skeleton, his countenance is altered, his cheek bones are prominent, his eyes look hollow and languid, his hair falls off, his nails are much incurvated, and his feet are afflicted with dropsical swellings, but to the end the mind retains its vigor. There is a peculiarity attending this disease. The patient is full of hope, flattering himself with the idea of recovery; nor is he aware of danger till the very last.

To effect a cure, when the disease has not progressed too far, the patient must be washed down every morning in cold water, with a little vinegar, with a handful of salt and a teaspoonful of cayenne, and then rubbed briskly with a coarse cloth. The object of this is to stimulate the skin and remove the night sweats; this will be very refreshing. An emetic of lobelia, with a little valerian, must be taken once a week, or as often as the strength of the patient can bear, and the following medicine must be taken:

Wild Cherry Bark 2 ounces.
Horehound 2 ounces.
Vervain Blue 2 ounces.
Centuary 1 ounce.
Boneset 1 ounce.
Licorice Root 2 ounces.

Add two quarts of water, boil down to three pints; strain, then add half a teaspoonful of cayenne and two ounces of raspberry tincture of lobelia. Take a wineglass full four times a day, and take four of my cough pills, one each time you take the medicine. To quench the thirst, drink slippery elm tea, sweetened with a little honey. Take this medicine for about 10 days, and then change to the following:

Comfrey Root 2 ounces.
Mouse Ear 2 ounces.
Columba Root 1 ounce.
Wild Cherry Bark 2 ounces.
Ground Ivy 1 ounce.
White Poplar Bark 1 ounce.

Boil these in the same manner, and add the cayenne and raspberry tincture, not forgetting the cough pills, as above, and a poultice composed of barley meal mixed with warm vinegar, and applied to the chest. This treatment must be persevered in to the very letter, for the patient may depend upon it that no half measures will effect a cure; and the reason why many fail is because they expect to be cured by magic. They take a few doses, and it is either too nauseous, or some kind friend tells them it will kill them. They abandon the treatment, and the botanic system is blamed for not having cured cases where the failure is altogether attributable to the patient. Lobelia emetics are of the utmost importance, as they cleanse the whole system, removing the tough and ropy phlegm, and breaking up the ulcers; the medicines are healing, and while they correct the circulating fluids they also improve the general health. The diet must be light and nourishing- beef tea, chops grilled, sago, tapioca, and fruit jelly, instead of butter, and exercise in the open air. Removing to a dry climate from low, damp atmosphere is of the utmost importance. Intoxicating drinks must not be taken, as they inflame the lungs and aggravate the symptoms. When the patient feels languid, a dose of our composition, strained and sweetened, will have a very good effect; and now let me repeat that no half way measures will do. You must follow this advice to the letter, and with the assistance of your will power, and the medicine prescribed, combined with the rubbing morning and night, we have no fear of the result.

MORTIFICATION

The parts affected have a constant pain, and the patient suffers great anxiety; the parts soon become a livid color, and afterwards black, with a very bad. smell. If the event proves favorable the mortified parts are completely surrounded by a white line, and the dead part loosens and separates from the ulcer. If, on the contrary, the termination be fatal, the mortification rapidly extends, and,unless speedily arrested, death soon ensues. If inflammation is properly treated it seldom terminates in mortification, but when called upon to treat it, our object should be to arrest and prevent any further extension of it, by means both local and constitutional. The strength of the patient must be supported by stimulants, tonics, and nutritious diet, and take a wineglass full of brewer's yeast three or four times a day. For local application use the slippery elm powder, mixed with sufficient quantity of yeast, to the proper consistency; apply warm, and often renew. This will correct the fetidness of the parts, and assist nature to perform a cure. Wash the parts frequently with bayberry bark and white pond lily root, made into a strong decoction. Then prepare the following medicine:

Balmony 2 ounces.
Bayberry Bark of Root 1 ounce.
White Poplar Bark 1 ounce.
Cayenne Pepper .25 ounce.

Boil in three pints of water down to one quart, and add, when cold, one ounce of tincture of myrrh and half-pound of loaf sugar. Give half wineglass full every hour and apply the vapor bath to keep up the internal heat. Follow this treatment; it will never fail.

GRIPPE

This is an epidemic disease which occasionally prevails. It first makes its appearance with pains in the head, thirst, lassitude, loss of appetite, pains in the limbs, sore throat and difficulty of breathing.

Treatment: Give a Turkish or vapor bath every other day, and take the following:

Yarrow 2 ounces.
Vervain 2 ounces.
Mullen 2 ounces.
Boneset 1 ounce.
Red Sage 2 ounces.

Add two quarts of water, boil down to three pints; strain, then add one ounce fluid extract of ginger; sweeten with honey or molasses. Take a wineglass full three times per day, hot; keep the bowels open, and let the diet be light.

AMAUROSIS

Amaurosis is a partial or total loss of vision, arising from paralysis of the optic nerves or retina; and this is produced by congestion of the vessels of the part or minute alteration of its structure. The eyes look almost natural, the pupil is generally dilated and motionless. There is frequently the sensation as if a cloud was before the eyes. This disease, like cataract, is extremely difficult to cure. Means must be used to excite a healthy action in the system, by the aid of vegetable tonics and stimulants. Take tincture of cayenne, gum myrrh and blood root, of each a quarter of an ounce. Mix these in a full gill of strong raspberry leaf tea; when cold, strain through a thick cloth; drop 10 drops in the eye three times a day, and take the medicine recommended under inflammation of the eyes.

LUMBAGO

This disease is a species of rheumatism that is more particularly concentrated in the small of the back, or the lower part of the spine. It causes great weakness or pain, with difficulty of stooping and often of walking. Treatment: Rub the back with tincture of cayenne and prickly ash berries, and take the following:

Pinus Canadensis 2 ounces.
Uva Ursi 2 ounces.
Tansy 2 ounces.
Juniper Berries 2 ounces.

Add two quarts of water, boil down to one; strain; then add a teaspoonful of cayenne. Take a wineglass full four times a day, and wear a belt next to the skin, made of two parts of red flannel, with a piece of manila paper, sewn between the parts.

INVOLUNTARY FLOW OF URINE

When this affection is not a symptom of another disorder, or debility in the system, such as stone in the bladder, palsy, etc., it can be easily cured. Prepare the following:

Bistort Root 1 ounce.
White Pond Lily Root 1 ounce.
Sumac Berries 1 ounce.
White Poplar Bark 1 ounce.
Rock Candy 2 ounces.

Bruise the roots and berries, and put down in three pints of water; simmer gently down to one quart. Pour this on one ounce of bethroot powder; strain when cold, and take a wineglass full three times a day. The patient should be rubbed across the loins every morning with salt and water. Let the patient accustom themselves to sleep either on their side or face downwards.

CROUP

Cynanchi Trachealis

This is an inflammatory affection of the windpipe, or trachea, which extends in most instances to the air passages of the lungs. Children are mostly subject to it, but occasionally it attacks adults. Croup is mostly sudden in its attacks, usually coming on in the night, but there is often cough and hoarseness impeding respiration. When the disease assumes its ordinary violence the cough is loud and ringing, the breathing much oppressed, accompanied with a wheezing sound: There is often danger attending this disease, as a large quantity of lymph is poured out into the windpipe causing an obstruction to the passage of air to and from the lungs. Let the feet be put in warm water and mustard; apply a flannel wrung out of hot cayenne tea; a teaspoonful to the pint of boiling vinegar and water, giving at the same time a teaspoonful of croup syrup, which will be named in the compounds, and which every family will do well to have by them, as a very few doses is sufficient to ensure a cure even in the most difficult cases.

ASTHMA

This disease is of the same class as the last; it is spasmodic, and generally seizes the patient after the first sleep. All sorts of remedies have been tried in vain for the cure of this most distressing disease, but we have found no better remedy than the lobelia herb, prepared in the form of an acid tincture, which will be named in the compounds. The smoking of stramonium leaves with a few aniseeds often gives relief, alone, but we depend principally on the tincture acid of lobelia.

WHOOPING COUGH

This is a disease generally confined to childhood. It seldom proves fatal under proper treatment, excepting, there is a weak constitution, and a relaxed habit of body. It commences with difficulty of breathing, thirst, fever, etc., and ofttimes will remain, despite the most active exertion. The causes are numerous, and in the cure of this disease we must begin by seeking to restore the balance. Immerse the body in a warm bath for about five minutes. It should then be wiped perfectly dry, and put to bed with hot bottles of water, placed to the feet and sides, and a poultice of barley meal and ginger put around the throat, giving the compound lobelia cough syrup three or four times per day.

DIPHTHERIA

This disease, which has devastated so many families- proving fatal in such numerous instances- is one of the most alarming of those arising from the inhalation of putrefaction into the system combined with cold, or when the system is in a debilitated condition. In its treatment we commence by placing the feet of the patient in hot water and mustard, bathing up to the knees, for half hour, twice a day; and gargling the throat with the following gargle every half hour.

Blood root, powdered 1 ounce. Put in half pint boiling water, stir till cold, and then add half pint best cider vinegar, give the patients strong sage tea to drink until they perspire freely.

COW POX, OR VACCINATION

The origin of this disease is both curious and interesting, and would of itself be sufficient for our book if the prejudices, persecution, and opposition connected with it were fully recorded. As our purpose is only to speak of the pathology and cure, we cannot find space to dwell further on the matter. It is an eruptive disease, but of a much milder form than the small pox, although the symptoms are sometimes nearly as severe, and bear a striking resemblance to it, so much so, that the most observant may often mistake it. The pustules generally fall off earlier, nor do they pit the skin in the same manner. There is no doubt, in the present state of society, some advantages connected with vaccination, and most certainly some disadvantages. In the first place, it is acknowledged by many old school practitioners to be uncertain. The worst forms of scrofula and venereal are often transmitted by this process of inoculation, and therefore on this account object to it. The treatment in this disease is to keep up a gentle perspiration on the surface, attend to the bowels, and give a gentle emetic or two. If there be fever, restlessness, and itching, give a bath in the same way as recommended for small pox. The milder mode of treatment answers here also; proper attention should be paid to ventilation and cleanliness; where this is attended to there will be no danger.

CHICKEN POX

This is a mild form of disease, and one most common to children. It is generally preceded by slight fever similar to that of cow pox, and the eruptions make their appearance about the third day, in small dark colored inflamed spots, about the breast and back; a small vesicle or pimple rises in the center, with a whitish transparent covering; about the second day after the eruption, the spots appear like small bladders; filled with a thin fluid of a soft nature, and these change again and become turbid and hard about the fourth day; and afterwards assume a crusted appearance, and begin to break, and about the eighth or ninth day gradually fall off altogether. The only thing necessary is to attend simply to the bowels and skin, keeping up a gentle perspiration. Should it require a more active treatment, let it be carried out. Pennyroyal, ground ivy, or hyssop tea, stimulated with Mrs Matteson's fever powder, will generally throw off the disease in a few days. If the bowels fail to move, give the slippery elm and ginger injection, and be careful not to expose the child too early in the open air, for if it takes cold when the body has been previously weakened, there will probably not be sufficient power remaining to throw it off; this should always be looked to,

SMALL POX (Variola)

There are two species of this disease- the distinct and the confluent. The distinct are when they appear singly on the body; confluent when the pustules run into each other. This disease makes its appearance with a considerable degree of drowsiness, loss of appetite, cold hands and feet, thirst and nausea, redness of the eyes, soreness of the throat, and pain in the head, back and loins. In children, convulsions sometimes take place previous to the eruptions, which generally show themselves about the third or fourth day, though sometimes it is longer before they appear; they first appear in small red spots, similar to flea bites, on the neck, breast and face, and continue to increase in number; the face swells considerable; with hoarseness and difficulty in swallowing, and a discharge of saliva from the mouth. From the appearance of the pustules, generally about the fourth day to that of the eleventh, they pass through different stages; first, filling gradually with a whitish matter, which changes as it advances to a yellow cast. In the more violent cases they turn brown, with little black spots in the center. This is an unfavorable sign, particularly if the tongue be covered with a thick brown crust, and cold shiverings with delirium and grinding of the teeth supervene. The mode of treatment should be as follows: Place the patient in a clean, warm bed, in a well ventilated room. The bedding should be changed every day, with bedding dried in the open air, if possible, and prepare the following:

Wood Sage 1 ounce.
Clivers 1 ounce.
Vervain 1 ounce.
Ground Ivy 1 ounce.
Marigold flowers 1 ounce.
Saracenica root 1 ounce.

Simmer in two quarts of water, down to three pints; pour this boiling hot upon one ounce of bayberry powder. Give a wineglass full every hour; keep the bowels moderately open; do not purge until the disease has passed the height, about the eighth day. Keep clean with a warm wash twice a day; water and castile soap; be sure and keep your patient warm day and night, with a fire in the room. When the pustules are full, apply with a feather, cream and fine oatmeal gruel in equal parts; on the hands and face often; this treatment will prevent pitting. Then mix equal parts of lime water and olive oil. This is excellent when the pock is shelling off the body. If they fester and bleed apply Fuller's earth, with warm water. Cover the parts with it often. It will take away any inflammation and heal the wounds and prevent pitting. Give slippery elm tea to drink, when thirsty, with light diet.

SPECIFIC AGAINST SMALL POX

The Saracenica root is considered by the Indians of Nova Scotia and others as a specific for this dreadful disease. The Saracenia root, or Indian Cup, is a native of Nova Scotia, found in swamps and mossbogs. It is supposed to act by neutralizing the virus in the blood, rendering it inert and harmless; and that this is its action may be gathered from the fact that if either vaccine or variolous matter be washed with an infusion of larrachria, it is deprived of its contagious property. Moreover, the eruption, even if confluent, on its disappearance leaves no trace behind. The root of the plant is the part employed. The dose of the powder is a dessert spoonful, simmered in a pint of water down to half pint. Make two doses of this and drink through the day. Sugar should not be used.

MEASLES (Rubeola)

This is an inflammatory disease, and is often communicated by contagion, and if not properly treated, other symptoms make their appearance, such as dropsy, asthma, sore eyes, running of the ears, and many other complaints. They make their appearance over the face and body, but particularly about the neck and breast, the eruptions are similar to flea bites, and produce a little swelling of the face, with redness of the eyes, soreness of the throat, sickness and vomiting. About the sixth or seventh day from the time of sickness; the eruptions begin to turn pale, and by the tenth or eleventh day the skin assumes its natural appearance; but if care is not taken the symptoms will return with redoubled violence. When the eruptions suddenly fall in, and the patient is seized with delirium, or the measles too soon turn pale, the patient becoming restless, extremely weak, and, experience great difficulty in swallowing, the symptoms are unfavorable. A tea made from marigold and tormentil root should be given freely, applying the quinsy embrocation, about the throat, and the feet placed in hot water and mustard.

When black spots appear among the measles, the case assumes a serious aspect. Those who die of measles generally expire on the ninth day; but often this disease is followed by pneumonia, or inflammation of the lungs. In which case treat the patient as under that head in this book. Since measles are highly infectious, and often prevail epidemically; it would be well to take a wine-glassful of vervain tea three times a day, as a preventative among members of families. When this disease shows itself, place the feet of the patient in warm water and mustard, and give plentifully of vervain and marigold or saffron tea, keep the patient warm; keep a fire in the room to prevent chills, and be sure to attend-to the bowels; if costive, give a dose of senna and ginger tea. And if the above treatment is carried out, we have no fear for the result.

FEVERS

GENERAL REMARKS

Fever constitutes the largest proportion or class of diseases that assail the human family, and it seems to be regarded by the medical profession as a profound and impenetrable mystery. Many treatises have been written on fevers that have been simply works of imagination. Fancy sketches, or profound metaphysical abstractions, filled with subtleties and hypothetical reasonings. From a retrospective glance over the history of our science, says some writers of the old school, we are forced to acknowledge that there is perhaps no subject which is more eminently calculated to humble the pride of human reason than fever in relation to itself. Pathology has been in a continual state of revolution and instability. The human mind has been engaged with it for over three thousand years. Theories have risen and fallen in a continued and rapid succession, and its votaries to yield it faith. But the stream of time has hitherto overturned ail those unsubstantial, though often elaborate fabrics. We may compare the old school physician to a blind man armed with a club, who comes to interfere between nature and disease. If he strikes the disease, he kills the disease; if he strikes nature, he kills nature or the patient. "Fever has baffled the learned college of physicians who have tried all their efforts and spent all their skill in vain. It must run its course, is the common sentiment. If one mode of treatment fails they try another and another, till the exhausted imagination, the worn out resources of the *Materia Medica,* and the dying patient arrest the hand of the experimenter (and we might have said tormentor),or nature triumphs over medicine and disease."

THE OCCULT FAMILY PHYSICIAN

The practice of medicine is perhaps the only instance in which man profits by his blunders and mistakes. The very medicines which aggravate and protract the malady bind a laurel on the professor's brow. When at last the sick is saved, by the vitality of the patient, or the living power of nature struggling against death and the physician, he receiving all the credit of a miraculous cure, he is lauded to the skies for delivering the sick from a detail of the most deadly symptoms of misery, when he himself had caused them, and out of which they never would have arisen but by the restorative efforts of that spirit power which at once triumphed over poison, disease and death. With the acknowledgments of the medical profession, that they are totally ignorant of the nature of fever, how are they to prescribe for it with safety or success? It need not surprise or astonish us, at the explanation of some of the learned professors, who state that fever and febrile diseases constitute the great outlets of human life, and continue to be almost as fatal as in the time of Sydenham, who estimated that eight out of every nine of all the deaths occurring in the human family were caused by febrile complaints. Is it any wonder that fever should be the scourge of the human race? Many of these professors must have visited the Indian camps, and have observed how, in the space of a single day, intermittent and other fevers have been broken up by their practitioners with such mathematical precision and certainty that if the same cures had been performed by the college professor, he, no doubt, would have been granted a diploma of merit for the wonderful discovery he had made. The mode of treatment adopted by the Indians was always in accord with nature's law. Purging, sweating and vomiting is the usual course adopted by them. What is fever? In nearly all cases it is a last effort of nature to restore the body to health. The fevered body is in a state of fermentation-incipient putrefaction By fermentation you deprive barley of its vitality, and it would then soon become rotten. By the action of heat, however, you arrest the putrefaction, and with certain chemical combinations you produce beer.

When you have a joint of meat in danger of becoming tainted, you put it in the oven, and by thus subjecting it to the greater heat than the fermenting fever heat, which is destroying its vitality, you preserve it sweet for a time. You have, therefore, to do the same with fever. The normal temperature of a person's blood is 98 degrees. Fever heat is 112 degrees. All you have to do, then, to kill the fever is to subject the patient to a greater heat than 112 degrees.

Furnace men, sugar bakers and others who are subjected to great heat, and who drink large quantities of meal and water, or milk and water, instead of beer, are not subject to fever. It cannot fasten on them. They, as a rule, are strong, healthy and vigorous. On careful inquiry you will find this correct. We could continue to enumerate cases of this kind, but will close our remarks by giving one more: Take for instance the person whose lungs are ulcerated and congested and whose stomach is almost powerless. In fact, he is a miracle to his medical attendant and others who know him, he is kept alive solely by his Turkish bath, wherein his body is daily subjected to a heat of from 200 to 250 degrees. The greater the heat the purer the atmosphere; and whilst the greatest heat can be most easily endured, there is no danger from it. It may seem almost incredible, but it is so, and no fever can touch the case in point, nor any infectious disease. Fevers are caused by cold, and the inhalation of putrefaction into the system. It is necessary that there should be a certain temperature of the body to maintain a healthy state of the system. Persons, however, will bear a great degree of heat or cold if applied to the system gradually, but, on the contrary, if suddenly applied, the most serious effects follow. Cold brings a torpid or inactive state of the capillary vessels, by which the pores of the skin are closed, morbific matter retained and a deviation from health follows. The symptoms of fever are often mistaken by the average physician for some other. The mournful list of names of over fourteen hundred diseases, so difficult to be understood and remembered, or distinguished, is another source of uncertainty in practice. Theories constructed on false principles mislead the physician, and often direct him to the use of wrong medicines; for false theories make a false practice. Combined with errors of judgment, and medicines that are of the most dangerous nature, poisons of the rankest dye, and most fatal tendency are often the cause of sudden death, all tend to confuse the practitioner and destroy all confidence in the established practice. We have no time to search for names. The name is out, the cause is out, and the remedy is out; and in a few hours the patient is relieved and restored, requires food, recovers strength, sleeps, rises, and returns to the business of life. In concluding these remarks we would ask our readers and friends to persevere in the mode of treatment laid down, follow it out to the very letter, and the result will be a speedy recovery of health, and the fever will disappear as if by some miracle.

If you survey the several grades oi society you will find that the class of men who enjoy the highest degree of health, and are the most free from fevers, are those that are the farthest removed from a high degree of refinement- it is that state of society which most nearly approaches, in habits and conditions, to primeval simplicity- I mean the tillers of the soil, the bushman or seaman. This alone is surely a strong argument that the habits of refined society are not friendly to health and strength. Again, as a proof that man, in a state of primeval simplicity, inhabiting the temperate latitudes, living almost entirely in the open air, supporting life by the simplest fare, his mind undisturbed by the harassing anxieties consequent on ambitious pursuits, and the thousand other perturbing causes inseparably connected with a highly cultivated state of society, enjoys almost an entire immunity from disease. But, from the moment he begins to emerge from primitive simplicity of his habits, and seek to live by his wits, rather than by the sweat of his brow, from that moment his intellectual and physical energies are at perpetual war with each other, since he can only increase the former at the expense of the latter. As he advances in refinement and knowledge, he retrogrades in physical strength. The very means, therefore, which are necessary to educate and polish the mind under the old system, have also a strong tendency to injure it. "Forced intellectual cultivation" sow the seed of physical deterioration; and the evils thus inflicted on the flesh, fail not to retaliate with interest on the spirit.

INTERMITTENT FEVER (Febris Intermittens)

This disease may be divided into three stages, viz: First, the cold stage; second, the hot stage; third, the sweating stage. It is called intermittent because of its regularly leaving and returning at stated times, sometimes every day, or every second, third or fourth day. The causes which produce this disease are various, Marsh miasma, or the effluvia arising from stagnant water on marshy ground. It may be induced by sleeping on damp ground, damp houses, or removing from high locations to low ones. In a word, whatever relaxes the solids, diminishes the perspiration, or obstructs the circulation in the capillary vessels, disposes the body to this disease. It is necessary in the treatment of intermitting fever, first, to cleanse the stomach and bowels by a lobelia emetic, as the liver and stomach are in a very morbid condition, viscid phlegm and bile being discharged by vomiting. Emetics not only cleanse the stomach, but increase the perspiration and all other secretions, which render them of such importance that they often cure without any other medicine. After the emetic has operated, make up the following:

Meadow Sweet .5 ounce.
Virginia Snake Root .5 ounce.
Chamomile .5 ounce.
Peruvian Bark .5 ounce.
Fever Powder .5 ounce.

Pour on them one quart of boiling water and continue the boiling for ten minutes; strain, and take a wineglass full every two hours. Take a vapor bath going to bed and rub the whole body down with vinegar and water in the morning, and then continue the rubbing with a coarse cloth. Let the food be light and nourishing, eat no fat or greasy matter, keep the bowels moderately open with a little senna and rhubarb. An emetic, with the fever powder alone, wall be sufficient for children.

BILIOUS OR REMITTENT FEVER

Febris Remittens.

This disease is most prevalent in hot weather, and in low marshy grounds and swamps. It generally commences with languor, drowsiness, bitter taste in the mouth, pain in the head, back and extremities, followed by chills, fever, thirst, nausea, and ofttimes a vomiting of bilious matter. The eyes, skin, and urine, from the wide diffusion of bile in the system, become of a yellow color. The bowels are generally costive, the tongue is dry, and covered with, a white or brown coat, breathing is oppressed, and a sense of weight and fullness is experienced in the right side, and in the region of the stomach, delirium sometimes occurs; the bowels become distended with wind sore or tender on pressure. The stools are sometimes watery and reddish, and at others black and offensive, resembling tar. There is a remission of febrile symptoms in the morning or afternoon of each day, which lasts for an hour or two, when the fever returns with its previous violence; and hence the term remittent fever. Bilious fever is caused by intemperance in eating and and drinking, irritating substances in the bowels, consuming animal fat that is not digested, breathing impure air, and the use of a poor unwholesome diet. Give an emetic of lobelia, and a vapor bath at the same time, and then prepare the following medicine.

Barberry bark .5 ounce.
Yarrow .5 ounce
Raspberry leaves .5 ounce.
Clivers .5 ounce.
Agrimony or Bitter bur root .5 ounce.
Ginger .5 ounce.

Pour on them one quart of boiling water, and continue the boiling for fifteen minutes, and strain, pouring it boiling hot upon half ounce of fever powder. And if the bowels are confined, give a dose of bilious powder with a little senna tea. Wash the body down with vinegar and water, rubbing well with a coarse cloth, all fatty matter must be avoided, as well as intoxicating drinks.

SCARLET FEVER (Scarlatina)

Scarlet fever commences with a chill and shivering, like other fevers; with nausea and often vomiting, succeeded by thirst and headache. Sometimes the symptoms are mild and other times violent. The eyes are red and much swollen, an eruption appears in the form of a stain or blotch of a fiery redness. As the disease advances the whole neck swells, and assumes a dark red color; the tonsils become ulcerated, and the throat and mouth are often much inflamed. The breath is often very offensive, rattling and oppressed breathing, great prostration of strength, copious discharge from the bowels, deafness, and stupor prevail almost from the commencement of the attack. Children are more subject to this disease than adults. The causes of this disease are numerous, independent of contagion, unwholesome food, filthy and damp houses, uncleanliness, putrid animal and vegetable effluvia, etc. Scarletina must be considered as a high state of fever, and treated in the same general way. Always remember that the heat must be raised internally by the use of stimulants, in order that by circulating the blood the morbid matter may be thrown to the surface. If the patient be a child, bathe the feet and legs in hot water and mustard for ten minutes. If an adult give a vapor bath. If the throat is sore, with an accumulation of mucus, impeding respiration, an emetic will have a most beneficial effect. If the patients throat continue sore, and a tough ropy phlegm so impedes respiration, saturate a cloth with crude oil, or as common oil as you can procure, and lay over the chest and throat, and cover with oil paper to prevent soiling of clothes, let remain until a blister has formed, be careful in opening the blister that the contents are disposed of as soon as possible, and the vessels disinfected. In fact, let all refuse be disposed of and the utensils and clothing be thoroughly washed and cleaned. After the bath, put the patient into dry warm linen, and prepare the following medicine.

> Fever powder .5 ounce.
> Sumac Berries .5 ounce.
> Vervain Blue .5 ounce.
> Pennyroyal .5 ounce.
> Meadow sweet or bayberry powder .5 ounce.

Boil the above in three pints of water for half hour, strain, and sweeten as you take it, a wine-glassful every two hours, the bowels must be relieved with senna and ginger, steady perseverance will have the desired effect.

TYPHUS FEVER

The word typhus is derived from a Greek word, which signifies stupor, this being the characteristic symptom of the disease. If the disease appear under the form of the severer or Malignant typhus frequently called putrid fever, its attack is more sudden and violent, its progress more rapid, and all the symptoms of debility and putridity appear earlier, and in an aggravated form. The slow or nervous is distinguished from malignant typhus by its effect on the nervous system, by a torpid state of the brain, prostration of muscular power, and more or less delirium. It commences with great debility in all its symptoms, loss of appetite, restlessness, giddiness in the head, depression of spirits, heats and chills, and often with vomiting; bowels generally confined although diarrhea sometimes accompanies it. There is often a cough, red and watery eyes, with bleeding at the nose, and difficulty of swallowing; as the disease advances, red spots appear on the abdomen, with often a loss of blood from the mouth and bowels; the memory becomes imperfect, delirium sets in, then follows great prostration, a black crust covers the lips, teeth and tongue; the stools are watery and oppressive; the patient, if the symptoms are unfavorable, becomes lost in stupor, and a black gangrenous thrush appear about the mouth and throat, the pulse sinks and intermits, the extremities grow cold, and death ensues.

We should commence immediately, by giving an emetic of lobelia and nerve powder, prepare a vapor bath, administer while on the bath, bayberry and a little bitter root, one ounce of each to the quart of water, boil down to one pint, and give freely with a little cayenne or ginger to each dose, rub the body down, with equal parts of cold vinegar and water, and then place a hot brick or stone to the feet, with cloths wet with vinegar; cover with dry flannel, be sure and raise the internal heat, and let down the external (raise the fountain above the stream) sufficient to produce a natural action. If the patient should continue vomiting so as to throw up the medicine given; the doses should be repeated until the stomach retains sufficient quantity to enable the patient to bear the steam, bear in mind, the higher the heat can be raised in the system, the more free and thorough will be the operation of the medicine. When the stomach contains sufficient medicine, and the patient has been put to bed with the hot brick to the feet, administer another emetic with the bayberry and cayenne, sufficient to thoroughly cleanse the stomach, three doses will generally be sufficient.

If the process has been conducted to the best advantage, the patient will, soon after the commencement of the vomiting begin to run down, that is, grow pale and weak, as it were, until he has not strength to move or even speak; the breathing will be short and soft, to long and loud, and from the most free and easy, to the most laborious jerking, in short, every symptom and appearance, calculated to alarm those who are unacquainted with the true cause and effect; yet those experienced, behold those scenes with pleasure, because they know these are favorable symptoms, to the recovery of the patient. We have known some instances where practitioners, who were acquainted with the full operation of the medicine, have become alarmed, when, as a matter of course, consternation would seize the mind of the friends of the patient, and an old school physician would be sent for, and by the time he arrived, the medicine given would have completed its operation, and the patient being on the turn, would soon revive, and finding themselves perfectly relieved, is easily persuaded to believe that the old school physician, had arrived just in time to save his life, the practice has suffered much in this way.

We have dwelt much longer upon this part of our subject than may be deemed necessary by some, yet the importance which we attach to a knowledge of the wonderful operation and effect of the emetic, lobelia, must be our apology, if, indeed any is required. We will suppose our patient, to have gained sufficient strength to converse, when a dose of the following medicine may be prepared, and some oatmeal gruel or other light food may be given.

Bayberry bark 1 ounce.
Bitter Root 1 ounce.
Vervain 1 ounce.
Peruvian bark .5 ounce.
Rosemary .5 ounce.
Cayenne pepper 1 ounce.

Boil the above in. two quarts of water down to three pints, and give a wine-glassful three times per day, (not forgetting light food) when necessary, give cold water with a little lemon juice, and if the disorder returns, repeat the vapor bath, and give a teaspoonful of brewers yeast, in the dose of medicine for several days. In order to restore the strength of the patient after the disease has entirely subsided, give such food, as will digest easily, be careful not to overload the stomach with hard, indigestible kinds of food, give plentifully of boiled milk and water for a few days, until the stomach is sufficiently strong to take more solid food, beef tea, soft boiled eggs, with light puddings, etc., until nature itself demands more solid food, by this means their strength may be materially increased until restored to health.

DISEASES OF FEMALES WITH TREATMENT AND MODE OF CURE

RETENTION OF THE MENSES

GREEN SICKNESS

Symptoms: When the monthly evacuation does not appear at the proper period of life the constitution becomes very much disordered. Then follows a disturbance, first in the stomach, general debility, costiveness, nervousness, and every organ of the body is in a torpid state; there is a sallowness of the countenance, and in some instances it is of a greenish tinge, which has given to the disease the name of green sickness. There are pains in the back or loins, or both, swellings of the ankles at night, palpitation of the heart, and sometimes a distressing cough. Attention must be paid to the general constitution, but strong forcing medicine must not be given, unless nature is making some effort, which may be known by the pains pressing down about the hips and loins. The same treatment under the head of painful menstruation is all sufficient.

WHITES (Leucorrhea)

This complaint is attended with loss of appetite, general debility, and costiveness, pains in the back and discharge from the vagina of a white or milky color. As the disease advances the color of the discharge becomes dark, and a scalding sensation is experienced when passing urine. Treatment: Inject into the vagina, with a female syringe, a tea of bistort or beth root, and cranesbill, night and morning, and take the following, night and morning, in wine-glassful doses:

White Pond Lily Root 2 ounces.
Unicorn root 2 ounces.
Wahoo Bark 1 ounce.
Gold seal 1 ounce.
Cinnamon 1 ounce.

Add three pints of water, simmer down to one quart, and pour boiling hot upon one ounce of grated nutmegs, half ounce of ginger, powdered, and half pound of granulated sugar. And be sure and take open air exercise, which is indispensable, combined with a nourishing diet.

PROFUSE MENSTRUATION (Menorrhagia)

This complaint occurs generally in those of full habit of body, general debility with a determination of blood to the womb, will also cause this disease. The discharge may be profuse and of short duration, or it may continue for ten or twelve days, exhausting the patient; or it may return every two or three weeks. Treatment, Take:

Cudweed 1 ounce.
Cranesbill 1 ounce.
Bistort root 1 ounce.
Tormentil root 1 ounce,

Add two quarts of water, boil down to three pints, and pour boiling hot, upon one ounce each of queen of the meadow and raspberry leaves, cool and strain. Take a wine-glassful three times per day, keep the bowels regular with the liver pills.

PAINFUL MENSTRUATION (Dysmenorrhea)

Painful menstruation may be relieved by sitting over the steam of a strong decoction of tansy, wormwood, and yarrow, and fomenting the abdomen with the same.

Then take the following in wine-glassful doses:

> Ground pine 1 ounce.
> Southernwood 1 ounce.
> Tansy 1 ounce.
> Catmint 1 ounce.
> Germander 1 ounce.

Simmer in two quarts of water down to three pints, and pour boiling hot on one ounce of pennyroyal herb, strain when cold, and take as per dose above.

SOOTHING SYRUP, OR MOTHER'S FRIEND

Take:

> Cramp bark . 2 ounces.
> Blue cohosh 2 ounces.
> Slippery elm 2 ounces.
> Raspberry leaves 2 ounces.
> Squaw vine 2 ounces.
> Orange peel 2 ounces.
> Bitter root 2 ounces.

Simmer gently in sufficient water to keep the herbs covered, for two hours, strain, and simmer gently down to one quart, let it stand to cool, then add one cup of granulated sugar, and four ounces of alcohol. Dose: Take a tablespoonful two or three times per day, for several weeks before birth of child, This preparation has been used extensively by me for a number of years in cases of difficult and protracted labor, as well as for pains which are frequently experienced after the birth of the child. Too much cannot be said in favor of this preparation as it assists mothers both before and after confinement, causing an easy birth, where difficulty had often been expected.

CHANGE OF LIFE

This is generally considered the second critical period of woman's life, as in reality it is, and, although some writers contend that disease is a necessary consequence of the change, nevertheless we are not of that number; our our opinion is, that as the first critical period is made so, more from artificial than natural causes, that so also is the second. If the general health can be sustained, there will be no danger attending it. If it cannot, there will be a breaking down of the constitution.

So far, then, as regards the change or "critical period of life," we can only say, whatever form of disease may manifest itself, either then or at any other time, the one object should be to seek a remedy in time. This will be a safe and certain way of sustaining the body, and preparing it for whatever changes it may be naturally compelled to pass through. Of one thing we are certain, and that is, that the change will take place without danger if the body is in health, but if dyspepsia, disease of the liver, general debility, or disease of any kind, exist when the body has commenced its passage down the hill of life, the difficulty becomes greater, and we must also remember, that in such a condition, the difficulty of throwing off a disease is greatly increased. In concluding our remarks upon this important subject, we can only add that proper attention to the body in its earlier stages is the best and surest preventative against disease in its later stages; and if our book should become, as we believe it will, the domestic friend of the mothers of America, we hope it will be found worthy of their patronage; nor have we a single doubt but that it will (if followed) be the means of enabling many a poor mother to prevent the fearful ravages made upon the constitution of herself and children, and teach them to understand the conditions established in nature for the preservation of that great and inestimable blessing, health; and if our efforts can be made available for this purpose, we ask no greater reward than their blessing.

APOPLEXY

Apoplexy, is a sudden suspension of the powers of sense of motion, from some diseased affection of the brain, or nervous system, the respiration being generally laborious, and frequently attended with a great noise. It is strictly a disease of the nervous system.

Symptoms: We are sometimes warned of the approach of apoplexy by a dull pain in the head, with heaviness, giddiness, drowsiness, frequent fits of nightmare; fullness and redness of the face and eyes; faltering in the speech, loss of memory, and bleeding from the nose; but its attack is more frequently sudden, and the patient falls to the ground with scarcely any warning, and lies as if in a deep sleep, from which he cannot be roused. In this state the face is red and puffed, the veins of the neck are distended, the head is hot, the eyes are prominent, blood-shot, and sometimes half open. The pulse, at first strong and full, soon becomes weak and irregular. The duration of the fit is various, but generally lasts from eight to twenty-four hours, and occasionally to thirty-six hours, or still longer. It is very doubtful, whether the sudden deaths we so frequently hear of, ought to be ascribed, as is common, to apoplectic seizure, since genuine apoplexy very seldom destroys life in less than two hours. They appear to depend upon some violent affliction of the heart, or stomach, or upon the rupture of some blood vessel larger than those of the brain.

Causes: First, drunkenness and habitual use of exciting liquors; second, gluttony; third, indolence; fourth, mental anxiety and the excessive use of tobacco. This disease may happen at any age, but is most frequent about the middle, or in the decline of life, especially in persons of a plethoric habit, who have short necks, and who are indolent, who eat and drink to excess. It differs from epilepsy, or falling fits, since there are no convulsions and contortions of the limbs, as in the latter.

Treatment: Our first object should be to put the feet in hot water with mustard, rub the calves of the legs with a course cloth, as briskly as possible, giving immediately two table-spoonful of cayenne tea, and if possible give a vapor bath, or spirit bath, and prepare the following injection: lobelia, skullcap, gum myrrh, rhubarb, and ginger, one ounce of each article, pour a pint of boiling water on the mixture, let it stand for fifteen minutes, strain, and when about milk warm, throw this up the bowels, make two doses of the above, and repeat the second time if it does not produce an evacuation. Our object is to cause a copious perspiration, and this done the patient is saved. The patient should be careful not to indulge in rich wines or heavy food; all excitement should be avoided; and the system strengthened with the stomach bitters, and we have no fear for the result. The following may be taken in wine-glassful doses:

Bitter herb, or balmony 2 ounces.
Bayberry bark 2 ounces.
Poplar bark 2 ounces.
Ginger root 1 ounce.
Licorice root 1 ounce.

Simmer in three pints of water, down to one quart, strain, and add one gill of alcohol, to keep it. This preparation may be freely used, to restore the digestive powers, and correct the bile, as well as create an appetite.

SCROFULA AND SCURVY

Scrofula has been known to exist for nearly twenty centuries, yet with all the chartered wisdom of the medical colleges they have not yet found out the cure, nor even the cause. The many opinions of the so called regulars, are as conflicting, with regard to the cause, and cure, as in most other diseases. Almost every article of the *Materia Medica* has been tried and abandoned. Some of their number, go so far as to state, that the disease often yields to old women and quacks. And what, we would ask, is the reason of this signal failure of the diplomatised practitioners, and the vexatious success of those whom they call quacks? The reason is obvious; they use those means which are rational, and which act in harmony with the laws of nature- herbs, from nature's laboratory.

These aid the powers of nature, assimilate with and purify the fluids, stimulate the absorbents, and expel morbid matter; while the learned quacks use poisons to drive poisons out. Is not the system already surcharged with poisoned matter? Is it not the height of madness to suppose that what will produce a disease will also, cure it? The symptoms that first appear are small tumors, or knots below the ears, or under the chin; they are, in general, two, three or four in number, but often still more numerous, and are movable, soft, and slightly elastic, of a globular or oval figure, without pain or discoloration of the skin. These gradually increase in size and number, till they form one or more hard tumors, which continue a long time without breaking, and when they do break they discharge a thin watery humor, matter and blood, other parts of the body are liable to its attacks, as the arm-pits, groin, feet, hands, or legs. This disease requires much patience and perseverance, as it is slow and sluggish. Let the patient have out door exercise, and plenty of it; abstain from all greasy substances, and intoxicating liquors. Take a cold bath or sponge bath, with a little vinegar in the water, every morning, and once a week, a turkish bath. If the tumors are broken, wash with an infusion of Bayberry and White Pond Lily, or Marsh Rosemary, and prepare the following medicine.

Burdock root 2 ounces.
Sumac berries or bark 1 ounce.
Bitter sweet root 2 ounces.
Clivers 2 ounces.
Red clover blossom 2 ounces.

Put in two quarts of water, boil down to three pints, strain, and pour boiling hot upon one ounce of scurvy powder, and take a wine-glassful three times a day; use the ointment recommended for wounds, to be spread on cotton, change the cloth twice a day, persevere with this treatment, and change the medicine to the following after having given the stomach a few days rest:

Red clover blossom 1 ounce.
Sarsaparilla (Jamaica) 2 ounces.
Stillinger 1 ounce.
Sassafras 2 ounces.
Mezerion 2 ounces.
Licorice juice 1 ounce.

Prepare the same as the first course, and take the same as above, continue alternately, taking the above preparations, and a cure will be the result.

ASIATIC CHOLERA

The first we have any knowledge of this disease, was at Jessore in India about the year 1817, where it committed great havoc among the inhabitants; from whence it passed into this country, and thence phto Europe. We do not intend to give a history of the disease, as this will do but little towards enabling us to cure it. Suffice to say it has carried off millions since the above mentioned year, with the introduction of the microscope, it has been shown that the deadly microbe- insects so small that millions cover one cubic inch of water, has been the cause of all the trouble.

Chemical analysis proved the presence of nitrogen, an infectious deadly poison; these microbes being inhaled into the lungs, contaminated and poisoned the blood in the living organism, deranging the vital principle in the body, and producing the disease named Cholera. The evacuations from the alimentary canal and the contents of the stomach, all become surcharged with the same minute insects. The heat of the sun acting upon putrid vegetable and animal matter causes an exhalation from the creeks and rivers, as well as from the putrid decayed matters of the earth, and brings into existence this deadly microbe, inducing this pestilence. They move in myriads in our atmosphere, and thus by the mere act of breathing this epidemic is inhaled into the lungs, poisoning the vital fluid, the blood. There is no disease incident to the human family that has spread so much terror and desolation as the Asiatic Cholera. It attacks people in good health, without any notice of its approach. It appears to be a more malignant type of the common cholera. It is characterized by frequent discharges from the stomach and bowels of a watery fluid, resembling rice or barley water.

The patient is seized by a spasmodic pain of the bowels, cold sweats, great coldness of the surface, the features contract and shrink; the lips are blue, the heat and pain in the stomach, extreme. The spasms of the patient are dreadful, beginning like cramps in the feet; sudden attacks of pain run up the legs and arms, as though they were breaking, to the trunk. At the approach of death these spasms leave the system. The action of the heart, pulse, and organs of respiration rapidly diminish; the system loses all power to retain its heat; the blood thickens, the large veins are black and marked, even the tongue is cold. The eyes become closed; there is complete suppression of bile and urine, yet the patient often continues sensible to the last. Treatment: There is no disease that so strongly exhibits or so clearly proves the theory of the Botanic practice. "Heat is life; the absence of heat death" Patients suffering from this disease become so void of that life-giving principle, oxygen, that there is not sufficient stimulus or heat; therefore the blood recedes from the surface, and is thrown upon the vital organs, which have not the power to throw off the extra amount of work. Our great aim is to restore the circulation and check the diarrhea; to accomplish this the following means must be used: Place the patient in hot water and mustard up to the knees, rub well, at the same time giving a tea-spoonful of cholera powder in hot water, strained and sweetened, every quarter of an hour, and 20 drops of anti-cholera drops every two hours. If thrown from the stomach, repeat again, and again, until it is retained in the stomach. After a ten minute bath, put to bed, with a hot brick to the feet, and one to each side, wrapped in cloths wet with vinegar, to be repeated as often as they become cool. Then prepare the following medicine:

    Tormentil root 1 ounce.
    Cranesbill root 1 ounce.
    Bayberry bark, ground 1 ounce.
    Cayenne pepper .25 ounce.
    Carbonate of soda. .25 ounce.

Simmer one hour in two quarts of water, when cool, clear, and add two ounces of tincture myrrh, keep up the steaming, and give the patient a wine-glassful of the mixture every fifteen minutes until perspiration flows freely. Remove to a safe distance all matter coming from the body, and use freely of disinfectants, cut several onions in two and place them around the sick chamber, as they absorb disease very readily, and tend to purify the atmosphere; or, powdered charcoal, placed around the room will answer every purpose. Let this treatment be persevered in, and when the pain and purging have subsided, give bitters, combined with gum arabic, comfrey, or slippery elm bark; these soothe the stomach and bowels, and remove the irritation.

EXCESSIVE DISCHARGE OF URINE (Diabetes)

This disease appears to arise from a general derangement of the system, in which the digestive and assimilative processes are but imperfectly performed; and the lungs are more or less disordered, which causes a peculiar condition of the blood, and a perverted action of the kidneys. It is treated by medical men under two heads, according to the nature of the urine- diabetes, mellitus. In this form of diabetes, the urine is voided in large quantities, far exceeding all the fluids which the patient takes. It is sensibly impregnated with saccharine matter, and is accompanied by a very urgent thirst, craving appetite, dry skin, wasting of the flesh, great debility, some degree of inflammation about the prepuce and glands, especially about the external orifice of the urethra. In the latter stages of this disease, there is a coldness of the feet, vertigo, head-ache, and difficulty of breathing.

Diabetes Incipidus: This disease is similar to the other, only the chemical nature of the urine is different. Under this head are included all excessive discharges of urine, not characterized by the presence of sugar in the water voided. Treatment: As perspiration is almost suppressed, it is of the utmost importance that a reaction should be produced; commence by giving a vapor bath once or twice a week; and after the bath, rub the body well with cayenne, salt, and vinegar, as (recommended in the gargle for sore throats,) every morning, and take the following:

Prickly ash berries 2 ounces.
Agrimony 2 ounces.
Meadow fern berries 2 ounces.
Bistort root 2 ounces.

Bruise the root and berries, boil in three quarts of water down to two quarts, and strain; then add half a tea-spoonful of cayenne pepper, sweeten with licorice juice, and take a wine-glassful four times a day; regulate the bowels with the bilious powder. Great attention must be paid to diet. No article containing sugar in any form must be allowed. The patient must be restricted to animal diet as much as possible, with very little to drink. Many have found relief, and even been cured, by taking the hoofs from a pigs foot, clean, and bake to a dark brown, pulverize to a fine powder. Give to an adult, a tea-spoonful once a day. This may be considered a singular remedy, but it has often cured many of this singular disease.

BLEEDING OR SPITTING OF BLOOD FROM THE LUNGS

Hemoptysis.

This arises from a debilitated state of the lungs. It may rise from injuries done to the lungs, or may be symptomatic of some other disease. It may be distinguished from bleeding from the stomach by observing that it is raised by coughing, and the blood is of a florid color and frothy, whereas in bleeding from the stomach the blood is vomited in larger quantities, and is of a dark color. Bleeding from the lungs is usually attended by heat, pain, and tightness of the chest, and a short tickling cough, with inflammation in the throat, and a salty taste in the mouth. The patient should place the feet in hot water with a table-spoonful of mustard in the water, and take the following:

Bistort root 2 ounces.
Tormentil root 2 ounces.
Oak bark 2 ounces.
Comfrey root 2 ounces.

Boil in three quarts of water, down to one, strain; then add a table-spoonful of ground ginger. Give a half wineglass full every half hour until relieved, keep the bowels gently open with a little senna and ginger tea, and if necessary, give the vapor bath; follow these directions to the letter, and a cure will be the result.

HOARSENESS

Take two ounces of fresh scraped horseradish root, infuse in a close vessel, in a half pint of cold water, for two or three hours; then add four ounces of acid tincture of lobelia and half a pound of honey, boil all together for half an hour, clear, and take a tea-spoonful four times a day.

DROPSY

The general causes of the disease may be fairly considered to arise from a loss of power in the body. We often find it connected with other diseases; sometimes it arises from a wrong treatment of other diseases, such as inflammation, fever, measles, colds, or obstruction, or in fact anything that disarranges the circulation may cause dropsy. Both sexes at certain periods of life, are subject to it. It is sometimes seated in the chest, sometimes in the abdomen or bowels, and at other times in the feet and legs. If in the legs and feet, press your fingers into the parts, and if the marks are left in deep indentations, you may be sure there is water there; where it is very bad the parts will appear very glossy, and much swollen; if in the abdomen or bowels, place the palm of the left hand on the parts, and gently tap the back with the knuckles of the other, when the water will be distinctly felt and heard, if in the chest, tap with the ends of the fingers, and a dull heavy sound will be heard; besides this, there always accompanies dropsy in the chest, tightness in breathing, cough, and a difficulty in lying down, through a feeling of suffocation. Medical men have classified them, or divided it into parts, and their treatment is made to correspond with the part where the disease is located. In our treatment we have no such classification; we venture to assert that the same general treatment will be found applicable and equally successful in all. In the treatment of this disease, the following course must be followed if you wish to effect a cure.

Treatment: Give a steam bath three times a week, and apply hot bricks with cloths wet with vinegar, to the feet and sides, and give a lobelia emetic once a week. Whilst in the bath drink freely of smartweed and ginger tea, and after the bath let the body be rubbed well with a coarse cloth. Be sure and keep the bowels open with the hepetic pill, and take the following:

Agrimony 1 ounce.
Clivers 1 ounce.
Parsley pert 1 ounce.
Juniper berries 1 ounce.
Dandelion root 1 ounce.

Add two quarts of water, and boil down to one; strain, add a tea- spoonful of cayenne. Take a wine-glassful every three hours, and two cayenne pills after each meal. Take a dose of diuretic powder at bed time, drink as hot as possible. It will keep the kidneys well stimulated.

DEAFNESS (TO CURE)

As our work professes to describe the nature and symptoms of disease, as well as the remedies suited to each complaint, we here insert a mode of treatment, for the cure of deafness. Many cases of long standing having yielded to the following mode of treatment, viz:

Take of sulfuric ether, and drop f/om four to eight drops into the aural conduit, every day, for about 20 days, when the application is suspended for several days, and again applied, lessening the dose by several drops, and again suspended at the expiration of 14 days. There are few cases that will require even the second treatment, except where there is malformation. But where there is much pain experienced in the application of the above remedy, the treatment must be suspended.

CRAMP IN THE LEGS AND FEET

Persons subject to cramp should first rub the parts well with some stimulating liniment; if that does not cure in half an hour, bathe the legs with mustard and water, and apply a cloth saturated with tincture of capsicum, and tincture of myrrh, made hot with equal parts of vinegar. Woolen stockings should be worn during the day, and the feet kept warm and' dry, as the circulation is sluggish. Take half a tea-spoonful of each composition, prickly ash, and cramp bark, all powdered, in warm water, sweetened, three times a day, keep the bowels regular with our liver pills.

DISEASES OF CHILDHOOD

HICCOUGH

Hiccough arises from many causes, and when it is found, the parent should endeavor to find the cause. It has its origin from an impurity in the milk, acidity of the stomach, or from the mother, who may have taken too much stimulating drink, or indigestible food. The following medicine may be prepared, and given with the greatest advantage:

Rhubarb, powdered 1 ounce.
Cinnamon, bruised 1 ounce.
Aniseed, bruised .5 ounce.

Boil gently in one pint of water, for one hour; strain, sweeten with honey, and give half-teaspoonful when the symptoms are most troublesome.

SNUFFLES, OR STOPPAGE OF THE NOSE

The nostrils of infants are often stopped up, or plugged with a thick, accumulation of mucus, the result of cold, irritation, and inflammation. A little lard or fresh butter rubbed in night and morning, or a bit of soft rag dipped in a little warm milk and applied inside the nose, and and a little balm or pennyroyal tea, given to promote a gentle perspiration, will generally be found sufficient. If it still continues after a night or two, give a warm bath, and repeat the same treatment.

SOOTHING SYRUP

For Colic, Wind, or Flatulence

Children are often troubled with gripes, pains in the bowels, and wind upon the stomach, generally accompanied with restlessness, crying, and drawing up the legs towards the chest, purging of a greenish matter, etc. It will be necessary to relieve the bowels of the irritation, as soon as possible; for this purpose, give freely of a medicine made as follows:

Spearmint .5 ounce.
Ladies slipper .25 ounce.
Rhubarb .5 ounce.
Cinnamon powder .25 ounce.

Pour half pint of boiling water on the whole, mix, let it stand to boil for fifteen minutes, strain, and sweeten well, with syrup or honey, and give a teaspoon full every half hour, diminishing as the pain subsides.

VOMITING

This is very common with small infants, and should be attended to. When the milk is thrown off in an unaltered state, or very little changed, it may be expected to arise from an overloading of the stomach, or from the richness of the milk itself. To avoid this, regulate the supply by considering the quantity the child can digest comfortably. If it arises from an irritable stomach and constipation, it will be well to relieve the bowels by gentle laxatives. The soothing syrup under the head of colic will have the desired effect, by adding half ounce of ipecachuana wine to the preparation, and given in a tea-spoonful dose every hour, until relieved.

LOOSENESS OF THE BOWELS

This is is frequently brought on by feeding the dear little one too often, believing the child to be in want of food, when the reverse is more often the case, keeping the child in a close, ill-ventilated room, want of cleanliness and general attention, cold, etc., but whatever the cause may be, the remedy is clear enough. First give a little of the soothing syrup, to relieve the irritation; then, if the child is sick at the stomach, give a tea-spoonful of the emetic syrup, then prepare a syrup as follows:

Burnet herb .5 ounce
Wild mint .25 ounce.
Cranesbill 1 ounce.
Ginger powder .25 ounce.

Simmer in a pint of boiling water for one hour, strain, pour boiling hot on one grated nutmeg, and half pound white sugar, give a tea-spoonful five or six times a day, until the symptoms abate, give freely of rice water to drink.

ONANISM (SELF-POLLUTION)

This subject is not generally treated by medical writers, yet there is no subject that is of more importance to the general health than this, as it involves consequences of the most serious kind. The semen is the most subtle, vital, and ethereal part of the human body. It contributes to the support of the nerves, as well as the reproduction of the human species. The emission of this fluid enfeebles the whole constitution more than the loss of twenty times the quantity of blood, producing a debilitating effect on the whole nervous system, on both body and mind. Physiologists say that the greater part of this refined fluid is reabsorbed and mixed with the blood, and imparts to the body sprightliness, vivacity, and vigor; which, if wasted by emissions imprudently, it fails to do- and there is lassitude, relaxation, and nervous depression. It should never be wasted only in a state of superfluity, and then never unnaturally. Self pollution prevails among both sexes to an alarming extent. We could disclose cases that would harrow up the feelings of every parent. It produces a whole train of diseases, and it has been shown by reports of lunatic asylums that it often causes insanity in both sexes. During the twenty years of my experience in examining patients, it has fallen to my lot to witness, examine, and mark the progress of a great many, who have been the victims of this debasing habit; and may safely say without fear of contradiction, that no cause whatever which operates on the human system, prostrates all its energies, mental, moral, and physical, to an equal extent. And I aver that more cases of idiocy, occur from this cause alone than from all other causes of insanity. It is opposed to moral purity and vigor; it keeps up the influence of unhallowed desires; fills the mind with lewd and corrupt images; and transforms its victim to a filthy and disgusting reptile. The evil is common, but its danger little known. Let the young take warning, and those that are in danger flee from it. We would advise the young to read such works that are alike moral, elevating and instructive.

Symptoms: Mental derangement, dyspepsia, hectic fever, weak eyes, nervous headache, and general debility. It matters not whether it is discharged naturally or artificially, it has the same effect, when carried to excess. And we would advise parents to throw off all mock delicacy, and warn their children, if they suspect danger.

Treatment: Abandon the practice immediately, and bathe the parts in cold water night and morning. Apply the tincture of cayenne to the back and loins. The diet must be entirely vegetable, but nutritious. Exercise in the open air. Intoxicating drinks must be avoided. Let the body be washed down in cold water and salt every morning. And take a tea-spoonful of the fluid extract of Buchu, and Priory Breava in a half cupful of hot water, sweetened, twice a day. Take also tonics recommended under that head in this work.

HYDROPHOBIA

In the human species it is always the result of specific virus, or contagion, received from the bite of an animal laboring under the disease.

Treatment: The vapor bath is a valuable auxiliary in the treatment of hydrophobia. The Indians of our country, when any of their number are bitten by a mad dog, generally secure their patient, and lay them over a vapor of hot steam, caused by building a fire and heating a number of large stones, and then by throwing water over them; the patient being covered with a wicker basket, covered with skins of animals, to retain the steam. The heat being raised to about 150 degrees. It has never been known to fail; more particularly, if a table-spoonful of the acid tincture of lobelia be administered when the attack comes on, or still better; give a tea-spoonful of the anti-spasmodic drops, while in the vapor bath, and repeat every twenty minutes till it operates. Then follow, by giving an injection of lobelia, cayenne, skullcap, and rhubarb, half a tea-spoonful of each, in a pint of warm water, with a tablespoonful of tincture of myrrh added, if the symptoms are violent. Repeat this every six hours. Wash the wound with tincture of lobelia, tincture of cayenne, and tincture of gum myrrh; keep the part constantly wet with it At night, apply a poultice made of slippery elm and lobelia, equal parts mixed with yeast.

EPILEPSY, OR FALLING SICKNESS

Epilepsy, this disease also called falling sickness, is a sudden deprivation of sense, accompanied by unusual motions and violent convulsions of the whole system. It occurs in paroxysms, which, after a period, leave the patient nearly in his or her former state; they are generally succeeded by languor, debility, stupor, and drowsiness, It takes place more frequently among young people, than those of mature years. In the fit, the involuntary muscular power is often excessive; the body is bent forward, or backward with great force; the eyes roll furiously; the lips are convulsed, and covered with a frothy saliva; the tongue is thrust violently from the mouth, and is sometimes shockingly lacerated; the pulse irregular; the breathing oppressed, and occasionally highly laborious; and in some cases, bilious matter in large quantities is ejected from the stomach. These symptoms sooner or later gradually give way, and the unhappy patient falls into a profound sleep.

Causes: The most frequent causes are irritation in the stomach and intestines; a diseased state of the spinal marrow, sudden fright, excessive grief, great loss of blood; the suppression of accustomed discharges, excessive drinking, and the imprudent use of calomel. Upon examination of those troubled with this disease, I find the small part of the brain, situated at the base of the head, the cerebellum, so called, more or less in a diseased condition, and no mark of disease to be found in any other part of the body. The involuntary laughing or weeping, and the sensation of a globe rising in the throat. Mall sufficiently distinguish the disease from hysteria.

Treatment: As soon as any of the above symptoms show themselves, means must be used to restore the equilibrium of the circulation. Place the patient in a hot bath, or a steam bath, take a table-spoonful of the anti-spasmodic tincture, while in the bath, or the following:

Mugwort Root 2 ounces.
Valerian root i ounce.
Black horehound 1 ounce.

Peony root or blue vervain 2 ounces.
Pellitory of the wall 1 ounce.
Wood bettany 1 ounce.

Steep in two quarts of water, in the oven, covered up, for two hours; pour boiling hot upon one ounce of skullcap. Give two table-spoonfuls four times a day; and give 20 drops of anti-spasmodic drops three times a day. Should worms be suspected, treat them under that head. If caused by the suppression of the monthly discharge, administer the medicine recommended under that head. And if caused by nervous prostration, give the medicine prescribed under that head, combined with electricity, and the Turkish bath, endeavor to find the cause, before attempting to remedy the effect, otherwise it is only time and labor wasted.

FAINTING AND VERTIGO

In fainting the motion of the heart and lungs becomes feeble and imperfect, the sensibility and perception are diminished, the pulse is small and weak, the voice uniformly lost, and the face pale. It may occur suddenly, and ceasing without any tendency to recurrence, or it may recur at periods more or less regular, with occasional palpitation of the heart during the intervals, and impeded respiration during the fit. The causes are fatigue, fright, long fasting, sudden loss of blood, acute pain, excessive eating and drinking. It may arise also from some structural disease of the heart, or the large arteries issuing from it; during the paroxysm, the breathing is obstructed, or feeble, the face livid, with a tendency to restlessness. In common cases it is only necessary to place the patient in a recumbent position, apply ammonia, strong vinegar, or any other pungent odor to the nostrils, and to use friction to the arms and legs. When the patient is capable of swallowing, a little wine and water should be administered; and the occasional causes sedulously avoided in future. In females, it often proceeds from difficult or obstructed menstruation. By bathing the feet in hot water and mustard at night; and taking the medicine recommended under the head of obstructed menstruation; and abstain from eating all fatty matter for a time, will be sufficient to effect a cure.

TETANUS, OR LOCKED JAW

This disease is often the effect of other diseases lurking in the system and terminating in locked jaw. It is sometimes caused by sleeping in the open air, or the use of narcotic poisons; but it more frequently occurs from wounds in the hands or feet. Where a nerve has been partly divided or lacerated, without being completely severed, the muscle of the lower jaw becomes contracted and hard, and at length the patient cannot open the mouth at all. Under the old school practice, there are as many different applications as there are physicians, none of which seem to have much effect. But under the Botanic practice is never known to fail to effect a cure. Cases have occurred within my own jurisdiction where the jaws of the patient was firmly set, resisting all efforts to open them with a spoon. The attending physician having exhausted his skill declared, that nothing could be done for the patient, as quinsy would burst in a few hours, that would cause suffocation. The family were much alarmed, and the patient being impressed with the hopelessness of her case, thought it useless to try other remedies, but her friends prevailed upon her to try my remedies; with the following result. The patient was given half a tea-spoonful of anti-spasmodic tincture, and one tea-spoonful of the acid tincture of lobelia. This was poured between the teeth several times, and in less than twenty minutes the nerves and muscles of the face relaxed, the quinsy burst, she vomited freely, and a few days after, attending her household duties. But to be sure of making a thorough cure, use the following injection in connection with the anti-spasmodic tincture, viz:

Lobelia, powdered .5 tea-spoonful.
Gum myrrh .5 tsp
Cayenne .25 tsp
Rhubarb .5 tsp
Valerian .25 tsp

Pour one pint of boiling water on one ounce of raspberry leaves, let it stand for ten or fifteen minutes, strain, and pour boiling hot on the above ingredients; and when milk warm, inject into the bowels. If caused by a wound, apply tincture of myrrh, and poultice with slippery elm, lobelia, and cayenne mixed with yeast.

PALPITATION OF THE HEART

This though a distressing affection, is only a symptom of other disease, such as disordered stomach, nervous debility, hysterical affections, great anxiety, and mental exertion, without sufficient exercise. Treatment: All exciting causes must be carefully avoided; attention to diet will be necessary, and intoxicating drinks must be avoided. Where there is organic disease, all that can be done is to mitigate the severity of the symptoms. The following will be found necessary:

Marigold flowers 1 ounce.
Mugwort 1 ounce.
Motherwort 1 ounce.
Centuary 1 ounce.
Dandelion 1 ounce.

Put in two quarts of water, boil down to three pints; pour boiling hot upon half ounce of valerian and half ounce of skullcap, Take a wine-glassful three times a day. Let the bowels be kept moderately open, and live principally upon vegetable diet, with plenty of out door exercise.

THRUSH

This is a complaint which few infants escape, it is by no means dangerous, but causes the child to be very restless. It may be known by observing the tongue, which is coated with little pustules; which if left to themselves, spread throughout the mouth extending into the stomach, and intestines. When first observed; swab the mouth out with a little borax and honey, and occasionally a little raspberry leaf tea, keeping the bowels moderately open with the soothing syrup.

CONVULSIONS OR FITS

These are very common with children, and are always connected with other forms of disease, The causes are various; such as internal irritation, acidity of the stomach, teething, inflammation, fever, constipation of the bowels, water on the brain, determination of blood to the brain, worms, etc. In treating convulsions it will be necessary to know the cause from whence they arise; from whatever the cause first relieve the bowels, with the soothing syrup, then prepare the following medicine:

Pellitory of the wall .5 ounce.
Angelica .25 ounce.
Wood betony .5 ounce.
Anti-spasmodic powder .25 ounce.

Boil in a pint of water for ten minutes, strain, sweeten, and give a tea-spoonful four to six times a day.

SCALD HEAD, TETTERS, AND NETTLE RASH

Scald head is a disease called chronic inflammation of the skin of the head, in which a peculiar matter is secreted. At first the eruption is confined to a small portion of the head, but by degrees its acrimony is spread over the whole scalp. It is accompanied by a troublesome itching, and the discharge of a thick offensive matter, which glues or mats the air together, and forms into a green or yellowish scale. It extends to the neck, ears, and eyes.

Treatment: To accomplish a cure, take two ounces of raspberry leaves, and boil them in a quart of water for twenty minutes; pour the liquor boiling hot upon one ounce of lobelia, and bathe the head with this night and morning, but not twice in the same liquor, after which apply the white ointment. Keep the head covered during the day with a cap. As this disease results from a disordered state of the body, means must be taken to purify the blood and strengthen the system. Of the compound decoction of sarsaparilla give a table-spoonful four times a day. If the disease commences in the spring, give a table-spoonful of the expressed juice of clivers or nettles three times a day.

NETTLE RASH

This is an eruption resembling the rash produced by stinging the skin with nettles. The skin is raised, and there is more or less inflammation, attended with painful tingling or itching. It disappears and re-appears suddenly, sometimes in one part and sometimes in another. This disease proceeds from an impure condition of the blood, and is usually connected with a disordered state of the stomach and bowels. Obtain, if you can, the juice of nettles, and give a tea-spoonful three times a day, and lay a little on the parts as well. Do not give so much as to purge the bowels too much, and it will cure at once. Wash the body down night and morning with water and marsh mallow soap. Give a dose of purgative powder every other night, if required, and drink freely of the antiscorbutic medicines, if the above cannot be got.

RINGWORM

This consists of a number of very small vesicular blisters close together, and forming a circle. The eruption is attended with itching and a tingling sensation.

Treatment: Give the compound decoction of sarsaparilla, rub the parts affected with tincture of blood root; or, what is better, a slight touch with aromatic vinegar every other day, once only each time, wall always cure in six days.

INFLAMMATION OF THE CHEST

It arises from cold, or obstruction, and begins with tightness of the chest, fever, cough, and difficulty of breathing, etc, and if not attended to, often terminates in death. Give freely of pennyroyal and hyssop tea, with a little plantain, sweetened with honey, and if the bowels are confined, relieve with the soothing syrup, after which give a teaspoonful of the emetic syrup. If the child be very young, a few drops will be sufficient; keep the child warm, and anoint the chest with goose oil, or sweet oil, and give a little cough syrup occasionally.

SYPHILITIC SORE, OR CHANCRE

This species of venereal commences with the formation of a small pimple, which in a few days breaks into an open sore, when it is either situated upon the glands or in the skin that covers it. When this has been badly treated or neglected, it assumes a malignant character; sometimes it is slow in its progress, at other times it spreads with great rapidity, occasioning extensive sloughing of the parts, and is contagious. To effectually cure this disease, it is necessary to keep the parts clean, apply the tincture of blood root, and fill the ulcer with blood root powder. This may be changed for a poultice mixed with slippery elm, lobelia, and bayberry, three times a day, and a lobelia emetic once a week for three weeks. Take the medicine recommended under the head of gonorrhea. The most loathsome cases may be cured by this treatment, and if followed out to the letter, it is a never failing remedy.

MIXTURE FOR GONORRHOEA

Take of spirits of nitric ether and sweet oil, of each two fluid ounces; copaiba and oil of turpentine, of each one fluid ounce; mix well together. Dose: A small tea-spoonful three times a day, in water, thin gruel, or mucilage. This preparation is very useful in gonorrhea, gleet, scalding of urine, etc., but must be followed by continual bathing the parts in warm water, in fact thorough cleanliness is absolutely necessary.

ON STEAMING, FOR THE CURE OF DISEASE

Steaming is a very important branch of our system for the cure of disease, which would in many cases, be insufficient to effect a cure without it. In all cases where the heat of the body is so far exhausted as not to be rekindled by the use of medicine; it is then of the utmost importance, to apply the vapor bath, for the purpose of re-animating the system. To add heat, as it were, to the decaying spark. Heat caused by steam, is more natural in producing perspiration, than any dry heat that can be applied to the body in any other manner, which will only serve to dry the air and prevent perspiration in many cases of disease, where a steam by water or vinegar would promote it, and add a natural warmth to the body, and thereby increase the life and motion which has lain dormant, in consequence of the cold. Many persons apply heat to the body by dry vapor, caused by burning spirit, which they call a vapor bath; it may answer in some cases and stages of disease; but in settled fevers, and cases where there is a dry inflammation on the surface of the body, it will not answer any good purpose, without the use of such medicines in large doses as are conducive to a free perspiration, for when the surface of the body is dry, the patient cannot bear it, as it will cause distress, having the same effect as a hot stove in a tight room, and will bring on difficulty of breathing. The proper method, and the only safe and reliable way of applying the vapor bath; is to allow the patient to stand, or sir over steam raised by heating a stone or brick to a red heat, and immersing it in half water, half vinegar, to about two-thirds its bulk, and be sure and have others ready as soon as the sharpness of the steam flies off, to take their place, let your patient be undressed, and a blanket put around them so as to shield the whole body from the air, then place them over the steam. Change the stones or bricks as often as cool. If your patient grows faint, bathe the face and chest with a little cold water and vinegar, which will restore the strength, after fifteen or twenty minutes, or during the time your patient is on the bath, give a dose of composition, yarrow or plantain tea, with a little ginger, or capsicum, sweetened to be drank hot, then at the expiration of the above time, wash down with cold water and vinegar, equal parts. Then wrap in dry warm clothing and put to bed. The use of steaming is good in preventing sickness as well as curing it. When a person has been exposed to the cold and is threatened with disease, it is one of the best preventatives. It is also one of the best remedies for cleansing the skin of the many impurities that adhere to and under its surface. This may be done without medicine, when it cannot be had; but it is much better to take something to raise the inward heat at the same time. Such as may-weed, summer savory, or ginger, etc., with hot water sweetened. This advice is for the poor people, who have no knowledge of medicine; and will many times save them much trouble, long sickness, and many dollars. Steaming is of the utmost importance in suspended animation.

Spotted, or scarlet fever, small pox, severe falls and

bruises, etc., and is far better than bleeding, as is the common practice, which only tends to destroy life, instead of promoting it. If the advantages of this mode of treatment were generally known, bleeding in such cases, or any other to remove disease, would never be resorted to by the wise and prudent. To clear off the obstructions caused by the disease, when the operation of medicine is insufficient to restore the balance of heat in the system. For as the natural heat of the body becomes lower than the natural state of health, it must by art be raised as much above as it has been below, and that may be accomplished by the use of steaming the body, and this must be repeated until the digestive powers are restored sufficient to hold the heat by digesting the food; then the health of the patient will be restored by eating and drinking such things as the appetite shall require. In this way the medicine removes disease, and food, by being properly digested supports nature, and continues that heat on which life depends.

THE TONGUE

As An Indicator of Disease.

A white fur on the tongue attends simple fever and inflammation. Yellowness of the tongue attends a derangement of the liver, and is common to bilious and typhus fevers. A tongue vividly red on the tips and edge, or down the center, or over the whole surface, attends inflammation of the mucous membrane of the stomach and bowels. A white velvet tongue attends mental diseases. The description of symptoms might be extended indefinitely, taking in all the propensities and obliquity of mental and moral condition. The tongue is a most expressive as well as unruly member.

DRYING AND PRESERVING ROOTS AND HERBS

Gather herbs, when the weather is fine, and the

flowers are in full bloom, or the seed getting ripe. Roots, should be dug in the spring when the sap is rising, for extracts; or in autumn, when they have ceased to vegetate; to dry for winter use, they should be sliced and dried, and kept from the air. Barks should be stripped when the tree is in full leaf, and dried in the shade; the bark of the roots should be taken in the fall, when the sap has descended, when nature takes her rest, flowers should be gathered when free from dew, and in full bloom, and when dried should be kept free from exposure to the air. All aromatic herbs should be kept in the same manner. A great deal depends on knowing how to keep herbs, as well as time of gathering.

MISCELLANEOUS

MEDICAL AND OTHER USEFUL RECIPES

ACETOUS POULTICE

This is made with vinegar and bran only, or with the addition of oatmeal, or bread crumbs. Very useful for sprains and bruises. As it becomes dry, it should be moistened with vinegar.

APERIENT FOR INFANTS

Rhubarb, powdered 5 grains.
Magnesia 3 grains.
White sugar .5 teaspoonful.
Manna 5 grains.

Mix with a few drops of water to the consistency of dough. Dose: from a piece half the size of a sweet pea, to a piece the size of an ordinary pea. Magnesia is very useful in acidity of the stomach, more when combined with rhubarb.

TO CURE A COLD WITHOUT MEDICINE

The following plan is very efficacious in curing most colds, but not all: Let a person fast for two days, providing he is not confined to bed, because by taking no carbon into the system by food, and by consuming the surplus which caused the disease, by respiration they soon carry off the disease by removing the cause. This will be found more effectual by taking copious draughts of water to continued fasting. By the time a person has fasted one day and night, he will experience a freedom from disease, and a clearness of mind, in a delightful contrast with mental stupor, and physical pain caused by colds. How infinitely better is this method than the old practice of depleting the system.

BURNS AND SCALDS

A few raw potatoes scraped or grated, and beaten in a bowl, then add a drachm of laudanum; apply to the affected parts, as you would a poultice. Very efficacious in burns, scalds, and other inflamed surfaces.

CHARCOAL

Fresh burnt charcoal, is one of the best remedies known for offensive breath, and will remove offensive odors from intestinal and renal discharges. It removes those local pains about the right shoulder, which are usually attributed to obstructions of the liver, it speedily removes heartburn, combined with bi-carbonate soda in equal parts. Charcoal is a powerful anti-septic removing or checking decay. Is useful in incipient consumption.

ACID TINCTURE OF LOBELIA

Lobelia herb and seed, two ounces; best malt, or cider vinegar, one pint, dissolve in bottle for a few days, shake once or twice a day, and at the expiration of one week, strain. Dose: A tea-spoonful in a little warm water, sweetened, for asthma, croup, and other complaints of the chest and lungs; for nervous affections, add a tea-spoonful of valerian; singers will find this tincture an excellent remedy for clearing the voice, and strengthening the vocal chords, by taking a few drops on a piece of lump sugar occasionally; mixed with tincture of capsicum, and tincture of myrrh in equal parts; is one of the most valuable medicines ever compounded. It will cure fits, lockjaw, suspended animation, and where the vital spark is nearly extinct, it has no equal; give a tea-spoonful for a dose, and repeat until relief is obtained; for children the dose must be regulated according to their age. If very young, reduce the quantity to one half, and give pennyroyal or raspberry leaf tea to drink, until it operates.

CAYENNE TINCTURE

This is a medicine of great value in the practice, and may be safely used in all cases of disease, both externally and internally. It is a valuable external application for rheumatic joints, and parts that have lost their sensibility. It is useful in palsy and wasting of the limbs, a flannel moistened with it, and applied to the side in pleurisy, will generally afford relief.

TINCTURE OF MYRRH

Take two ounces of gum myrrh, bruise and infuse in a pint of alcohol, stand in hot water bath until the gum has dissolved, and use the clear. This is applied to fresh wounds and offensive ulcers. Diluted with two-thirds of raspberry leaf decoction, it is good for a gargle, for ulcerated sore throat, and a tea-spoonful mixed with a little china tea, will cure sore mouth, spongy gums, and makes a good wash for inflamed and weak eyes.

RASPBERRY TINCTURE

Take half pound of honey and a cupful of water; let these boil: take off the scum;.pour boiling hot upon half an ounce of lobelia herb, and half ounce of cloves; mix well, then strain and add a gill of raspberry vinegar. Take from a tea-spoonful to a desert-spoonful four times per day. This is good for asthma, croup, hooping cough, inflammation of the lungs, dry and tickling coughs, and is very pleasant to take.

FOR BLEEDING AT THE LUNGS, ETC

Take of herb Robert, and St. John's wort, of each

one ounce, simmer gently in one quart of water for one hour; strain, and drink freely, every hour until relieved. This is also one of the best remedies known for bloody flux, more particularly if one ounce of tormentil root be added. It also makes a splendid ointment for scrofulous swelling, and will heal sore nipples.

TO CURE DRY SCURVY

Dandelion roots, two ounces, yellow burdock, two ounces of clivers, one ounce; put down in two quarts of water, boil down to three pints, sweeten with licorice juice, give a wine-glassful four times per day.

TINCTURE OF CATECHU

Take of powdered catechu two ounces, cinnamon bark in powder, one ounce, alcohol one pint: macerate for a few days, and strain. This is used for diarrhea, and a liniment for indolent swellings.

OIL TINCTURE

Saltpeter: Nitrate potassa .5 ounce.
Spirits of turpentine .5 ounce.
Spirits of sal ammonica .5 ounce.
Oil of vitriol .5 ounce.
Vinegar 8 ounces.

Mix the whole together; but be careful of the vitriol as it burns that which it comes in contact with. This is good for carbuncles, moles, freckles on the face, pimples, blights or gatherings, and will often give relief when other remedies fail, moisten a cloth and lay on part twice a day.

TINCTURE OF BLOOD ROOT

Take of blood root pulverized, two ounces; sweet

niter one pint; macerate for ten days, shake once or twice a day. This is very useful for polypus, proud flesh, and all fungus swellings, venereal ulcers, etc.

TINCTURE FOR TOOTHACHE

Peppermint water, half ounce, sweet niter, quarter ounce, chloroform, one drachm, ether, one drachm, oil of mustard ten drops. This is a remedy that will give relief when all others fail, not only for toothache, but neuralgic pains in any part of the body, apply with your fingers or moisten a cloth with it and lay on the parts affected, continue until you find relief.

RHEUMATIC DROPS

Take one quart of the best brandy, or any kind of high wines, quarter of a pound of gum myrrh, pounded fine, half ounce cayenne pepper, put the ingredients into a stone jug and boil it for a few minutes in a kettle of water, leaving the jug open. When settled, bottle it for use. These drops will prevent pain and mortification; they may be taken internally, or applied externally, or may be used in injections. One or two tea-spoonfuls of these drops may be given alone, or the same quantity may be put into a dose of medicines prescribed under that head. It is an excellent remedy for rheumatism, by taking a dose, and bathing the parts affected with it. It is also good for bruises, sprains, swelled joints, and old sores, as it will allay the inflammation, bring down the swelling, ease the pain, and produce a tendency to heal; in fact there is hardly a complaint in which this useful medicine cannot be used to advantage. It is the best preventative against mortification that can be found in nature's laboratory. I would say, that one quarter part of spirits of turpentine may be added, in bathing for rheumatism, itch or other humors, or in any kind of swelled joints. If the parts are bruised, add a little gum camphor.

BREAST LINIMENT

Take one pint of raw linseed oil, and four ounces tincture of camphor, mix, and apply a cloth saturated in the liniment to the affected parts, taking care the whole surface of the inflamed parts is covered with the liniment. Cover with several folds of cloth, or oil skin to prevent the liniment from staining the bed clothes. When the breast becomes swollen or painfully inflamed, apply the liniment often, to prevent gathering; but even when the breasts have gathered, it is an excellent outward application. It allays pain and is extremely soothing, and very seldom fails to effect a cure.

RHEUMATIC LINIMENT

Opodeldock 1 ounce.
Tinct. cantharides 3 drachms.
Spirits sal ammoniac 3 drachms
Rectified oil of amber 3 drachms.

Mix: This forms a valuable liniment for rheumatic, and other pains in the limbs, after rubbing, wrap the limb in fine, soft flannel, and keep warm. If persons who are troubled with the rheumatism, would abstain from the use of malt and spirituous liquors; and indulge more in the use of lemonade, or would occasional eat a lemon or two, it is one of the best remedies known, or I may say preventative, which is better than the cure.

CURE FOR HARD OR SWELLED BREASTS

Chamomile flowers 1 ounce.
Marshmallow roots 1 ounce.

Bruise and boil, in one quart of water, down to a pint. Foment the breast with the liquor, as hot as can be borne; and then place the flowers and roots in a cloth, and apply as a poultice.

TO PREVENT HYDROPHOBIA

When Bitten by a Dog.

Immediately wash the parts with clear water; then take leaf, or cut tobacco, and bind over the part bitten, changing it two or three times a day for a week. This effectually absorbs the poison. It is a good preventative, even if the animal is not mad, when bitten.

CURE FOR CHILBLAINS

Fresh lard 2 ounces.
Venice turpentine .5 ounce.
Gum camphor 1 ounce.

Melt together, stirring briskly, when cold it is ready for use.

OINTMENT FOR BROKEN CHILBLAINS

Sweet oil .5 pint.
Venice turpentine 1.5 ounces.
Fresh lard .5 pound.
Bees wax 1.5 ounces.

Simmer gently together, in a water bath until the bees wax is melted, stirring until cool, when it is ready for use. Apply going to bed, on a soft rag.

CATARRH SNUFF

Canella powder 4 drachms
Bayberry powder 6 drachms
Blood root powder 2 drachms

THE OCCULT FAMILY PHYSICIAN

Valerian, powdered 2 drachms
Golden seal, powdered 2 drachms
Oil of lavender 3 drops
Oil of lemon 10 drops

Mix thoroughly, and keep in stoppered bottle or free from the air. This preparation, is a valuable remedy for those troubled with catarrh, and by persistent use, has cured many difficult cases of long standing; more particularly, if the nasal douche, with warm water, is used every morning and evening.

SMOKING TOBACCO FOR ASTHMA

Stramonium leaves 4 ounces
Skunk cabbage leaves 4 ounces
Coltsfoot leaves 2 ounces
Lobelia leaves 2 ounces

Rub to a course powder. Mix, and dissolve two ounces of nitrate of potassa, in one half pint of water; mix well with the powder; dry thoroughly, smoke in ordinary clay pipe morning and evening.

PREPARATION FOR WORMS IN CHILDREN

Santonin 8 grains
Fluid extract of pink root 1 drachm
Simple elixir, to make 1 ounce

Mix a teaspoonful, morning and night.

MRS. MATTESON'S EXPECTORANT

Tincture tolu 2 ounces
Tincture camphor 1 drachm
Tincture lobelia 1 drachm
Wine of ipecac 2 drachms

Syrup of poppy 2 drachms
Syrup of squills 2 ounces
Essence of aniseed 1 drachm
Fluid extract of licorice 1 ounce

Mix, add sufficient water to make a ten ounce mixture. In all cases of tightness of the chest, difficulty of breathing, colds settling on the lungs, coughs, and in fact, most all chest and lung affections, arising from cold, give a table-spoonful three or four times per day; children half quantity.

MIXTURE FOR RECENT COUGH

Take of honey, five ounces; New Orleans molasses, four ounces; best malt vinegar, seven ounces. Mix them, and simmer in a preserving pan or earthen jar for fifteen minutes; after removing it from the fire and the mixture has become lukewarm, add one drachm of ipecacuanha wine, one drachm of acid tincture of lobelia, and one drachm tincture tolu, when it is ready for use. The dose is a tablespoonful every four hours for adults, half quantity for children. In our opinion, this is one of the best mixtures now known for recent cough. On account of its pleasant taste, it is particularly eligible in the coughs of children and infants of all ages.

MRS. MATTESON'S COMPOSITION POWDER

Pleurisy root, powdered 2 ounces
Bayberry powder 2 ounces
Cinnamon powder .5 ounce
Ginger powder 1.5 ounces
Cayenne pepper .25 ounce
Cloves, powdered .5 ounce

Mix: This composition is intended for colds, chills, cramps, and in the less violent attacks of disease. It is a remedy of much value, and may be safely used in all complaints of male or female, as well as for children. It will remove all obstructions caused by cold, or loss of inward heat. By taking a dose on going to bed, and putting the feet in hot water, with a little mustard thrown therein, will generally throw off the first attack of disease, and if repeated, will cure a bad cold. If the symptoms are violent, with much pain, add to each dose of the composition, a tea-spoonful of tincture of myrrh. In nervous symptoms, add a teaspoonful of nerve powder. To prepare the medicine, take a full tea-spoonful of the powder, with a tea-spoonful of sugar, rub together in a breakfast cup, fill with boiling water, stirring the while, and when cool enough, drink the clear. If this will not answer the purpose, the patient may depend there is something more serious the matter, and may have to go through a regular course of medicine, consult the oracle is our advice, same as the Greeks of old.

BILIOUS POWDER

Senna leaves 2 ounces
Jalap root 1 ounce
Mandrake root .5 ounce
Cloves .25 ounce
By-Carbonate of Soda .25 ounce

All in fine powder, well mixed, and passed through a fine sieve: Take a tea-spoonful in a cup of boiling water, sweetened, once a day; children according to age, and as required. This is an efficient purgative, and very useful in every stage of costiveness, headache, and bilious complaints. It removes all offensive accumulations without causing costiveness after its operation.

FEVER POWDER

Peruvian bark .5 ounce
Pleurisy root 1 ounce

THE OCCULT FAMILY PHYSICIAN

Skunk cabbage 1 ounce
Lobelia herb .25 ounce
Ginger .5 ounce

Mix, and sieve the same as the others. This preparation rarely or never fails in producing moisture of the skin; in fevers it operates mildly and gently upon the system, and will frequently produce moisture in from five, to ten minutes. It allays excitement, regulates the pulse, and predisposes to sound and natural sleep. The dose is from a quarter to a whole tea-spoonful, in half cup of hot water, sweetened, repeat the dose every hour, till relieved.

SCURVY POWDER

Stillenger powder .5 ounce.
Sarsaparilla root 1 ounce
Mezeieon root 1 ounce
Sassafras bark of root 1 ounce
Princess pine 1 ounce
Ginger .5 ounce
Licorice powder 1 ounce

All finely pulverized, well mixed, and pass through a fine sieve. This preparation is an excellent remedy, to enrich the blood, and will remove blotches, pimples, scorbutic, and cutaneous diseases.

COUGH POWDER

Beth root 1 ounce
Pleurisy root 1 ounce
Black cohosh 1 ounce
Elecampane root 1 ounce
Lobelia herb .25 ounce
Licorice 1 ounce
Ginger .25 ounce
Celery seed .5 ounce

Mix thoroughly, and pass through a fine sieve. This is a superior remedy, and gives speedy relief in asthma, hoarseness, shortness of breath, difficult in breathing, pleurisy, and all diseases of the lungs of a chronic nature, Dose: A teaspoonful, sweetened with honey, in half cup of boiling water, drink the clear.

COLIC POWDER

Sweet flag root 2 ounces
Marsh mallow root 1 ounce
Ginger powder .5 ounces

This preparation, is one of the best for those afflicted with pain and cramps in the stomach and bowels. It gives almost instant relief, and seldom fails, where the dose is repeated. Take a tea-spoonful in half cup of hot water, sweetened. It may be given to children, only in less quantity.

FEMALE RESTORATIVE POWDER

Cranesbill root 1 ounce
White poplar bark 2 ounces
Bistort root 1 ounce
Golden seal 1 ounce
Cinnamon .5 ounce
Cloves .5 ounce
Ginger .25 ounce
Ground sugar .25 pounds

Mix: This compound is excellent for complaints of weak females, such as whites, bearing down, or profuse menstruation, etc. Dose of the powder, is a tea-spoonful, in half cup of boiling water, three times a day, drink the clear only.

INDIAN PILLS

Sarsaparilla extract .5 ounce
Turkey rhubarb powder .5 ounce
Socotrine aloes .5 ounce
Cayenne pepper .25 ounce
Curcuma powder .25 ounce
Valerian powder .25 ounce

Mix in sufficient bullock's gall to form into pill mass, and and make into medium size pills, two, or more, may be taken at bed time. Persons who have weak stomachs, as well, as those who are inclined to dyspepsia, will find this pill very grateful. Females will find great benefit by taking two or three a day, when near confinement.

BUTTERNUT (JUGLANS CINERA)

Butternut is a valuable cathartic, being one of the few laxatives that may be employed to overcome obstinate constipation. It also allays irritation of the mucous membrane, and is useful in some cases of dyspepsia. Use either the bark or solid extract.

TONIC AND LIVER PILLS

Podophyllin 2 grains
Powdered rhubarb .25 ounce
Cayenne pepper 1 drachm
Extract of dandelion .5 ounce
Blood root, powdered .25 ounce

Mix thoroughly, and divide into about three grain pills, very useful in weak stomachs, and inactive liver. Take two to four, twice a day, gradually reducing as the case may require.

INDIGESTION PILL

Powdered aloes, (socotrine) .25 ounce
Powdered rhubarb .5 ounce
Oil of caraway 20 drops
Solid extract of gentian .5 ounce
Solid extract Butternut .25 ounce

Mix thoroughly, and divide into three grain pills. Dose, two before dinner. This pill is a very useful formula for those troubled with dyspepsia, more particularly, those compelled to sit at their daily labor.

AROMATIC AND PURGATIVE PILL

Aloes socotrine 1 ounce
Myrrh, powdered .5 ounce
Cinnamon, powder .25 ounce

Molasses, quantity sufficient to make into pill mass, divide into about three grain pills, Dose: two to four. This pill is useful for those troubled with costiveness combined with what is known as a windy digestion, we only recommend it as a temporary remedy.

COUGH PILLS

Gum ammoniac 1 ounce
Lobelia powdered .5 ounce
Ipecac, powdered .5 ounce
Black hellebore .5 ounce
Extract balm of gilead .5 ounce
Cayenne pepper .5 ounce
Gum arabic powder .5 ounce
Oil spearmint 20 drops.

Bruise the gum ammonica, and dissolve in a little

water by heat, and when dissolved add the ingredients, with a sufficient amount of syrup of squills to form into pill mass, and roll down in licorice powder, into regular sized pills. Dose: Two to be taken three times per day. Good in affection of the lungs, asthma, coughs, etc., as they promote a free expectoration. The use of these pills may occasion in some instances, more or less uneasiness and pain in the bowels, until a more natural warmth and action are restored to the bowels, and then they will cease to produce pain, unless taken in large quantities.

RHEUMATIC PILLS

Extract of sarsaparilla .5 ounce
Poke root powdered .5 ounce
Gum guaiacum, powdered .5 ounce
Cayenne pepper .25 ounce
Macrotin .5 ounce
Xanthoxylin .25 ounce
Iodide of pottas .25 ounce
Extract henbane .25 ounce

Mix thoroughly with a little warm water, if required, roll in licorice powder into common sized pills. Dose: Take two twice a day, about an hour after eating.

BLACKBERRY SYRUP OR CORDIAL

To one quart of blackberry juice, add one pound of white sugar, one table-spoonful of cloves, one of allspice, one of cinnamon, and one of nutmeg. Boil together for fifteen minutes; add a wine-glassful of best whiskey, or brandy. Bottle while hot, cork tight and seal. This preparation is almost a specific in relax of the bowels or diarrhea. One dose, which is a wine-glassful for an adult- half quantity for a child- will often be sufficient to cure diarrhea. It may be taken three or four times a day if the case is severe. This is an invaluable remedy, and should be kept ready, in case of an emergency, more particularly in large families. It might save you much trouble and many dollars.

BALSAM, FRIARS

The old monks knew what was good. This balsam is the same as used by them, from which it takes its name.

Gum benzoin 15 ounces
Strained storax 1.25 ounces
Balsam tolu 5 drachms
Aloes 2.25 ounces
Rectified spirits 1 pint

Mix thoroughly, and let it stand for fourteen days, shaking well occasionally, and always before using. Very useful in chronic asthma, catarrhs, and consumption with a languid circulation. Dose; half a drachm in mucilage, dropped on lump sugar, or a little honey. It is also good for wounds, it stimulates and heals them.

ASTHMA

Milk of gum ammoniac 3 ounces
Syrup of squills 2 ounces
Acid tincture of lobelia .5 ounce
Syrup of licorice .5 ounce

Mix: A dessert-spoonful to be taken when relief is required. It greatly relieves by copious expectoration.

BITE OF MAD DOG

Wash well with a strong decoction of tobacco, and then bind wetted tobacco on the wound- or, take a pound of salt, dissolve in a quart of water; squeeze, bathe, and wash the wound with this liquid for one or two hours; then bind some salt upon it for ten or twelve hours.

SYRUP FOR DYSENTERY

Take of:

Poplar bark 4 ounces
Bayberry Bark 4 ounces
Tormentil root 3 ounces

Simmer gently in four quarts of water, down to three, strain, and add two pounds of granulated sugar; let it come to boiling point; skim, and add half pound of blackberry, or peach jelly and half pint best brandy, bottle, and keep in a cool place. Take a half wine-glassful three or four times per day, or more often if required. This syrup is very good to strengthen the stomach and bowels, and restore weak patients, and is particularly useful in dysentery, which generally leaves the stomach and bowels sore. In a relax, or first stages of dysentery, by using this syrup, it will generally effect a cure.

COUGH SYRUP NO. 2

Take one pint of clarified molasses, one ounce of the tincture of lobelia, quarter ounce of spearmint, one drachm essence of pennyroyal, half drachm essence of oil aniseed, four ounces syrup of red poppy, and one gill of vinegar; mix, and shake thoroughly. Dose: A dessert-spoonful for those above twelve years of age, and upwards, three times per day, a tea-spoonful down to six; the same proportion younger, for children under two years, dilute with a little water. This preparation is one of the best for, coughs, croup, hooping cough, and all affections of the lungs.

LUNG BALSAM

Tincture blood root 4 ounce
Acid tincture lobelia 4 ounce
Tincture red poppy 2 ounce
Tincture capsicum .5 ounce
Essence Sassafras .5 ounce
Essence Anise .5 ounce
New Orleans molasses. 1 quart

Bring the syrup to a boil, and add cautiously, the other ingredients. Dose: One to two tea-spoonfuls.

REMEDY FOR THE EFFECTS OF POISON IVY

Bromine 10 to 20 drops
Olive oil 1 ounce

Mix, rub the mixture gently into the affected parts, three or four times a day The bromine being volatile, the solution should be freshly made.

MRS. MATTESON'S PAIN CURE

Spirits of wine 8 ounces.
Spirits of lavender .5 ounce.
Oil of origanum 1 drachm.
Saltpeter (or niter) 1 drachm.
Gum camphor .25 drachm.

Crush the saltpeter fand camphor, then mix, shake well, and as soon as the saltpeter and camphor are dissolved, it is ready for use. This preparation is good for pains, cramps, and inflammation of the stomach. For what is known as painless colic, and in fact for colic in either man or beast. The dose, is a tea-spoonful in a table-spoonful of water, every half hour until relieved. For horses or cattle with colic, give one once in a pint of oatmeal gruel.

ANTI-SPASMODIC POWDER

Burdock seed, powd. .5 ounce
Ginger, powd 1 ounce
Lobelia herb powd. .5 ounce
Skullcap, powd. .5 ounce
Carraway, powd. .5 ounce
Golden seal, powd. .25 ounce
Cayenne pepper .5 drachm.

This preparation is exceedingly good in spasms, and cramps, of the stomach and bowels. Mix thoroughly, and take for an adult, a tea-spoonful to a cup of boiling water well sweetened, drink the clear only.

TOOTH POWDER, No. 1

Cream tartar, pure 2.5 pounds
Powd. Alum 1 pound
Carb. Magnesia .5 pound
Powd. cuttle fish bone 1 ounce
Powd. Cloves 1.5 ounce
Powd. cassia 1 ounce
Powd. cochineal 3 ounce
Oil peppermint 1 drachm.
Oil burgamot 1 drachm.
Oil geranium 1.5 drachms.

Powder very fine; rub the perfume with the magnesia; then mix, and sieve thoroughly. This is a good preparation for the teeth and gums.

MRS. MATTESON'S TOOTH POWDER

Cream of tartar, powdered 3 ounces.
Cochineal, powdered 1 drachm.

Alum, powdered. 4 drachms.
Myrrh, powdered 1 drachm.
Cinnamon, powdered 1 ounce.
Sugar, powdered 1 ounce.

Mix and pass through a sieve. This is a preparation that has no superior for cleaning, preserving, and whitening the teeth. It has been used extensively by the ancients as well as the people of our time, and has no equal as a cleanser.

PILE POWDER

Black pepper 1 ounce
White poplar bark 1 ounce
Elecampane 1 ounce
Fennel seed .5 ounce
Ground loaf sugar .25 pound

Mix well, and sieve as before. Dose: A tea-spoonful in hot water three times a day, and a half tea-spoonful of the extract of senna in the dose on going to bed. Use a pile ointment in connection with the powder, prepared in the following manner, viz. Take grated horse-chestnuts, two ounces, fresh lard, four ounces, simmer until the grated nuts are well browned, strain through a cloth while hot, when cold, apply to the parts. This is a good pile ointment.

STOMACH BITTERS

Balmony 2 ounces
Bayberry 2 ounces
White poplar bark 1 ounce
Ginger 1 ounce
Cinnamon .25 ounce
Cloves .25 ounce

Mix thoroughly and run through a sieve. This is

designed to correct the bile and create an appetite. It is an excellent tonic, and will be found very useful for those brought low by disease or old age. Dose: A tea-spoonful sweetened, in a cup of boiling water, drink the clear.

COMPOSITION POWDER

Bayberry powder 2 ounces
Hemlock bark, powder 2 ounces
Ginger root, powder 2 ounces
Cayenne pepper .25 ounce
Cloves, powdered .25 ounce

Mix. The above must be all in fine powder, sifted through a fine sieve, and kept well corked in a bottle. For a dose take a tea-spoonful of the powder, with an equal quantity of sugar, to a cupful of boiling water; to be taken when cool, drink the clear only. Useful in the first stage of disease, for colds, relax of the bowels, and to remove obstructions, caused by cold, or inward heat.

TOOTH POWDER, No. 2

Bayberry, powder .5 ounce.
Alum root, powder .5 ounce
Gum myrrh, powder .25 ounce
Orris root, powder .5 ounce
Cuttlefish, powder. .5 ounce
Carbonate of soda, powder .5 ounce
Oil of rosemary .25 ounce

Mix thoroughly, and pass through a sieve. This is a very good preparation for whitening the teeth, as well as sweetening the breath. It is also useful for sore and spongy gums.

COUGH POWDER

Skunk cabbage 1 ounce.
Wake robin 1 ounce.
Bayberry bark 1 ounce
Valerian .5 ounce.
Lobelia 1 drachm.

The above must be all in fine powder, thoroughly mixed and sifted through a fine sieve. The dose is a tea-spoonful in boiling water, sweetened, going to bed. This preparation is very useful, and will relieve a cough when other remedies fail.

FOR NERVOUSNESS

Valerian root, powder 1 ounce.
Skullcap powder 1 ounce

Mix a tea-spoonful in boiling water, sweetened; for all nervous disorders.

WEAK EYES

Take of sulfate of zinc, eight grains, tincture of opium fifteen drops, rose water, one ounce; Mix and apply with a cloth to the eyes night and morning, or bathe with the tincture of camphor, twice a day. A good eye water is prepared in the following manner: Take three ounces of Lisbon wine and half a drachm of lapis calaminaris, in powder; shake them well together, and use this to weak and sore eyes, bathing with a cloth twice a day,

INFLAMMATION OF THE EYE

Spring well water, one pint; sulfate of zinc, half a drachm, mix. Bathe eyes several times per day.

HOARSENESS

Take of fresh scraped horseradish, two ounces, infuse in a half pint of cold water, for two hours, in a close vessel; then add two ounces acid tincture of lobelia and a quarter of a pound of honey, simmer the whole for ten minutes, strain, and take a tea-spoonful three times per day; apply outwardly, the cayenne liniment, going to bed at night.

SMOKING HERBS

Many persons who have been accustomed to the use of tobacco, but who may have become asthmatic, will find the following compound, much better than the tobacco of commerce. As it possesses no nicotine properties. Viz:

Stramonium leaves 4 ounces.
Yarrow leaves 4 ounces.
Rose leaves 3 ounces.
Coltsfoot leaves 3 ounces.
Mullen leaves 3 ounces.

Dry moderately, cut fine, and scent with a little essence of musk. Mix ready for use.

SORE MOUTH

An invaluable remedy for sore mouth, spongy gums, loose teeth, fetid, or bad breath, and for gently correcting and cleansing the stomach, may be found by using the following. Infuse a handful of raspberry leaves, in a half pint of boiling water, for fifteen minutes, and when cold, strain, and add two ounces of the tincture of myrrh, rinse the mouth with a little of it two or three times per day, swallowing a little each time, until relieved.

BLEEDING PILES AND BLOODY FLUX

Take of wood sanicle, two ounces, tormentil root, two ounces, boil in three pints of water, down to one quart, and add one ounce of the tincture myrrh. Take a wineglass full three or four times a day

SCURVY IN THE GUMS, TO CURE

Make a strong tea of sage, and dissolve therein a little alum, dip a cloth therein and rub the gums with the same. If you wish a good tooth wash, mix a little burnt alum with two ounces of honey, and two spoonfuls of the juice of celendine, and rub your teeth with the same.

TO CURE - SCURF OR DANDRUFF IN THE HEAD

Into a pint of water drop a lump of fresh quick-lime, the size of a walnut; let it stand all night, pour off the clear, strain, and add one gill of the best vinegar, wash the roots of the hair with the preparation. It is a good remedy, and harmless.

TO CURE WARTS

The juice of the marigold frequently applied is effectual in removing them, wash them with tincture of myrrh.

TO CURE CORNS

Pare the corn, and apply the tincture of iodine with a camel hair brush, repeat several times, or, touch the corn with the strong acetic acid on going to bed, after several applications, pick out the corn. Soft corns will disappear if treated in this way.

THE OCCULT FAMILY PHYSICIAN

TO CURE WHITLOWS

Take a lemon, cut a hole in it, and wear it on the finger like a thimble, the whitlow being encased in the fruit it will soon disappear.

FOR CORRECTING THE BILE AND CREATING AN APPETITE

The following preparation will be found useful to those who are bilious, and dyspeptic, and for creating an appetite:

Bitter herb 2 ounces
Bayberry bark 2 ounces
Poplar bark 2 ounces
Balmony 2 ounces
Ginger- 1 ounce
Licorice juice .5 ounce

Simmer in two quarts of water, down to three pints, strain, add four ounces of spirit, and take a wine-glassful three times per day.

GONORRHEA AND GLEET

Bathe the parts morning, noon and night, for ten minutes, in hot water, and take two capsules of docuta sandal wood two hours after each meal. Use no injections, but bathe freely. Also let the patient take a tea-spoonful of of peacocks bromides, containing about five drachms of the active principle of yellow jessamine, or gelseminum. The patient should continue the capsules twice daily, for ten days after discharge has ceased. Keep the bowels moderately open with stomach pills.

PLASTERS

CANCER PLASTER

Take of red clover flowers sufficient to fill a brass kettle, and boil them in water for one hour; then take them out and fill the kettle again with fresh ones, boil as before in the same liquor; strain, and press out all the juice, then simmer the liquor over a slow fire, till about the consistency of tar, when it is fit for use; be careful not to let it burn. When used it should be spread on a piece of bladder, split and made soft. It is an excellent remedy for the cure of cancers, and old sores in any part of the body.

STIMULATING PLASTER

Take cumin seeds, caraway seeds, laurel berries, of each, one ounce; dried pitch one pound; yellow wax, one ounce. Melt the pitch and wax together, then add the ingredients in fine powder, and mix thoroughly. This is a stimulant and discutient plaster, very useful for coldness between the shoulders, and likewise for indolent tumors.

POOR MAN'S PLASTER

Take of litharage plaster, twenty-four parts; white resin, six parts; yellow wax, olive oil, of each three parts; red oxide of iron, eight parts. Rub the red oxide of iron with the oil, and adding the other ingredients melted, mix the whole together. This plaster is applied with advantage in case of muscular relaxation, weakness of the joints, sprains, and strains, pains in the back, etc., spread on stout linen or thin leather.

STRENGTHENING PLASTER

Take burdock leaves and mullein leaves, bruise

them and put them in a kettle, with a sufficient quantity of water, and boil well; then strain off the liquor, press or squeeze the leaves, and boil down to the consistency of thin molasses; then add three parts of resin and of turpentine, and simmer them well together, until the water is evaporated; then pour it into cold water, and work it well with the hands; if two hard put in more turpentine, when it is ready for use. Spread on soft leather, and apply to the parts affected; is good to strengthen weakness in the back, and other parts of the body.

HAIR TONIC AND DYES

The practice of dyeing the hair, by way of personal adornment, has been universally follow^ed, among the people of every country, both civilized, and uncivilized. The practice in eastern Europe, is to blacken the edge of the eye-lids, both above and below, for this purpose they use a powder called Kohol. It becomes our duty, to say that, as a rule hair dyes ought to be avoided; as personal beauty is often spoiled by the inharmonious application of colors. But the use of hair tonics, we would strongly recommend, for strengthening, and cleansing the scalp, and overcoming the cankerous diseases which cause the hair to fall off, hence, we give a few valuable formula.

PREPARATION FOR DESTROYING HAIR

Hydro-sulfate of soda, crystals 2 drachms.
Quick lime, (powdered,) 10 drachms
Starch, (powdered,) 11 drachms

Powder the soda and mix quickly. To apply: Make the powder into a paste with a little water, and spread it on the place to be deprived of hair. As, on pulling one hair, it comes off readily, the paste is to be washed off with water and some simple cerate, or cold cream applied.

BARBER'S OIL FOR THE HAIR

Castor oil 1.5 pints
Alcohol .5 pints
Oil of bergamot 1 drachm
Oil of lavender drachm

Mix. This is a good preparation for strengthening the hair, as well as feeding it.

HAIR OIL, OR CREAM

Alcohol 1.5 gallons
Castor oil 1.5 gallons
Coconut oil 2 pounds
Oil of lavender 3 ounces
Oil of bergamot 3 ounces
Oil of white thyme ounce

Melt the coconut oil in the castor oil; warm the alcohol over a water bath, and add the oils when it is cold; lastly add the perfume.

SHAMPOO WASH

Borax (powdered) 4 drachms.
Bay rum 2 ounces.
Water of ammonia 1 ounce.
Rose water 13 ounces.

Mix: This is a first-class preparation, and one that cannot be surpassed for the purpose which it is intended.

TEA HAIR DYE AND TONIC

Strong infusion of black tea 1 pint.

Bay rum 4 ounces.
Oil of lavender 1 drachm.
Alcohol 4 ounces.
Glycerin 4 ounces.

Mix: This is a simple but good dye, as well as tonic; to be rubbed on the head two or three times per day. In using hair dyes, be sure and use the mordant for cleaning the hair, and when the hair is dry, then apply the silver solution.

QUICK HAIR DYE (Mordant.)

Acid pyrogallic 1 drachm.
Water, distilled 5 ounces.
Alcohol .5 ounce.

THE DYE

Nitrate of silver, crystals 1 drachm.
Water, distilled 6 drachms.
Water of ammonia 2 drachms. or quantity sufficient to make clear.

Mix: Clean the hair with the mordant, then apply the dye, with a comb. If any of the surrounding surface becomes stained with the dye, remove with the following:

Sulphuret of potash .5 drachm.
Distilled water 1 ounce.

This preparation will remove the stains.

A VALUABLE HAIR TONIC AND DYE

Sugar of lead 1 ounce.
Borax 1 ounce
Lac. sulfur 1 ounce

Water of ammonia .5 ounce
Alcohol 4 ounces

Mix, and let stand for fourteen hours- then add:

Bay rum 4 ounces.
Table salt 3 drachms.
Soft water 3 pints.
Essence of bergamot 1 ounce.

Remarks: It will turn gray hair to a dark color, and will cause the hair to grow. When the hair is thin, or the head bald, apply twice daily. For gray hair, one application daily will be sufficient,

INDIAN HAIR TONIC

Oil, castor 3 ounces.
Oil, bergamot 3 drachms.
Oil, cinnamon 15 drops.
Oil, cloves 15 drops.
Oil, lavender 1.5 drachms:
Tinct. cantharides 2 drachms.
Water of ammonia 4 drachms.
Alcohol sufficient to make 2 pints.

Mix: This is a splendid preparation; and one, that has been the means of saving many heads of hair to their owners. Rub in with the hand, once or twice a day; the hair will not only be invigorated, but will gradually resume its original color.

ROSEMARY HAIR WASH

Rosemary 2 ounces.
Southernwood 2 ounces

Boil in one quart of water for half an hour, strain

when cold. Add the following, and mix well together:

Rosewater 6 ounces.
Olive oil 12 ounces
Spirits of ammonia. 4 ounces
Spirits of cantharides 2 ounces
Otto of rose 20 drops.

Shake well, and apply the wash night and morning to the roots of the hair, the brush being freely used before and after each application.

ENGLISH FACE WASH

English precip. chalk 3 ounces.
Powd. borax 1 drachm.
Bay rum 1 ounce.
Glycerin .5 ounce.
Ex. Violet. 1 drachm.
Distilled water 1 pint.

Rub the chalk and glycerin to a smooth paste, then add the rest. This preparation has been used extensively in England and other parts of Europe, for hiding a coarse skin, freckles and other blemishes, etc.

DISINFECTANT

Sulfate of iron 5 pounds
Carbolic acid, (crude) 4 ounces
Water 5 gallons

Mix: To be used as a disinfectant in time of epidemics, or contagious disease. Powdered charcoal, is also very useful, where there is contagious disease. It should be kept in every room in a box, uncovered. It is a great absorbent of disease germs, and sweetener of the atmosphere.

A VALUABLE FAMILY SALVE

For burns, scalds, cuts, and wounds, of every description, a valuable remedy. Take:

Yellow dock root 2 ounces.
Dandelion root 2 ounces.
Celendine herb 2 ounces.
Plantain leaves 2 ounces.

Cover with water, allowing the ingredients to steep for several hours, then simmer gently for one hour; strain, and press the juice out as dry as possible. Then simmer the liquid with fresh butter and mutton tallow, or you may take sweet oil and mutton tallow. Simmer until no appearance of the liquid remains, strain through a coarse cloth, and bottle for use.

ALTERATIVE, OR PURIFYING POWDER

Sassafras bark 1 ounce
Rhubarb root 1 ounce
Sarsaparilla .5 ounce
Cubebs .5 ounce
Comfrey root 1 ounce
Stillenger .5 ounce
Dock root .5 ounce
Cayenne .25 ounce

All of the articles must be ground fine. Mix well, give a tea-spoonful in a cup of boiling water, sweetened, three times a day. Excellent in purifying the blood, and cleansing the system in old scorbutic cases,

FEMALE RESTORATIVE POWDER

Balmony .5 ounce

THE OCCULT FAMILY PHYSICIAN

White pond lily .5 ounce
Cloves .5 ounce
Bistort .5 ounce
Comfrey root 1 ounce
Tormentil root 1 ounce
Cayenne 1 drachm

Mix well, and take in wine-glassful doses, well sweetened. This will be found a most excellent remedy for leucorrhoe (whites) and all excesses of menstruation, etc.

A GOOD SUBSTITUTE FOR COFFEE

Clean and cut up parsnips in thin slices, after which hang to dry, and roast in the oven, grind to powder, and use as coffee. This is a most excellent substitute, cheaper, and more healthful. Make as you would coffee, with sugar, milk, etc.

FEMALE CORRECTIVE POWDER

Excellent in obstructions of the monthly periods, debility, loss of appetite, etc.

Poplar bark 2 ounces.
Ginger .5 ounce.
Bayberry 1 ounce.
Cinnamon .5 ounce.
Aniseed .5 ounce.
Golden seal .25 ounce.

Mix well, and give a teaspoonful in a cup of boiling water, sweetened with sugar, two or three times a day.

PILE OINTMENT

Take of horse chestnuts, grated, and the green plant of celendine, quarter of a pound of each, and simmer in one pound of leaf lard, until the nuts are a rich brown; or say, for about two hours, strain through a coarse cloth, and it is ready for use. This ointment has cured many inveterate cases of bleeding and inward piles of long standing, for inward piles, smear a tallow candle with the ointment and push into the anus. But be sure and keep the bowels regular with a mild aperient pill, and eat but little meat, in fact, live principally on a vegetable diet, and it will never fail to cure, even the most chronic cases.

ROSE CREAM, OR LIP-SALVE

Oil of sweet almonds 1 ounce.
White wax 4 drachms.
Spermaceti 1.5 drachms.
Oil of rose 3 drops.
Carmine 3 grains.

Heat the oil of almonds and carmine together, filter; melt wax and and spermaceti; add to the above; remove from the fire; add oil of rose, and stir till cold. This is a very useful preparation for chapped hands, cracked and dry lips, dry scurvy, and for softening, beautifying, and cleansing the skin generally.

A GOOD FAMILY OINTMENT

White wax 4 ounces.
Bayberry wax 1 ounce
Spermaceti 3ounces
Olive oil 1 pint.

Mix them together over a slow fire, taking care to stir it briskly until cool. This is an excellent ointment for mothers when troubled with sore nipples; it moistens the skin and keeps it soft; it is good for dry scurvy, chapped hands, blotches on the face, and all sores which require a mild ointment, but should be assisted with internal medicines, when the case requires it.

OINTMENT FOR OLD SORES

Honey 8 ounces.
Beeswax 8 ounces
Spirits turpentine 1 ounces
Oil of wintergreen 1 ounce
Tincture opium 2 ounces
Fluid extract lobelia .5 ounce
Lard 1.5 pounds

Mix by the aid of gentle heat, stirring well at the same time. This is a very useful ointment for healing of wounds and old sores. A smaller quantity may be prepared by reducing the quantity of each article in proportion. For those who may have used the German remedy, known as "Brust Thee," Breast tea, we give the formula.

BREAST TEA

Marsh mallow root 4 ounces.
Orris root 1 ounce
Coltsfoot leaves .5 ounces
Red poppy flowers 2 ounce
Licorice root. 1 ounce
Mullen leaves 1 ounce
Star anise seed 1 ounce

Cut fine and mix well, this is a good mixture for colds, coughs, and cases where a quiet soothing medicine is needed, it is a good general remedy, for those who are subject to relax in the sudden changes of temperature.

LINIMENT FOR CHRONIC RHEUMATISM

Olive oil 1 pint.
Sassafras oil 2 drachms.

Camphor gum 2 ounces.
Chloroform .5 ounce.

Dissolve the camphor in the oil, and when dissolved, add the chloroform, and four ounces oil of turpentine or rosemary. Rub the parts well night and morning. If the limbs are very sensitive to cold, add to the mixture two ounces of the tincture of capsicum.

LINSEED OIL AND LIME WATER

Raw linseed oil 8 ounces.
Lime water 8 ounces

Mix by shaking well until the oil has thoroughly amalgamated with the oil. This preparation is very useful for burns and scalds.

PAIN KILLER

Spirits of camphor 2 ounces.
Tincture of capsicum 1 ounce
Tincture of guaicum .5 ounce
Tincture of Myrrh .5 ounce
Alcohol 4 ounces.

Mix, used as a pain killer internally or externally A teaspoonful in a little water, is the dose internally, and rubbing the parts externally.

MRS. MATTESON'S PAIN RELIEF

Oil of cajeput 2 drachms.
Oil of Sassafras bounce.
Oil of origanum 1 drachm.
Oil of hemlock 1 drachm.
Oil of cedar 1 drachm.
Powdered capsicum 80 grains.

Alcohol, quantity sufficient for 1 pint.

Mix: This preparation is a veritable pain killer, and may be used internally, as well as externally. It is excellent for rheumatic pains when used outwardly, as well as pains in the back, sprains, cramps in the legs, and headache, and internally for colic, cramps in the stomach, etc. The dose is two tea-spoonfuls in a wineglass full of water.

INDIAN LINIMENT

Linseed oil 1 quart.
Aqua ammonia 1 ounce
Tincture of capsicum .5 ounce.
Oil origanum .25 ounce.

Mix: This is one of the old fashioned liniments that has been used extensively throughout the United States for many years, and makes a good local application for sprains and bruises, etc.

KEROSENE LINIMENT

Kerosene oil 2 ounces.
Tincture of opium 4 drachms.
Tincture arnica 5 drachms.
Tincture Stramonium 6 drachms.
Aromatic spirits of ammonia. 6 drachms.
Spirits of camphor 5 drachms.
Oil origanum 4 drachms.
Chloroform 8 drachms.

Mix: This is a very valuable preparation for sprains and bruises, from any cause. Rub in twice during the twenty four hours.

LINIMENT FOR NEURALGIA AND ALL NERVOUS PAINS

Essential oil of mustard 1 drachm.
Aconitin 1 grain.
Glycerin 1 ounce.
Alcohol 4 ounces.

Mix, and shake well before using. This remedy is a valuable external preparation for all nervous and neuralgic pains, rub twice a day until relieved.

MRS. MATTESON'S CELEBRATED TOOTH WASH

Soap bark, (Quillaya) 3 ounces.
Star Anise 1 ounce
Cloves 2 drachms
Cinnamon 2 drachms
Oil Peppermint 12 drops
Carmine, No. 40 5 grains.
Diluted alcohol 28 ounces.

Macerate the drugs with the alcohol until the strength is exhausted, let the drugs be in coarse powder, then add the carmine, and oil of peppermint; filter, and bottle for use. This makes a very superior wash for the teeth, and one that is not alone a great cleanser, but is also a sweetener of the breath, which alone, is saying a great deal, for what is worse than a foul breath? It is a harmless preparation, as it contains nothing that is in any way injurious to the teeth or gums. When cleaning the teeth, use a few drops on the brush, each time, and rinse with cold water. This preparation may be had of the author at her residence, see title page.

VETERINARY PRESCRIPTIONS

We propose to give a few valuable prescriptions for some of the diseases to be found among horses. They are reliable and will be found safe in those diseases for which they are designated.

WHITE OINTMENT

Take:

Fresh butter 1 pound.
Tincture iodine 1 ounce.
Oil origanum 2 ounces.

Mix well together, and apply every night, rub in well with the hand. This ointment is well suited for swellings of all kinds.

STOPPAGE OF THE BOWELS

Take piece of lime the size of a hens egg, and stir into a half pint of molasses; give in one dose, followed by a quart of boneset tea, to be given warm. This is a grateful preparation where the horses bowels have become so costive, and dry, that they cease to move naturally. Follow the dose with another quart of boneset tea, in one hour. If the first does not operate.

FOR BELLY-ACHE AND COLIC

Powdered colycinth 1 ounce
Alcohol .5 pint

Mix: give ten or twelve drops in a little water; if necessary repeat the dose in a half hour,

FOR FRESH WOUNDS, KICKS, AND COLLAR GALLS: GREEN OINTMENT

Pine pitch .5 pound.
Verdegris 2 ounces.
Fresh lard .5 pound.

Mix, and apply to the parts, keep well covered with a cloth.

CHRONIC COUGH

The following will be found very useful in chronic cough, take:

Balsam fir 2 ounces
Balsam copabia 2 ounces
Tincture lobelia .5 ounce

Mix, and give a table-spoonful once a day. Keep your horse dry; and give the blood purifier at the same time.

WORMS IN HORSES

Take the following in one dose, and repeat if necessary, viz:

Santonine powder 10 grains.
Castor oil 4 ounces.
Whiskey 2 ounces

BLOOD PURIFIER

Use the following, all in fine powder, viz:

Gentian root 2 ounces.
Sassafras bark 2 ounces.

Elecampane 2 ounces.
Skunk cabbage 1 ounce.
Cream tartar 1 ounce
Saltpeter 2.5 ounces.
Ginger 2 ounces.
Sulfur 6 ounces.
Blood root 1 ounce.
Buchu leaves 1 ounce.
Juniper berries 1 ounce.

Mix: If your horse is in bad health, give a table-spoonful once a day, for about fifteen days.

FOR HOOF-BOUND, HOOF-EVIL, OR ANY DISEASE OF THE FOOT

Balsam fir 2 ounces.
Venice turpentine 2 ounces.
Oil tar 11 ounces.
Oil hemlock 1.25 ounces.
Tincture iodine 1.25 ounces.
Alcohol 1.5 ounces.

Mix: Turn up the foot, and put a tea-spoonful in the crease of the frog; and also in the heel of the frog, once a day for twenty to forty days, as may be needed. Hold a hot iron near the foot for a short time.

FOR BLOOD OR BOG SPAVINS, WINDGALLS, ETC

Take of:

Oil hemlock 2 ounces
Turpentine 3 ounces
Oil wormwood 1 ounce
Iodide potassium 4 drachms
Tincture cantharides 2 ounces
Alcohol 8 ounces

Mix thoroughly, then bathe the affected parts with smartweed or wormwood tea, warm, and rub the parts every other day with the liniment, until the liniment has been used six, or eight times; wash the parts well before using, be sure and shake the medicine well before applying. If too much soreness is produced, omit the medicine, and grease well.

OINTMENT TO MAKE HAIR GROW ITS NATURAL COLOR

Soot .5 ounce
Gun powder .5 ounce
Fresh lard .5 pound

Mix thoroughly, and apply to the injured, or exposed parts. Let the soot be from pipe or stove that has been burning wood.

OINTMENT FOR INFLAMMATION OF THE KIDNEYS

Take of fresh lard one half pound, the whites of a half dozen eggs, and mix them thoroughly together, and apply over the region of the kidneys, be sure and cover up with a blanket.

EYE WASH

The following formula is a good remedy for inflamed and sore eyes.

Sugar of lead 2 drachms.
Sulfate of zinc .5 drachm.
1 Tincture opium .5 ounce.
Soft water 1 pint.

Mix, and shower the eyes with cold water for fifteen minutes, and bathe with the wash twice a day.

BOTTS

Mix the following. Give a dose, followed in a few hours, by half pint of castor oil.

Whiskey 5 ounces.
New Milk 7 ounces.

FISTULA AND POLL-EVIL

This preparation will cure what is known as the sweeny, by bathing the shoulder. Put in the pipes, by means of a syringe, twice in four days. Mix the following:

Alcohol 1 pint.
Spirits of ammonia 4 ounces.
Tincture iodine 1 ounce
Tincture cantharides ounce.
Oil of cedar 1 ounce.

HEAVES

Give three or four grains of tartar emetic, in wet food, until the horse is relieved; then use every time they return. Care is required in feeding. Wet food is always best. This remedy will give relief only.

RING-BONE – BIG-HEAD

Use the following, mix in an open vessel.

Quicksilver 2 ounces.
Tincture cantharides 2 drachms.
Nitric acid 2 ounces.
Oil of cedar 2 drachms.

Shave the hair from the spavin, and apply

occasionally for twenty-four hours; then wash the parts with castile soap and water. Follow after with some healing ointment.

COLIC

Mix the following and give at one dose. If not better in thirty minutes; repeat the dose. Use a tobacco injection if needed.

Laudanum 1 ounce.
Sweet spirits of niter 1 ounce.
Tincture capsicum 2 drachms.
Carbonate of soda 2 ounces.

A GOOD CONDITION POWDER

This condition powder is a good regulator of the system generally, and will restore the tone to the stomach, kidneys, and bowels; by the aid of friction externally, you may build a new horse.

Powdered Gentian 2 pounds.
Powdered Saltpeter pound.
Powdered Sulfur 2 pounds.
Powdered Resin 1 pound.
Powdered Fenugreek 1 pound.
Powdered Ginger 2 pounds.
Powdered Capsicum 1 pound.
Powdered Black antimony 2 pounds.
Powdered Flax Seed 5 pounds.
Powdered Slippery elm bark 5 pounds.
Powdered Blood root 1 pound.
Powdered Copperas 5 pounds.

Mix thoroughly, and give a dessert-spoonful twice a day, to be given in soft feed. A smaller quantity may be mixed by reducing each article in proportion.

NASAL GLEET

The following will be found very useful in nasal gleet:

Alum .5 pound.
Resin .5 pound.
Blue vitriol 2 ounces.

Grind to a fine powder, and then add ginger powder, half pound. Give a table-spoonful, every night and morning. Keep the animal dry, and do not work him for a few days.

PHYSIC BALL

Aloes, powdered .5 ounce.
Jalap, powdered .5 ounce.
Oil juniper 3 drops.

Make into one pill with molasses. Very useful where the bowels are costive.

GREEN OINTMENT, No. 2

Lobelia herb 2 ounces.
Cider vinegar .5 ounce.
Fresh lard 1 pound.

Simmer in brass kettle until the complete evaporation of the vinegar. This ointment is an excellent remedy for stiff joints, large and swelled joints, white swellings, etc., bathe the parts with warm water, and rub in well with the hand.

YELLOW WATER

Take:

Aloes, powdered 6 drachms.
Jalap, powdered 4 drachms.
Myrrh, powdered 2 drachms.
Oil juniper 1 drachm.
Ginger, powdered 4 drachms.
Molasses sufficient to make into a ball.

When the bowels have moved, stop the physic, and give one tablespoonful of spirits niter, in a pint of water, every morning for twelve days.

MISCELLANEOUS

BLACKBERRY WINE

Blackberries, crushed, 10 gallons
Boiling water 2.5 gallons.
Sugar 20 pounds
Alcohol 5 pints

Crush the berries, pour on the water, let it stand twenty four hours, stirring occasionally; then strain into a cask add the sugar, and alcohol, cork tight and let it stand for a few months, when it will be fit for use. This makes a delightful wine, very useful in relax of the bowels.

FRECKLE LOTION

Muriate of ammonia 1 drachm
Distilled water 1 pint
Lavender water 2 drachms

Mix. Apply with a sponge, several times a day.

TOILET CHAMPION

Chlorate of potass, powdered 1 drachm.
Rose water. 5 ounces.
Glycerin 3 ounces.

Mix, This is one of the best preparations known; being a valuable remedy for chapped hands, lips, dry scurvy, etc.

REMEDY FOR CHICKEN CHOLERA

Sulfuric acid 1 fluid ounce.
Sulfate of iron 16 ounces.
Water to dissolve 1 gallon.

Mix. Add one ounce of this mixture to a pint of water, and supply, in place of water, to drink ; or, mix with meal or other food. This is a valuable remedy, for those raising chickens, or poultry of any kind.

HOG CHOLERA CURE

Mandrake 2 pounds.
Charcoal 1 pound.
Resin .5 pound.
Saltpeter .5 pound.
Madder .5 pound.
Bi-carbonate soda 5 pounds.

All in fine powder. Mix thoroughly, give a table-spoonful daily in feed; as a preventative, give twice a week.

INSECT EXTERMINATOR

Quassia chips 3.25 ounces
Stavesacre seed 5 drachms

THE OCCULT FAMILY PHYSICIAN

Boil in eight pints of water down to about five, when cool, strain it and use with a watering pot. This is a very useful preparation for destroying insects that infest plants.

FLY POISON

Chloride of cobalt .5 ounce.
Brown sugar 3 ounces.
Hot water 1 pint.

Dissolve the cobalt in the water and add the sugar, saturate unsized brown paper in the solution, hang up and dry. When required for use, lay in a plate with a little water.

FRENCH SHOE DRESSING

Vinegar 2 pints.
Soft water 1 pint.
Glue, powdered 4 ounces.
Logwood chips 8 ounces.
Powdered Indigo 2 drachms.
Bi-Chromate potass 4 ounces.
Gum tragacanth 4 ounces.
Glycerin 4 ounces.

Boil together for a short time, strain and bottle for use. This makes an elegant shoe dressing, and one that in nowise impoverishes the leather.

PERSPIRATION POWDER, (to prevent)

Persons in the habit of sweating too freely in the hands or feet, will find the following formula a very good preventative:

Carbolic acid 10 drops.
Salicylic acid 10 grains.

Burnt alum, powdered 1 drachm.
Starch, powdered 2 ounces.
French chalk, powdered 2 ounces.
Oil of lemon 20 drops.

Mix thoroughly. To be dusted in the stockings or gloves.

ARTIFICAL HONEY

The manner in which it is prepared:

Clarified sugar 10 pounds;
Pure honey, strained 3 pounds.
Soft water 3 pints.
Cream tartar 1 drachm.
Essence peppermint 10 drops.

Dissolve the sugar in the water by the aid of gentle heat, take off the scum, add the honey and the cream tartar, previously dissolved in a little water, bring to the boiling point, stir well, then let it cool. We give this preparation for what it is worth, not that we would recommend it ill preference to the genuine article.

FRENCH ABSINTHE

Oil of wormwood 1 drachm.
Oil of melisa 15 drops.
Oil of anise 2.5 drachms.
Oil of star anise 2.5 drachms.
Oil of fennel .5 drachm.
Oil of coriander 3 drops.
Alcohol 14 pints.
Water 6 pints.

Mix: This is an elegant preparation.

THE OCCULT FAMILY PHYSICIAN

FOR REMOVING IRON RUST FROM CLOTHING, ETC

Cream of tartar 4 ounces.
Oxalic acid 4 ounces.

Mix; and apply with a sponge.

TRAPPER AND FISHERMAN'S SECRET

Oil of rhodium 1 ounce.
Oil cumin /bounce.
Tincture musk 1 drachm.

Mix: Used by putting a drop or two on the bait.

GREASE ERADICATOR

Castile soap, shavings 4 ounces.
Carbonate soda, powdered 2 ounce.
Borax, powdered 1 ounce.
Water of ammonia 7 ounces.
Alcohol 3 ounces.
Turpentine 2 ounces.
Sulfuric ether 2 ounces
Soft water sufficient for .5 gallons

Boil the soap with the water until dissolved, then remove from the fire and add the rest. This is a good preparation for removing all kinds of grease, paint, or tar spots from cloth or cotton goods, without in any way injuring the goods. Apply with a sponge.

TO MAKE A GOOD FLY PAPER

Castor oil 8 ounces
Resin 24 ounces
Sugar 4 ounces

Melt over a slow fire, stirring constantly; while yet warm spread upon unsized manila paper; paint your paper with a coat of common glue first, and allow to dry, then spread mixture.

LIQUID BLUING

Soluble Prussian blue 2 ounces.
Olalic acid .5 ounce.
Water 1 gallon.

Boil together for a few minutes, stir well, allow to cool and settle, then pour off and bottle.

TOLU CHEWING GUM

Balsam tolu 4 ounces.
Gum benzoin 1 ounce.
White wax 1 ounce.
Paraffin 1 ounce.
White sugar 1 ounce.

Mix by melting. While warm make into sticks, and wrap in paper.

WASHING POWDER FOR FAMILY USE

Carbonate soda, powdered 5 pounds.
Hypo-sulfite soda, powdered 1 pound.
Borax, powdered 1 pound.

Mix: Use a tea-spoonful to each gallon of water, when the clothes are boiled. It is a harmless preparation, and will save considerable labor.

DOMESTIC WINE MAKING

Wine making is an art; and while the process is too

complicated, and space too limited, to admit of all the details in being published in our work, still, as good domestic wine, from our own native fruits, are a healthful drink when not taken to excess; a few hints may be of value, and not out of place.

First: It is important that grapes or other fruit used should be gathered at the proper time, on dry, pleasant days; and carefully handled to prevent bruising and decay.

Second: After the fruit is crushed, the expressed juice
must) should be placed only in clean, sweet vessels, and closely watched during the process of fermentation.

Third: The practical production of proper regulation of the vinous fermentation constitutes the real art of wine making, as it is here the greatest difficulty is met, and the most careful attention and best judgment are required to overcome it. Saccharine fermentation first takes place, by which starch and gum are converted into sugar. Next, alcohol or vinous fermentation sets in, by which the sugar is converted into alcohol. If the fermentation proceeds too far, the alcohol is converted into vinegar and the wine is spoiled. Vinous fermentation proceeds most favorable at a temperature of from 68° to 80° F. If possible, the wort should be kept at about that, for if the temperature rises above 90 degrees, the fermentation takes place too fast. If the weather is too cool for the sugar to be decomposed, fermentation can be hastened by the addition of a small quantity of good yeast. Ripe grapes, or other sweet fruits, do not usually require this.

Fourth: After wine is sufficiently fermented, it may be racked off into another cask, and allowed to remain and ripen; or, it may be bottled at pleasure. Have the bottles clean and dry, cork well, and wire down; lay the bottles on the side, in a dry cellar, kept at a temperature of 48 to 60 degrees, F. It is best to let wine remain upon the lees and ripen for several months before bottling. If bottled too soon, the bottles will burst.

Fifth: If wine is clouded, it must be clarified by 'fining,' which is done by adding one or two ounces of it in glass, dissolved in boiling water, to each barrel, and mixing by agitation. White of eggs, beaten to a froth, will answer the same purpose.

Sixth: Inordinate fermentation, either primary or secondary, may be checked by racking off the wine into a cask, previously fumigated by burning a little sulfur in it. Another method is to put from one half pound to one pound of bruised mustard seed into each barrel. Either process will also remove mustiness from the wine or corks.

Seventh: Experience alone, can furnish the amateur wine-maker the knowledge required to insure success

GENERAL RULES

with quantities for making domestic wines, from ripe saccharine fruits:

Ripe fruit 24 pounds.
Soft water 1 gallon.
Loaf sugar 3 pounds.
Cream tartar, dissolved in hot water 1.25 ounces.
Brandy 1 quart

Mix: This must stand for one week before drawing off.

ANOTHER FORMULA

Is the same as the above, only using two pounds more fruit and sugar, this will be found excellent without brandy, but of course better with it, and to make it still better, one and one-half pounds of raisins may be added to each pound of sugar. The same directions must be used as in the above formula. By following the above formulas, excellent wines can be made from the following fruits:

Gooseberry, currant, cherry, elder, strawberry, raspberry, mulberry, blackberry, apple, grape, apricot, and other fruits.

ON HERBS AND THEIR APPLICATION

*"Herbs gladly cure our flesh because that they
Find their acquaintance there."*

-Herbert.

While a classification of herbs have been made scientifically by Linnaeus, who arranged them according to various rules, there is still a further classification needed. It is calculated that there are in the vegetable world, upwards of one hundred thousand species of plants, trees, etc. The object of systematic botany is to arrange this vast assemblage of the productions of nature into their various tribes, genera, and species, according to their forms and structure. Such knowledge is unquestionably of great use, and tends to facilitate the progress of the student in the study of medical Botany. Without some such arrangement as this, we should be at a loss in describing a plant, so as to make others understand us intelligently. So far the labors of Linnaeus have been of great service; but as I before stated, there is another object to be obtained, and that is the medical properties contained in many plants, their adaptation to the various diseases of man, as also the injurious nature of others. Here is indeed a great field to the inquiring mind. It would be advisable to select a certain number of the most useful plants, diligently examining them, obtain every information regarding them and their adaptation to the various diseases to which the human frame is subject. Exploration into the extensive field of medical science can be pursued by degrees, effecting good and dispensing benefits in the meanwhile. There is a fear in the minds of some people in applying for advice to the medical faculty. It would be thought very strange for a hungry person to fear applying to a baker or a butcher for food; but the fact is, letting alone the matter of confidence in the remedies prescribed, there is generally such a long account thrown in for payment at the close of their torturing treatment, that it becomes a matter of serious consideration, whether you are likely to have the means of paying the account. Many diseases that the human frame is subject to, that I have not treated in this work; the remedy may be found by searching through that part of the work devoted to *Materia Medica*. In most of the diseases, the human family are heir to; healthy stimulants are the chief remedies. As has been frequently enforced upon your attention in this work; heat is the principle of life, and is an indispensable essential to the system.

Nature has provided many stimulants for our use, chief among them is cayenne pepper, the most powerful of all known stimulants, hence the best, and may be employed without fear wherever a stimulant is required. For exciting a profuse perspiration, restoring and keeping up the vital heat, by quickening the circulation and driving the blood to the extremities. It has repeatedly scattered disease in the system, before it has had time to become seated in any particular organ. The parts cramped and contracted with pain are speedily relieved by the powerful heat of this stimulant, It is always well to keep a supply of this article on hand in case of emergency. There are other stimulants such as ginger, horseradish, camphor, mustard, and many others which may be found in another part of this work that may be more suited to the case in question, for which it is required.

YARROW

In the early stages of disease few herbs are more useful than yarrow. It is found in abundance in fields, etc. It is very useful for colds, rheumatism, and one of the most powerful diaphoretics, or sweating herbs in nature. It not only equalizes the circulation but acts as a mild strengthener, exerts an influence upon the kidneys, promoting urine. Therefore it is well to collect and have a supply always at hand. It has saved more doctors bills, than most any other herb we know of.

BLUE VERVAIN

Is another very useful herb to collect and store for use; there is no better remedy for the cure of small pox, than vervain. It is also emetic.

LOBELIA INFLATA

Is among the list of herbs we would recommend to have constantly on hand, as it has valuable emetic properties, is a sudorific, nervine, and anti-spasmodic, having no rival in the *Materia Medica*. It is a diffusive stimulant also, removes obstructions, equalizes the circulation, promoting at the same time a healthy action throughout the system. It is advisable to take a warm stimulant first, such as ginger or composition tea. Croup, and diseases of the chest and lungs yield to this herb alone, which are mentioned under their respective heading. Many medical writers of the old school have tried in vain to prove lobelia to be a poison. So far from being a poison it is an antidote to a poison, and wherever a poison exists, it will vigorously contend against and expel the intruder. Can that be said of a real poison? Lobelia has been given to a child who had taken sixty drops of laudanum through a mistake, and it was restored to life, though apparently at death's door. The same was the case with the green leaves of stramonium, which had almost killed a child. Poured into a snake's mouth it had killed it, but applied to the bite of one, the lobelia had cured the patient. A table-spoonful dose was given to a patient who had taken one hundred and twenty grains of arsenic, enough to kill several men, and though the patient was insensible, it restored him to life!

Away then with such ridiculous nonsense as the old

school of medicine would have us believe, viz: that lobelia is a poison, had it been such, thousands would have died from its effects, for from three to five thousand pounds have been consumed annually, for years, for medical purposes; which would have been more than sufficient to kill one half the population of the United States. The time is fast approaching, when all this unfounded prejudice will be swept away regarding the invaluable aid rendered by the use of vegetable remedies; as well as the system of locating and diagnosing disease. There are various other stimulants as will be seen by referring to another part of this work, I merely mention some of those that are the most important, and I now pass on to notice astringents.

AGRIMONY

Is a plant that is well known, having rather a bitter taste, the roots as well as the tops of the plant may be used. A decoction has been found very serviceable in looseness, being of a binding nature, as well as aromatic and tonic; it is very useful in canker; we use it in connection with others for dropsy and jaundice, in scarlet fever, it will be found very useful combined with raspberry leaves and ground ivy, which is an astringent and diuretic, it also has been found serviceable in cleansing the system of bad humors,

RED RASPBERRY LEAVES

Are astringent, tonic, and somewhat expectorant. They are useful in thrush, clearing away of ulcers and sores, excellent for children in looseness of the bowels, and while teething. Raspberry leaves make a good substitute for the ordinary tea of commerce, and would be found far preferable, it is a safe remedy and accords well with the human frame.

CLIVERS

Is another very useful herb, a powerful diuretic and alterative, and mixed with gum myrrh, cancers have yielded to it repeatedly. There is a great deal said and wrote about strengthening medicines; this is a mistaken notion, they should be called correctives, for let the system but be in a proper state, food is all the strengthening medicine that a patient requires.

BOGBEAN

Is a bitter herb growing in marshy grounds, and very useful in dyspepsia; and as a corrector of the bile, it has scarcely a rival. It is very like the common bean in appearance, which perhaps may have given rise to the name assigned to it.

SPEARMINT

Has already been described in another part of this work, and in fact many of the common herbs treated under this heading have received attention. Yet they are very efficacious in many complaints, that we claim it wise to extend our information, so that you may become a practical medical botanist, and that in turn you may be enabled to do for others, what they are unable to do for themselves, thereby becoming a more useful member of society. Spearmint tends to stay vomiting. If an overdose of lobelia should produce excessive vomiting, a strong infusion of spearmint will stop it, and ease the stomach.

PEPPERMINT

Promotes perspiration, and will disperse a cold, if drank just before going to bed. The essence, or oil in warm water relieves pains in the stomach and bowels.

SUMMER SAVORY

Is good for colds, and may be taken with benefit in sickness. The oil of the herb will cure tooth-ache.

HOREHOUND

Is an aromatic tonic and expectorant, and very useful in coughs and asthmatic complaints for loosening the phlegm, A syrup made with honey, ginger and horehound, is very useful for children troubled with chin-cough.

MAY-WEED

Drank in infusion upon going to bed, with a little ginger or cayenne, will cure a cold; or throw off the first attack of fever, and if there are symptoms of the grip, place a hot brick to the feet, with a cloth wet with vinegar, and wrapped in a dry flannel; drink freely of may-weed with cayenne; and in most cases it will effect a cure.

WORMWOOD

The green herb pounded, and a tincture made from the same, with spirit, is excellent for bruises and sprains.

CENTAURY

Is another of the so-called tonic medicines, and is met with in dry pastures. It has been found very useful in disorders of the liver and kidneys, it is somewhat useful for worms, and is used as an aperient.

BARBERRY BARK

Is an excellent tonic, and a corrector of diseases of the liver, beneficial in jaundice, slightly aperient. The bark used in connection with either cayenne or ginger, has always been found serviceable in indigestion. I have used the term tonic, because it is more frequently used among the public; but more properly speaking, the herbs so designated are correctives, and if you desire to be strengthened after the stomach has been previously prepared by such medicines; I would prefer that the butcher and baker have the credit of that. Pursue this course and you will need little of such medicines so designated by the faculty.

BITTER SWEET

Makes a good external application. The bark of the root with chamomile and wormwood, make an excellent ointment, simmered in fresh lard; very efficacious for bruises, sprains, swellings, corns, and bunions.

MULLEN LEAVES

When bruised and applied to swellings, are very efficacious, and also to restore contracted sinews. Apply them warm. It also makes a very good smoking tobacco for asthma, combined with stramonium leaves. And combined with marshmallow, is a good remedy in diseases of the kidneys and bladder.

CHAMOMILE

An infusion is good for bowel complaints, and externally applied, will relieve sprains, bruises, and swellings arising from inflammation, and restore sunken kidneys.

BURDOCK

The leaves are good applied to the feet in case of fever, to keep them moist and promote perspiration. The root possesses superior diuretic and alterative properties, useful to assist the urine, and as a blood sweetener. The seeds are very useful in stone and gravel. It should be taken in decoction, three or four times per day.

BRYONY

Is a tall climbing wild plant, grows in bushes and slashings, leaves are somewhat like the vine; the flowers white, and the berries are red, and very showy. The root is large, rough, and whitish; stalks tough and about ten or twelve feet long, with tendrils at the joints to hold themselves. The root is a very strong purgative, even if a small dose be taken. Caution should be observed in taking it. It is used for dropsies, hysterics, etc., given in small doses. An electuary made of the root with honey, proves a powerful expectorant. The root, leaves, and fruit boiled, are good to cleanse old sores, canker, and gangrene; and the decoction frees the face from freckles, black and blue spots, etc. The root scraped, and laid on to a bruise, will draw the discoloration out in a few minutes.

CHICKWEED

The plant chopped and boiled in lard, makes a fine green cooling ointment, and is good for the piles, ulcers, sores, etc. The juice taken inwardly, is good for the scurvy. A cloth saturated with the juice and applied outwardly over the region of the liver, reduces inflammation; it is also good for inflammation of the eyes, when dropped into them.

CORALWORT

Cleanses the bladder and provokes urine, and is one of the best diuretics we know of. It also expels gravel and stone: it eases pain in the sides and bowels, and is very good for inward wounds, especially when located in the breast and lungs. A drachm of the powdered root may be taken every morning in wine. An ointment made of it is good for wounds and ulcers. It is a good wound herb.

COCOA

Is a native of Southern countries, when genuine and properly prepared, is very wholesome and nutritious, containing a large quantity of oily or fatty matter, starch, etc. Cocoa does not effect the nervous system in the same manner as tea or coffee, and therefore it may be used where they are not proper. Cocoa can seldom be obtained in a perfectly pure state; the only way is to purchase the beans, crush and boil them over night, allowing it to stand and cool, and in the morning remove the fatty matter and reboil, it is then ready for use. The sick and weak, and those troubled with a weak stomach; will find that by adding a tea-spoonful of arrowroot, to the cup of cocoa, that it will not only increase its nutritive properties, but will make it easier to digest or assimilate.

CELENDINE (GREAT)

Is a common wild plant having large leaves, and yellow flowers. It grows nearly three feet high. They grow along way-sides and clearings; and flower all summer. It is a most valuable remedy for diseases of the eye, used as a decoction, or made into an ointment. The juice is the best way of administering it. It is also a very efficacious remedy for jaundice, scurvy, and all other obstructions of the liver and other viscera. The addition of a few aniseeds in making a decoction of it with wine, in creases its efficacy in removing obstructions from the liver and gall. The juice applied to warts soon removes them, also ringworms. An ointment made with the roots and fresh lard will cure the piles.

CARDAMON

Is a very grateful aromatic. It is an Indian plant, rather resembling our reeds. It produces a fruit or pod about the size of a horsebean. They strengthen the stomach and promote digestion. They are good for the headache, arising from bilious affections, and will also relieve the colic. Some dyspeptics will find relief by chewing the cardamon seed daily. The large cardamon or grain of paradise is an excellent tonic. Tincture of cardamon may be made as follows:

Cardamon seed, bruised 3 ounces,
Proof spirits 2 pints.

Mix, and digest for one week, then filter, or strain, it is then ready for use. The compound tincture of cardamon may be made as follows:

Cardamon seeds, powdered 2 drachms.
Caraway seeds, powdered 2 drachms.
Cochineal, powdered 2 drachms.
Cinnamon, bruised ounce.
Raisins, stoned 4 ounces.
Proof spirits 2 pints.

Digest for fourteen days, and strain. Dose of the tincture, two or three drachms, and of the compound tincture, from three drachms to half an ounce. In dyspeptic persons, a half wine-glassful before dinner will serve to rouse the nerves of the stomach, and to aid digestion.

CARROTS (WILD)

Grow together like the garden carrot, but the leaves and stalks are whiter and more rough. The stalks bear large tufts of white flowers; with a deep purple spot in the middle. The roots are small, long, and hard, and unfit for meat, being sharp and strong. They are useful to expel wind, and remove stitches in the sides. It will also promote urine, and assist menstruation, as well as remove stone in the bladder. The seed is very useful in dropsical cases, and an excellent diuretic, and anti-flatulent.

ERYNGO; OR SEA-HOLLY

Is a wild plant growing by the sea-side, and often cultivated for its medicinal virtues. The plant is prickly like the thistle, stalk firm, woody, round, straight and thick, leaves small, of a pale green, oblong, jagged and prickly. The plant is used for sexual apathy, and breeds seeds exceedingly; it is also good for yellow jaundice. The candid roots are most excellent for coughs, and general debility. They possess rare virtues as a diuretic.

FENNEL

One of the customs of boiling fennel with fish, is still adhered to by some, but to ask them why they do so is, because they don't know as a rule. Fennel boiled with fish consumes the phlegmatic humor, which fish copiously produce. Fennel is a good diuretic, hence a remedy for urinary diseases. The leaves or seeds boiled in barley water and drank, are good to increase the milk when suckling child. It will also remove nausea, etc.

FIG-TREE

Is so well known, needs no description. The decoction made from the leaves or branches when they are broken off, is good to wash sore head; there is scarcely a better remedy for the leprosy. It is one of the best blood cleansers in nature, The fruit of the tree grown in Spain, etc, grow larger there, and ripen better than in our climate. To make a very good syrup for costiveness, use the following:

One half pound of figs cut up, and stewed in one quart of water; with two ounces of senna leaves, strain, and add half ounce of the tincture of ginger. Dose for an adult, one half wine-glassful twice a day. Children half quantity.

FLAX (COMMON)

Is a most valuable plant producing oil, as well as fiber. The seed is known as linseed: The seed contain about one fifth of mucilage, and one sixth of fixed oil. Linseed is emollient and demulcent, therefore good as poultices. Linseed Oil mixed with an equal quantity of limewater is an excellent application for burns.

LILY (WHITE)

This is a well known garden flower, needs no description. It is good in pestilential fevers, the roots bruised and boiled in wine, and the decoction drank daily. The juice being mixed with barley-meal, baked, and eaten as ordinary bread, is an excellent cure for dropsy. An ointment made of the root with fresh lard is good for scald heads and for cleansing ulcers. The ointment will cure burns and scalds without leaving a scar, and will stimulate the growth of the hair on patches and thin heads of hair.

LICORICE ROOT

Grows wild in many parts of this country, its virtues are great. Its demulcent properties render it very useful in coughs and bronchial irritation, and in some stomach complaints, arising from a deficiency of natural mucus which should defend the stomach against the acrimony of the food, and the fluids secreted in it. Licorice also works gently by urine, and is very soothing to ulcerated kidneys or urinary passages.

LOOSESTRIFE (PURPLE)

A very useful herb with woody square stalks full of joints, three feet high. The stalks branch into long stems of spiked flowers, about six inches long, growing in bundles, one above the other, out of small husks, like the spiked heads of lavender, with fine round pointed leaves of a purple or violet color. Seeds are small and brown. It grows in wet ground, and flowers in July. It is one of the best remedies for preserving the sight, and for the cure of sore eyes. It is fully as valuable as eye-bright. It will cure blindness, provided the crystalline humor be not injured or destroyed. There are other species of this plant, the medical properties are much like the above.

MANNA

Is concrete juice, the product of the flowering ash, and is obtained by tapping the tree. It has a sweet bitter taste, and is a gentle purgative, so mild in its operation that it may be given with safety to children, persons of very weak habits; and in pregnancy.

MAJORAM (WILD)

It is a wild herb, its roots run much under ground, and continues sending up brownish square stalks, with small dark green leaves, very like sweet marjoram, but broader; at the top of stalk stand tufts of flowers, of a deep purple red color. It strengthens the stomach and head, and for those troubled with acidity of the stomach, there is no better remedy, taken in decoction. It is stomachic and restores the appetite, and will relieve cough, and weakness of the lungs. It is an antidote to henbane, hemlock and opium. It also provokes urine and the terms in women, and will relieve dropsy, and yellow jaundice.

MERCURY (DOG)

There are two kinds of mercury, male and female; this is a highly poisonous plant and must be guarded against. It is one of the most fatal, it is useful only as an outward application for green wounds of a scrofulic nature: The plant has a strong virulent smell.

MINT (HORSE, OR MOUNTAIN MINT)

Is a great purifier of the breath, will cure colic, and difficulty of breathing; snuffed up the nose, will cure headache. This plant taken in decoction, with pennyroyal is a good emmenagogue. All the family of mints have much the same medical properties, differing only in strength.

MISLETO

The leaves dried and powdered, are a splendid remedy for falling fits. They are good also in nervous disorders, and have cured many difficult cases, when other remedies have failed.

NIGHTSHADE (DEADLY)

Is a wild plant, four or five feet high; of a dark green color, with bell shaped flowers, of a deep purple color, they are succeeded by berries, violet black, glossy, sweet, and pleasant to the taste, hence they are often eaten by children ignorant of their very poisonous properties, with fatal results. Atropa is a generic name, from one of the fates, who was supposed to cut the thread of life. Belladonna signifies "beautiful lady", because the Italian ladies used the distilled water of this plant as a cosmetic. There is no doubt of its being a very useful herb in proper hands. The leaves were first used externally to to discuss scrofulous and cancerous tumors, and as an application to ill-conditioned

ulcers. This plant alleviates pain, nervous excitement, spasm, etc, But as nature is so bountiful in offering such a vast number of other plants, etc., for the cure of all known diseases, that are equally as efficacious, and even more so than the above, and much less dangerous to handle; we would prefer that the unskilled, confine themselves to the less dangerous class of
herbs than the above.

WOODY NIGHTSHADE

Its name is Latin, is dulcamara (*dulcis* sweet, *amarus* bitter.) In various countries it has different names; as bitter sweet, felon wort, etc. It is a climbing plant, often reaching six to eight feet. The stems bear many leaves, rather long and broad, pointed at the ends. The color of the leaves are a pale green; flowers purple with a yellow center, standing close together. The berries are a scarlet red. They taste sweet at first then slightly bitter. This is also a poison us plant, but not so much so as the deadly nightshade. It is a powerful medicine, increasing all the secretions and excretions, to excite the heart and arteries; and in large doses will produce nausea, vomiting, and convulsion. The plant is alterative, diuretic, sudorific, and mildly narcotic. The berries are extremely dangerous for children. To remove obstructions of the liver and spleen, take a half pound of the leaves and wood, bruised, and infuse in three pints of white wine over a gentle fire for three or four hours; and strain, this will also relieve difficulty of breathing, taken in half wine-glassful doses, two or three times a day.

NIGHTSHADE (Common)

This is a different plant from either of the other nightshades quoted. It has an erect, round, green hollow stalk, two feet high, with leaves broad and pointed, soft and full of juice, with edges indented; flowers grow in clusters, from six to twelve in a bunch; they are white with a yellow center, succeeded by round black berries. It must be used with caution, for like the other nightshades, it is somewhat dangerous. The juice mixed with vinegar, is good to wash an inflamed mouth and throat. The juice will cure ringworms, and foul ulcers. The bruised leaves applied to scalds, bruises, inflammations, and eruptions of the skin will relieve and cure them. The juice dropped in the ears, relieves pain.

OATS

As an article of diet, ground into meal has no superior, as we find the people of Scotland live almost entirely on oatmeal, proving its nutrition by their well knit, muscular and bony frames, clear and vigorous intellects, and ripe old age to which they attain. A poultice made of oatmeal and oil of hays, cure the itch and leprosy, fistula, and hard swellings. Oatmeal poultices are more stimulating, and draw more rapidly than those made of linseed meal.

ONE BLADE

So called, because it seldom bears more than one leaf, though sometimes it has a stalk, and in that case it has two leaves; but this seldom occurs. The leaf is of a bluish green color, pointed, with many ribs or veins, like plantain. At the top of the stalks grow many white flowers, star fashion, with a sweet smell; after which come small red berries. It is good, taken in drachm doses for syphilitic cancer. It is also a good wound herb, and enters largely in many compound balms for curing wounds, whether fresh or green.

ORCHIS

It is called dog stones, foal stones, and by others too tedious to mention. It is a beautiful plant, found in moist pastures, with a stem like that of the tulip, crowned at the top with a spike of beautiful purple flowers; the leaves are long and pointed and grow from the root. The root is a double tuber. A very nutritious and wholesome farina is obtained from the root, and when carefully prepared is one of the best articles of diet for the sick and weak. Wash the roots in hot water, and place in the oven for fifteen minutes; and then dried for use as a powder.

PARSLEY

The roots are the parts used in medicine. A strong decoction is a good remedy in jaundice. It operates on the urine, and good for the expulsion of wind. It gently removes obstructions of the liver and spleen. It is good for dropsy, stone in the kidneys, and jaundice taken in connection with fennel, anise, caraway seeds, burnt saxifrage, in equal parts.

COW PARSNIPS

It grows with three or four large spread-winged, rough leaves, lying often on the ground, with long, round hairy foot-stalks under them, of a whitish green color, smelling strongly; from which springs, a round, crusted, hairy-stalk, two or three feet high, with a few joints and leaves thereon, and branched at the top, on which stand large white and sometimes reddish flowers, and often with white winged seeds, two together. It grows in moist places, and flowers in July or August. The seed is a good remedy in coughs and shortness of breath, falling-sickness and jaundice. The root is available for the same purpose, and boiled in sweet oil and the head rubbed therewith, will cure headache and drowsiness, lethargy, etc. The juice of the flowers dropped into the ears that run and are full of matter, cleanses and heals them.

PELLITORY OF THE WALL

It grows with long, tender, weak and almost

transparent stalks; upon which grow at the joints two leaves, rather broad and long, of a dark green color, rough and hairy, as the stalks are also, from the middle of the stalks upwards stand many small, pale purplish flowers, in hairy rough heads, which bring forth small, black, rough seeds. The root is long, of a darkish red color. It is a good remedy made into a syrup; for dry coughs, shortness of breath, wheezing, and tightness of the chest. A decoction with honey will cure sore throat. The juice will cure toothache. The juice of the herb mixed with a little salt, is good to cleanse and heal fistula. A poultice made with bran, and the bruised herb, mixed with sweet oil; will remove pain from bruised parts and severe contusions. The juice of pellitory boiled to syrup with honey, and a spoonful taken twice a day for a week, is a safe and certain cure for dropsy.

PELLITORY

The common pellitory has a root of a biting taste, its stalks are small and brittle, two or three feet high, with narrow long leaves dented at the edges, one above the other. The flowers are many and white, and grow in tufts, with a small yellow thrum in the center. The seeds are small, grows in fields and clearings, and other places. It is a good purger of the brain, and will purge the head of phlegmatic humors, thereby relieving headache, catarrh, lethargy, coughs, and falling sickness, An ounce of the juice taken in a little light wine an hour before a fit of ague comes, will prevent the fit, and if continued several times, will mostly drive it away entirely. An ointment made with lard, and the herb bruised, will cure sciatica, and will remove black and blue spots occasioned by injury. The root chewed is a splendid remedy for toothache. It has cured the effects of salivation, has often cured the palsied tongue and throat, and given relief to diseased uvula and other parts of the throat.

ST. PETER S WORT

This herb is somewhat like St. John's wort. It grows with square upright stalks, brown, having two leaves at every joint, a little round pointed, with few or no spots in the leaves, and having some smaller leaves rising from the bosom of the greater, and a little hairy. The flowers are many and star-like, with yellow threads in the center, very like the St. John's wort, but larger. It grows in moist and damp places. Its medical virtues are much the same as St. John's wort. It is also a good wound herb.

PONDWEED

Also called water houseleak, crab's claw, etc. It roots in the mud at the bottom of the water, it has very narrow leaves, stalks have a forked head, like a crab's claw, out of which comes a white flower of three leaves, with yellowish threads in the center. Its medicinal properties are valuable, in weakness of the kidneys, bladder, and in reducing swelling of the testicle. It is very useful in erysipelas, and inflammations, etc. But it excels all others in disease of the kidneys.

ROSEMARY

We have also noticed this plant in the fore part of our book, but would say further that rosemary taken in strong decoction, will strengthen the stomach and expel wind. It also removes obstructions of the liver, and promotes digestion. It is a good remedy also for whites in females, if taken daily.

WILD ROSES

The wild rose is so well known it requires no description; the fruit is chiefly red. It is used principally as a vehicle to other remedies. It is pleasant and acidulous, and useful to allay thirst in fevers; using the pulp only; remove skins and seeds, and beat up with sugar. A strong tea made from the dried buds, or taken in powder, will check profuse menstruation. The seeds dried and powdered, correct irregularities of the urine, and good against gravel.

ROCK CRESS

It is a small wild plant, five or six inches long, the leaves, direct from the root are long, and deeply divided; those on the stalks are smaller, flowers small and white, standing among the leaves, at the top of the branches. The plant is a good diuretic, as well as a safe one. It is also good for jaundice, scurvy, and obstructions of the urine and kidneys.

YOUTH WORT (OR SUN DEW)

It is also called *rosa solis*. It has various small, round, hollow leaves, rather greenish, but full of red hairs, which give them the reddish appearance they have. The leaves are moist in the hottest day, among these leaves rise up slender stalks, reddish also, ten or twelve inches high, bearing small white knobs or flowers one above the other, after which, come seeds; it grows in wet places, and moist woods. It is a very good remedy for salt rheum distilling on the lungs, which induces consumption. The herb simmered in wine and water, equal parts, is a good remedy for all diseases of the lungs, as phthsis, wheezing, shortness of breath, cough, etc.

RICE *(Oryza Sativa)*

A tropical plant growing in the Southern states, and other tropical countries, a well known article of diet, very nutritious, easily digested, and therefore suitable for delicate stomachs. It has no laxative properties, and is therefore suitable for those who have tender bowels. For children troubled with the so-called summer complaint, which is a lax state of the system, it is a very useful article, ground and boiled in sufficient water; three pints of water to one half pound of rice, adding a little isinglass to render it more astringent, boil for one hour, and strain, sweeten with sugar, give often. It is not so nutritious as wheat, but more nutritious than most of the bread made from the high grade flour generally made in our own country. Rice affords sustenance to about three-fourths of the inhabitants of the globe. It should always be well-cooked, otherwise it is not so digestible.

RHUBARB

The species of rhubarb we here refer to, are the product of the rheum palmatum, undulatum, and other species growing in Chinese Tartary, and gathered from plants from five to six years old. A portion of this rhubarb goes to China, while a large quantity of it pass through Russia and Turkey, and known by the name of Turkey and Russian rhubarb. This is the best. It is in roundish pieces, of a yellow reddish color on the outside, soft and easily reducible, having streaks of bright red running through it. It has generally a hole in the middle, caused by stringing, when drying. Rhubarb has also been raised in India, and other countries, some of which are equally as good as the so-called Turkey; but so strong is prejudice against other than what is called the best, that very little of it would be sold; if sold under its proper name. Few medicines are more valuable or safer. It is one of the mildest aperients in nature, its action depending upon the amount of the dose. It rarely gripes; it seems to act as a tonic upon the stomach. It has astringent properties, it therefore has a tendency in its reaction on the coating of the bowels, to contract or constipate, after the purgative effect is past. We have treated of this root in another part of this work, to which we would refer our readers. But we wish to enlarge upon our treatment of this very valuable root as a medicine, for too much cannot be told of the medicinal properties of that, what belongs to it. Rhubarb is very useful in a lax state of the bowels, as it expels any acrid matter that may irritate and offend the bowels. When it is intended to act on the bowels, it should be given in conjunction with about fifteen grains of super-sulfate of potass, which covers its taste, and causes it to act more readily and with more certainty. For those who may be troubled with irregularity of the bowels, or an acidity of the stomach. Take the following:

Rhubarb .5 ounce
Calcined magnesia 1 ounce
Ginger, powdered ounce

A tea-spoonful in a cup of cold water is the dose, once in two or three days, or not more than once a day. Syrup of Rhubarb is excellent for young children, given in from one to two drachms, which may be obtained at your druggist, A favorite prescription of many physicians, who when called upon to visit a sick child, and unable to tell what ails the child; jumps at a conclusion, that the stomach and bowels are out of order, hence, the prescription; the cost of such information is from one to two dollars, and the price of the medicine from thirty to fifty cents. We of course use nothing but the language known to the common people. Compound Tincture Rhubarb, one ounce, Bi-carbonate of Soda, half drachm, Fluid extract of Licorice, one drachm; pure water, six ounces. Give from one to two tea-spoonful according to the age of the child; for an adult, take from one to two table-spoonful. The powder sprinkled on foul and indolent ulcers excites them to a healthy action.

REST HARROW

This is a small, tough and almost shrubby plant; common in dry fields, and by road sides. It is one or two feet high. The stalks are round and reddish, tough and woody. It has many leaves, three standing together on each stalk. The flowers are small, purple, and stand among the leaves toward the top of the stalks, shaped like pea-blossom, but flatter, each followed by a small pod or seed. It removes obstructions in the kidneys. The bark is a good remedy for stone in the bladder, when simmered in some light wine. The decoction is an excellent diuretic; and a powerful remedy for obstructions of the liver and spleen. It has cured many long standing cases of rheumatism, when all other remedies have failed.

POPLAR TREE

There are two kinds of poplars, viz. white and black. They are so common it is not necessary to notice them further, than state, that the buds of the popular are collected, and simmered in fresh lard, which make a valuable ointment for all kinds of inflammation, to be applied outwardly. It is much used to dry up the milk of woman's breasts, when they have weaned their child. This ointment is prepared from the buds of the black poplar. The white poplar is a good diuretic and tonic, as will be found in another part of this work, under the head of *Materia Medica*. But would say, that no better remedy can be found for those on the down hill of life, than equal parts of white poplar bark and buchu-leaves, say two ounces of each, simmered in three pints of water, down to one quart, strain, and take a wine-glassful two or three times a day, fasting.

RANUNCULUS

The various species of this family of plants, are so common in this country that they need no description. They are known by the name of butter flowers, butter-cup, or crowfoot. The whole family of this class, are very acrid, proved, by chewing a small portion of the leaves. Their action is emetic, in fact, it is not fit to be taken internally, on account of its poisonous influence. The juice of this plant when applied to the skin acts as a rubeficient; on thin and delicate skin it will act as a blister; and combined with wood sanicle, and ginger, is good for cough, shortness of breath, wheezing, and to relieve the bronchial passages when they become congested. The fresh roots beaten, or the powder of the dried roots mixed with honey, and applied to the nose, will cure polypus.

PURSLANE

This herb is so well known it requires no description. It is a superior remedy to allay heat in the liver, blood, and stomach, and in hot ague, there is nothing better. It restrains hot and choleric fluxes, the whites and gonorrhea, distillation from the head, and pains therein proceeding from heat, want of sleep, or frenzy. The seed is more effectual than the herb to cool the heat and sharpness of urine. The herb bruised and applied to any part, the seat of inflammation, will remove it. It is a good remedy for sore and inflamed mouth and throat. It will fasten loose teeth by rinsing the mouth with the juice.

POLYBODY OF THE OAK

This is a perennial herb of the fern tribe. It is a small herb consisting of nothing but roots and leaves, bearing neither stalk, flower, nor seed. It has three or four leaves rising from the root, each one single by itself, from eight to twelve inches high, and winged like fern leaves generally are. The root is small, and is a creeper; of a sweetish harsh taste. It grows upon old rotten stumps, or trunks of trees, as the oak, beach, hazel, willow, etc., as well as moist and mossy places. That which grows on the oak is considered the best. The fresh root is generally used; it is a safe and gentle purge, used as a decoction it promotes the flow of urine. It is a good remedy in jaundice, dropsy, and skin disease. It is also an expectorant, removing the tough phlegm in chronic cough. It will remove hardness of the spleen, if combined with mallows, and combined with a little ginger, it is a safe and gentle medicine, fit for children or adults.

PLANTAIN

Plantago Major: We have noticed this very useful herb in another part of this work, but we are anxious to let the reader know as much as possible concerning such a valuable plant. It grows almost everywhere. It is a very hardy plant, its leaves are bitter or tonic and astringent, and have been long held in popular esteem as a wound herb. They are used as an external application in green wounds, ulcers, indolent and scrofulous tumors. The juice taken internally will cure spitting and vomiting of blood, and prevent bloody urine. A strong decoction will answer the same purpose. It is also a good remedy in fever and ague. The bruised leaves make a good application for burns and scalds. The juice mixed with lard is a good pile remedy, the leaves make a splendid poultice to allay inflammation, where the bone is broken or out of place, and to bathe the head with in case of head-ache, as well as itch, ringworms, and breakings out on the body. It will also cure the bite of the rattle-snake, if taken in time, apply outwardly and take the juice inwardly.

OSIER (GREEN AND RED)

This plant is a native of the United States, extending from Canada to Virginia, growing on hill-sides, banks of creeks and rivers. It flowers in June and July. It is a shrub from six to ten feet high, with warty branches, large roundish pointed leaves, waved on their edges and downy beneath, it bears white flowers, which are very conspicuous in our forests when in bloom. The fruit grow in bunches of a light blue color. The bark when dried is of a whitish or ash color. It is tonic, astringent, and aromatic. The bark of the red osier when dried has a red cast, and the flowers are smaller than the green osier, but the medical virtues are much the same in all of the dogwood family to which they belong. The bark and small stems are the parts used medicinally, as well as the bark of the root. They are a superior remedy in low and intermittent fevers, and if combined with equal quantities of peruvian bark and St. John's wort, with a little ginger, sweetened; is a remedy that may be relied on to cure malarial and other fevers. It is also a very useful remedy in relax of the bowels, and also in debility of the stomach and bowels.

OPIUM

Papaver Somniferum, of the natural order papaveraceae Opium is the dried juice of the white poppy. There is no drug in the entire list of medical agents that is more extensively used by the medical fraternity than opium, it has probably yielded more relief to human suffering than any other physical means. Applied externally, it acts as a sedative, easing pain; in moderate doses, administered internally, its first effect is that of an excitant; it quickens the pulse, and increases the heat of the skin and induces a tendency to sleep; pain is abated or removed, irritation subdued, and the muscular system relaxed, the secretions of the bowels is lessened by it, but that of the skin is increased, and thus it acts as a sudorific. If small doses are continually taken, it intoxicates. If over doses, it acts as a narcotic poison, causing intense sleep, with contraction of the pupil of the eye, which results in coma and death. Opium should never be given to a person in a high state of fever, or inflammation ; a parched tongue and a dry skin should generally forbid its use. But if the fever is moderate and skin moist, with no cerebral disorder, it may be given to alleviate pain and subdue irritation. It is given in delirium tremens, and all neuralgic disorders. In convulsive disorders it is given as an anti-spasmodic, and in some cases a diaphoretic. It is dangerous where there is a determination of blood to the head. It is extensively used by the drug practitioners, in tetanus, St. Vitus's dance, hysterics and cholera morbus. Applied outwardly, opium subdues pain and spasmodic action. Applied by friction, it relieves cramp, tetanus, etc., and when rubbed over the abdomen it is good for spasmodic pain of the stomach and bowels. The remedies for an over dose of opium, are lobelia in emetic dose, lemon juice neutralizes the narcotic influence, or a half drachm of sulfate of zinc dissolved in water, or mustard, salt, or even strong coffee.

ORANGE

The chief medical use of the orange is derived from the rind, and the best for the purpose is the bitter orange, which yields an agreeable aromatic, stimulant, astringent and tonic bitter. A tincture or syrup may be used, it is often prescribed in combination with stronger bitters, such as gentian, Colombo or quassa wood, it forms a good vehicle for disagreeable and nauseous purgatives. A good infusion may be made as follows: One ounce of the bitter orange-peel, one pint of boiling water, simmer for fifteen minutes, and let it stand for an hour, then strain; a little lump sugar and lemon juice will make it more pleasant. It is stomachic; dose, a wine-glassful twice a day.

POPPY-HEADS *Papaver Album*

Poppy-heads, or dried capsules of the poppy, possess anodine properties: there are three kinds of poppy, viz. The white, black and red poppy. The white poppy has at first four or five whitish green leaves, compassing the stalk at the bottom, they are very large and with a rough edge; the stalk which attains a height of four or five feet, sometimes have no branches, usually but two at the most, each bearing one head, in a thin skin, the flower consist of four large white round leaves, with many whitish threads in the center, set about a small round green head, having a crown or star-like cover at the end thereof, which growing ripe becomes as large as an apple, from which is produced the opium of commerce.

BLACK POPPY *Papaver Nigrum*

There is little difference between this plant and the former or white poppy. The flowers are somewhat less, and of a black purplish color, the head of the seed is much less than the former, and opens a little round about the top, under the crown. The seed is black.

RED POPPY OR CORN ROSE

The botanical name *Papaver Erraticum*, is a very common species in this country and needs little description, it bears a scarlet red flower, very showy, in the center of which is a small green head, full of black seeds, when this plant, like the other two species are cultivated, they are much larger than in their wild state. The plant is a very useful anodyne. Syrup of poppy is made from the capsules. The heads of the red poppy used as a fomentation, render them valuable to soothe inflammation and pain. They should be crushed before boiling, the liquor only to be used. A flannel dipped into it, wrung out, and applied to the part affected, and renewed as it begins to cool. The decoction also taken in small doses, relieves pain and promotes sleep. The wild poppy or corn rose, is good to prevent falling sickness. The syrup made with the leaves and flowers, is effectual in pleurisy and erysipelas. The dried leaves decocted have the same effect.

PRUNES

The fruit of the *prunus domestica* of the natural order *rosaceae*. They possess much mucilaginous and saccharine matter. They abate heat and gently open the bowels, They are of great service in costiveness, of which parents should feed more often to their children. There would be less cause of sickness; where prunes are not sufficiently purgative in themselves, their action is promoted by combining with them a little senna or rhubarb They are the base of the lenative electuary sold by druggists. A very useful way of administering medicine to children for opening the bowels, is as follows: Take a few prunes and simmer for a half hour in sufficient water to cover them, with a half ounce of senna leaves, remove the prunes and allow them to dry. Give the child to eat of these prunes when costive. But prunes taken alone, in some constitutions, are sufficient to open the bowels and will generally relieve costiveness. The French prunes are the best.

QUININE

Is a chemical preparation from the yellow peruvian bark, by means of sulfuric acid. It is a white powder, partly soluble in hot water, and wholly so diluted sulfuric acid, and spirits of wine. The medical fraternity, have almost discarded the use of the bark, on account of the minute dose required. Eight grains are about equal to one ounce of the bark. But as we are not in the habit of using this preparation from the bark, we leave it to others, to state what amount of good, if any, has been gained by the use or abuse of this individual preparation. We still prefer to use the bark itself, believing that the various properties that the bark possesses, beyond that possessed by quinine, is more conducive to health, and in my experience has seldom failed to effect the purpose for which it was administered, which cannot be said of quinine. Although as a febrifuge or anti-fever remedy, there is possibly few remedies to excel it, in small doses.

RYE

Is one of the cereals that has been a great blessing to mankind. It produces a nutritious flour, having less bran and more farina than wheat has, though darker in color. It is not so nutritious as wheat, but is easier to digest, and it slightly promotes the action of the bowels. Ergot of rye, or smut rye, is a diseased portion which grows on the ear of rye. It is of a poisonous nature, this substance is greatly extolled by the medical fraternity as a remedy to assist child birth; but no two can agree upon that subject. There is no doubt of its influence over the uterine system, to rouse the energies of the womb, in case of lingering labor. We prefer to use the remedies that are in nowise dangerous in the hands of the people, and that are equally as efficacious and reliable.

RUPTURE WORT

This herb spreads upon the ground, about ten or twelve inches long, divided into many small parts, full of small joints, very thick together; the leaves are very small, nearly oval, of a pale green; two at each joint, tinged with yellow. The flowers are very small and yellow, scarcely discernible from the stalks and leaves. The root is very long and small, and deep in the ground, it grows in dry, sandy and rocky places, and is cultivated in gardens. It has been found by experience that its name is what it implies, for it has cured many cases of rupture in children, and sometimes in adults, if the disease be not too inveterate, by taking a drachm of the powder of the dried herb every day for a week, or more in wine, or a decoction will often answer the same purpose. The juice or distilled water of the green herb, wall cure inward fluxes and gonorrhea. It will relieve stone and gravel, and an excellent remedy in stranguary. It is also a good outward remedy for wounds and sores, the green herb being bound on the wounds.

WOOD SAGE

It is a plant similar to the garden sage, but smaller, and smelling very strong. It bears a spiked flower, heads are black and round, the root is long and stringy, growing in woods and clearings. The decoction of wood sage will increase the flow of urine and will stimulate the kidneys to action. The decoction is also a good remedy for internal injuries, or to stop inward bleeding. The juice of the herb, or the powder dried, is good for moist ulcers and sores, to dry them and cause them to heal more speedily. It is no less effectual in green wounds. It will disperse congealed blood in the stomach and intestines. It makes a good wash for the head, and will cleanse the dandruff from the hair creating a healthy action in the skin of the head, and thicken the hair.

SAMPHIRE

This plant is common along the sea coasts, something like fennel. It grows along the rocks that are often saturated with sea-water. It has a tender green stalk about two feet high, has round leaves, of a deep green color, the root is large, white, and long, and of a hot spicy taste. The juice of the fresh leaves stimulate the kidneys and urinary passages, and are a good remedy for suppression of the menstrual flow. It is excellent in promoting digestion. It was formerly highly esteemed as a pickle, but adulteration of the article has almost destroyed its sale.

WOOD SANICLE

A very pretty plant growing wild in the woods and shady places. It has many large round leaves, standing upon long brownish stalks, every one deeply cut, or divided into five or six parts, some of these are cut like the leaf of crows-foot, and finely dented at the edges, and of a dark shining color, and reddish about the brim; from which rise up small, round green stalks, without any joint or leaf, except at the top, where it branches into flowers. The flowers are small and white, starting out of a small round greenish yellow head, in a tuft, in which afterwards are the seeds, which are small round burs, almost like the leaves of clivers, and stick in the same manner. The root is fibrous. It heals green wounds speedily, ulcers or inward bleeding, it is also good for tumors. And when the disease settles on the lungs or throat, there are few herbs that will give relief quicker than this herb; combined with others of this class, which may be found in this work, almost all diseases of the lungs and their ramifications, if taken in time will surrender to their influence. It makes a splendid gargle for malignant ulcers in the mouth and throat, the gargle made with the leaves and roots in water, and a little honey.

WOUND WORT *Saracenia*

It is also called saracen's woundwort. It sometimes grows with brownish stalks, also green, to the height of five or six feet, it has narrow green leaves, rough on the edges, like those of the peach and willow. The tops of the stalks have many yellow flowers, standing in green heads, The seed is rather long and brown, downy when ripe, and is blown away. The root is fibrous. The taste strong and unpleasant, and so is the smell, it grows in damp ground by the wood side, and shady groves. This like the last, is one of the most useful wound herb, in the whole *Materia Medica*. It will reduce inflammation of the liver, when boiled in wine, and in decoction will cure yellow jaundice, dropsy, inward ulcers, etc. The medical virtues of this herb, are the same as those of sanicle, and very useful to combine with it.

SARSAPARILLA

Smilax is the *officinale* name. The sarsaparilla plant is a native of most warm countries, more particularly South America and the West Indian Islands, that grown in the Northern part of this country, is of little use as a medicine. It has a mild bitterish and glutinous taste, not disagreeable. The root is the part used, the bark of which, possesses the medicinal virtue. The kind having a reddish brown appearance is by far the best. It posses tonic, demulcent, and alterative properties; and sometimes diuretic and diaphoretic. It is given with advantage, combined with other alteratives in various obstinate internal chronic diseases, and in swellings, ulcerations, and other local maladies, depending upon constitutional indisposition. Under the head of alteratives, I have treated more extensively of the diseases for which sarsaparilla is generally used, as well as in the compounds for which it is prescribed. The compound form is the most convenient way of taking it.

SASSAFRAS

Is a beautiful tree, a native of North America, the bark of the root possesses the medicinal virtue. Sassafras belongs to the natural order *Lauraceae*. It has a sweet aromatic taste, and a strong odor, owing to the presence of a volatile oil, in which its virtues chiefly reside, though it contains fatty matter, resin, gum, albumen, wax, etc. It is best taken in infusion, or tea; and is a pleasant beverage, but should be combined with other alteratives which make it more effectual as a blood cleanser. As we have already spoken of this substance, and its uses, both under the head of alteratives, as well as in the compounds, it is unnecessary for further comment.

SAVORY

There are two kinds of savory, the summer and winter; summer savory is a good remedy for colic, it is also a very useful herb to expel wind from the stomach and bowels. It is very beneficial to take during pregnancy, and is a good expectorant, removing tough phlegm from the chest, and improving the breathing. The juice dropped into the eyes improve the sight, if it proceed from cold in the head. It is useful for those stung by bees or wasps, by tying the bruised herb over the part.

SAXIFRAGE (White)

The common white saxifrage has a few small reddish kernels of roots covered with skin, lying among small blackish fibers, which send forth round, yellow green leaves, grayish underneath, lying above the ground, edges rough and hairy, each upon a little footstalk, from which rise brownish, hairy, green stalks, two or three feet high, with round leaves, rather branched at the top, on which stand pretty, large, white flowers, of five leaves each, with yellow threads in the center, standing in a brownish green husk, small black seeds follow the death of the flower. It grows in dry meadows, and grassy sandy places, and flowers in June and July. Its *officinale* name is *saxifraga alba*. It possesses superior diuretic properties, and is very useful for those troubled with gravel and stone in the bladder, and to relieve stranguary. Taken in strong decoction, it cleanses the stomach and lungs from thick tough phlegm. There are few better medicines for stone, than this. The saxifrage burnet, I have already spoken of in another part of this work.

SCABIOUS

As I have already treated on scabious, it will be unnecessary to comment further than say, that scabious, when combined with others of this class, is one of the best medicines for cleansing and regulating the system that we know of. The juice of the scabious with the powder of borax and samphire, cleanses the skin of the face, or other parts from freckles, pimples, and other blemishes. The head washed with a warm decoction, cleanses it of scurf, sores, dandruff" and itch.

SCURVY-GRASS

The leaves of the scurvy-grass are flat, thick and oblong, smooth on the edges. The flowers stand in little clusters, they are small, white, and bright. It flowers in May and June. The plant possesses diuretic and anti-scorbutic properties. It has also superior powers in cleansing the blood of impurities, as well as the liver and spleen. The juice, taken every morning fasting, will answer this purpose. To mix the juice, with the juice of the bitter orange, is a more agreeable way of taking it.

SELF-HEAL

It has many names, such as hook-heal, sickle-wort, etc. It is a small low creeping herb, with small round-pointed leaves, of a dark green color, from which rise square hairy stalks, a foot high, the flowers are small, and of a bluish purple; they stand in short spikes or heads, the cups of them are often purplish. The roots have many fibers, and spreading strings, and flowers in May and June. This also is a good wound herb, which its name implies. Very useful for strains, and internal injuries, taken as a decoction, inwardly, and the juice of the root and herb, made into an ointment, for external application for bruises and sores. As self-heal is like bugle in form, so also is its medicinal virtues, if combined with sanicle, bugle, and scabious, it will be more effectual to wash or inject into ulcers outwardly. It is a special remedy for all green wounds, to close and heal them. The juice mixed with honey, will cure ulcers in the mouth and throat.

SENNA

Is the leaves of different species of cassia. It is a medicine that has come down through the ages, and is a native of upper Egypt. It is also cultivated in many parts of India, It is a useful purgative, its operation is mild, but effectual. It should not be administered when irritation and fever are present, nor during pregnancy. As we have already treated of this herb, we would refer the reader to that part of the work. But would say that a very good way of administering it is as follows, electuary of senna.

> Senna leaves, powdered 4 ounces
> Pulp of French prunes 1 pound
> Pulp of tamarinds 2 ounces
> Molasses 1.5 pints
> Essential oil of caraway 2 drachms

This herb has also many names. It is a very common plant, overrunning garden beds, farm, and court yards. The leaves are long, rather broad, indented at the edges. The stalks round and erect, nine or ten inches high, the flowers are in clusters, small and white. The seeds are small, yellowish, and roots are white.

Boil this in the syrup to the thickness of honey, then add the powder, and when the mixture cools, the oil; lastly, mix the whole thoroughly. A smaller quantity may be prepared by reducing its proportions to the above.

SHEPHERD'S PURSE

This herb has also many names. It is a very common plant, overrunning garden beds, farm, and court yards. The leaves are long, rather broad, indented at the edges. The stalks round and erect, nine or ten inches high, the flowers are in clusters, small and white. The seeds are small, yellowish, and roots are white. This plant is very astringent and glutinous, It is good for bleeding at the nose and spitting of blood, and in diarrhea, dysentery, and bloody urine. It makes a valuable ointment with fresh lard, for cuts and wounds.

SMALLAGE

Is a common wild plant, very much resembling celery. The leaves are many and large; stalks two feet and a half high, round, smooth, and branched. The flowers stand at the division of the branches; they are small and a yellowish white.

SOAPWORT

It is also called bruisewort. It grows wild in low wet grounds, by streams of running water. It flowers in July and August. It is one of the old fashioned remedies for skin disease. It possesses alterative and diuretic properties; it is very mucilaginous and will make a lather like soap, instead of which it is sometimes used; hence its name soapwort. A decoction of the roots and herb remove obstructions, and promotes a flow of urine, and perspiration. It is a great purifier of the blood. It will also expel or prevent the accumulation of water in persons disposed to dropsy. In syphilitic affections, it is more effectual than sarsaparilla, or guaicum. As a purifier of the blood, it is worthy of attention. But should be compounded with others of its class to make it more effectual.

SORREL

It is so well known it requires little description. It is useful to cool the blood in all hot diseases, in ague, sickness, and fainting in fevers, and procure an appetite, in debility, and weak stomach. It destroys worms in children, it is cordial to the heart. The seed is the most powerful, it is astringent, and very useful in bloody flux. The decoction of the roots is good in jaundice, and the gravel, and other diseases of the kidneys and bladder. The decoction of the flowers made with wine, will cure the black jaundice, and ulcerated bowels. A syrup made with sorrel and fumitory, is a good remedy for the itch; the juice combined with a little vinegar, is a good remedy for the tetters, ringworms, etc. It removes kernels and sores in the throat; to gargle with the juice. The leaves wrapped in cabbage-leaf, and roasted; and applied to carbuncles, boils, or plague sore, soon ripen and break them.

SPEEDWELL

This is a very common herb, growing in dry pastures in some parts of this country. It grows about six or eight inches high, leaves short and oval. Stalks trail on the ground, only rising at the upper parts. The flowers are small and blue, they grow in slender spikes, arising from the bosom of the leaf. The root is small and fibrous, the whole herb is used, and is best fresh. An infusion taken freely, opens all obstructions in the kidneys and bladder, also the pores of the skin. It is an excellent cleanser of the blood. It removes blotches and cutaneous eruptions. It is one of the best medicines for children in the spring, combined with some one of the medicines recommended under that head.

STAVESACRE

This herb is a member of the crow-foot family, its *officinale* name is *delphinum staphisaqria*. Its seeds are violently emetic and cathartic. They are seldom given internally; though the powdered seeds have been given in dropsy, in very small quantities at first, and increased until the effect is produced. Dose at first should not exceed two or three grains. It is a vermin destroyer, and will kill lice and other parasites, by washing or bathing with the liquor. It will cure the itch. The seeds are merely boiled in water.

ST. JOHN'S WORT

This is a common herb abounding in our fields and woods; but as we have spoken of this herb in the early part of our work, we refer our readers to that particular part for a description of it. But I will say further that wonders have been performed with this herb in intermittent fevers, and hemorrhages, it is equal to any herb of its class as a wound herb, made into an ointment.

SQUILL

Squill is a bulbous root of a plant growing on the sandy shores of Southern Europe. It is a stimulating expectorant, and diuretic; and is somewhat useful in chronic cough, and asthma. In large doses it vomits and purges, but is seldom given with either of these intentions It was early known as a remedy for cough and dropsy, and still retains its character as a remedy of efficacy when judiciously exhibited. It seems to possess a peculiar virtue for coughs, and difficulty of breathing, of old people, in which there is an accumulation of mucus within the chest. Its expectorant properties are increased by the addition of lobelia, or ipecacehuana. Warm demulcent and mucilaginous liquors, contribute in no small degree to its successful operation. It must not be administered when the skin is hot and dry, with a hard pulse, or where other marks of inflammation are present; as it then checks instead of promoting expectoration. The compound squill pill is a combination of squills with, ginger, hard castile soap shavings, and gum ammoniac. It is an old preparation, and is considered a valuable expectorant, in doses from five to eight grains, twice a day.

STONE CROP

Is a kind of house-leek, it grows with trailing branches upon the ground, with many thick, flat, roundish, whitish green leaves, pointed at the ends. The yellow flowers stand together, rather loosely. The roots are small and are creepers. The properties of this herb are astringent and anti-canker. It will stop bleeding, both inward and outward, tends to cure cancers, fretting sores and ulcers. It is a great preventative of the bile, and prevents diseases arising from bilious humors. It expels poison, prevents fevers, by removing obstructions. It is one of the most useful and harmless herbs we know of for the above mentioned diseases, and preventatives, which is often better than a cure. The decoction of it being used. The leaves bruised and applied to scrofulous sores, and piles, is an effectual remedy.

SUCCORY OR CHICORY

This is a species of Endive, and is a common plant. It has long leaves lying on the ground, much cut in on the edges, on both sides, even to the middle rib, ending in a point. From the leaves rise a hard, round, woody stalk, spreading into many branches, with smaller leaves on them to the top, where stand the flowers. The seed and root are harder and more woody than that grown by cultivation. It grows in waste and barren fields. It is of great service in all obstructions of the viscera, particularly of the liver. It is good where there is an excess of bile, or so-called bilious attacks; it is therefore useful as a remedy in jaundice, inflammation of the liver, and the gravel, as it works powerfully by the urine. It is good also in dropsy and ague, by stimulating the kidneys to action. A decoction of the leaves has the desired effect, in the above mentioned diseases if made strong. The distilled water of the herb and flowers is good for swooning and fainting.

SPLEENWORT

It is also called Harts tongue. The leaves are single, and long, arising from a black bushy root, indented on each side irregularly, and covered on the under part with seeds. The leaf appears more like some insect. The plant is an astringent, it is therefore binding in its nature, and especially a cleanser of the spleen, and removing by its superior medical virtues, stone in the bladder; is a good remedy for stranguary or obstructed urine; hence it is a valuable remedy to those whose vitality is waning, assisted of course by proper exercise. Elderly people of both sexes, will find the following a very useful preparation, viz. Buchu-leaves, spleenwort, balmony, of each one ounce; ginger, half ounce. Put down in three pints of water, boil gently down to one quart, strain, and take a wine-glassful two or three times a day, sweeten if desired. This is a very valuable preparation for the aged and infirm, as well as for those troubled with general debility; or where it may be stated, that no particular part of the system is diseased, but the languid, depressed, debilitated state, demands a remedy. The above is the remedy, needed.

TUTSAN OR PARK LEAVES

It deserves mention here, on account of its great medical virtues. It has brownish round stalks, about two feet high. The stalks are firm, smooth, upright, not branched, except from some young shoots near the tops. The leaves are two, at each joint opposite one another, nearly oval color brownish green, smooth. The flowers small, and a beautiful yellow, like those of the St. John's wort, full of yellow threads which stain the hands red. The fruit is a kind of a berry, and when ripe, black, containing many small seeds. The plant in Autumn frequently appears of a blood red color, very singular and beautiful. The root is small and red, and creeps under the surface. It grows in woods and clearings. The leaves are an excellent remedy for fresh wounds. There have been very singular instances of the efficacy of this herb; many other plants are celebrated for their curative properties; but the efficacy of this is surprising. A decoction of this herb is a good diuretic and very useful to promote urine. It is a superior remedy in stranguary and other diseases of the urinary canal, in either sex.

THISTLE (Woolen)

It is also called cotton thistle. It is a very common plant, with many large, crumpled leaves, covered with a down, and set with many sharp prickles, from which spring stalks, set with many heads of flowers, with crimson threads or thrums of a purple color, and sometimes white, but seldom. The seed is a down or cotton, and resembles the seed of the lady thistle, but paler. The root is large, thick, and spreading. The root is the part used medicinally. It is a good remedy for children whose nervous fiber is weak and seem to deter the growth of the child; it has that property of binding or contracting the nerves fiber, ligaments, etc. It is therefore good for rickets in children, and is also a good remedy in all nervous complaints.

THORN APPLE

It is called also stramonium. It is a common plant, growing plentifully in this section. It grows about three feet high. The leaves are large, and of a light green; the flowers are white and trumpet shaped. The seed oblong and the size of a large butternut, covered with soft thorns, hence its name. As I have already spoken of the medicinal virtues of this plant, further comment is unnecessary.

VALERIAN

It has a thick, short, grayish root, partly lying above the ground, shooting forth a number of small pieces of roots, which have many long green fibers running in the ground. The shoots are many, with large leaves. Stalks are long, with many leaves, dented at the edges. The flowers stand in tufts on top of the stalks, and are small and white, with a reddish cast. The root is of a whitish color, very fibrous, and with a strong and unpleasant odor. It is a good remedy to relieve stranguary or obstructed urine, prepared with aniseed and licorice. It is good for short-winded people. It is also very useful to relieve obstructed menstruation and pain in the sides. The juice of the herb is very useful for inflammation and dimness of the eyes. It is also one of the most useful nervines we have; as it is a good remedy in hysteria and spasmodic attacks generally. It is best given in substance with a little cinnamon to disguise the taste. The ammoniated tincture is a valuable remedy in all nervous disorders.

OUR COMMON GRAPE VINE

The leaves of the *Vitis Vinifera* being boiled, makes a good lotion for sore mouths; boiled with barley-meal into a poultice, it is cooling to inflammations and wounds. The ashes of the burnt branches make a very superior tooth powder, it will clean the blackest of teeth, if continued for a few mornings, to that of a pure white.

VIOLETS

This class of herbs are all cold and moist, when green, and are used to cool heat in any part of the body. Outward inflammation of all kinds yield to this plant alone, if applied as a poultice. The flowers and herb are demulcent and laxative, they are therefor very useful in choleric humors, more particularly in children, combined with hyssop and honey, it is very useful in cough and tightness of the chest.

VIPERS BUGLOSS

It is a common herb, and so well known requiring no description. This species has a large flower of a beautiful blue in color, with red stamens in the middle. The leaves and flowers of this plant are sudorific and cordial.

It is used in fevers- will cure the headache and is a good remedy in nervous disorders. A decoction of the roots will drive away melancholy and stimulate the heart. The whole herb is a blood sweetener, more particularly if taken when the plant is in full bloom, it is good to expel poison from the system. The juice or bruised leaves are very useful to cure snake bite, applied as a poultice.

WILLOW TREE

The leaves and bark of this tree are used to staunch bleeding wounds, spitting of blood, and other fluxes, and will stay vomiting when boiled in wine and drank. The bark is good for inflammation of the eyes, and dimness of sight. A good wash is made from the leaves and bark in wine, it will cleanse the head of dandruff, and take away scurf from the head, by washing the part with it.

INSATIS TINTORIA

A plant known by the name of woad, and at one time was extensively cultivated for the use of dyers. The herb is such a powerful astringent, it is not fit to be used internally. An ointment made from the leaves is good for severe bleeding in fresh wounds. It is an excellent remedy made into a plaster, and applied to the region of the spleen which lies on the left side, it relieves the hardness thereof. The ointment is good for moist ulcers and humors. It cools inflammations, and stays defluction of of the blood to any part of the body.

WORMWOOD (Roman)

This is a delicate plant of the wormwood kind. Its botanical name is *Artemesia Romanum*. It is often cultivated in our gardens. It is a plant about two feet high; the stalk is round, smooth, hard, upright, of a brownish color, and somewhat woody. The leaves stand very irregularly on it, and are small and divided into very fine segments; they are more like the leaves of the common southern wood in figure, than those of either of the other wormwoods. The flowers are small and brown, like those of the common wormwood, but much smaller; they are very numerous, and stand at the top of the stalks in a kind of a long and thick spikes. The root is thick and composed of fibers. The whole plant has a bitter taste, but not at all like that of wormwood, extremely aromatic and pleasing. The flowers are bitter, also as well as aromatic. The whole plant is used, green or dry. It is excellent to strengthen the stomach, but that is not all its virtues. Made into a strong decoction and drank freely, will remove obstructions of the liver and spleen, and has often been known to cure jaundice alone.

YARROW

This plant is known by the name Millefolium, and is so well known needs no description, having treated of this plant in another part of this work, further comment is unnecessary, with one exception, and would say that yarrow possesses more medicinal properties than most herbs, and possibly, has saved more lives, as well as dollars, to the poor man, than any herb we know of. It cannot be surpassed by any other herb for a common cold, taken in infusion with ginger upon going to bed.

DOCK YELLOW

The yellow dock is so common, it needs little description. The root is the part used, and when made into an ointment with fresh lard, or the root finely bruised and mixed with cream; kept warm for ten or twelve hours, and not scalded, will cure the itch. Rub on when going to bed. Three times using will effect a cure.

MEANS TO PROMOTE AND MAINTAIN HEALTH

EXTERNAL AND INTERNAL APPLICATIONS

HEAT

A certain degree of external heat is necessary to promote the vital manifestations of all warm blooded animals. It is frequently employed as a remedial agent externally. The Hot Air Bath, at a temperature of from 100 to 130 degrees, F. is a powerful stimulant, and valuable when the blood has receded from the superficial parts of the body, and the internal organs congested; as in some cases of fever, in spasmodic cholera, in drowning, stiffness of the joints, etc.

COLD BATH

The cold bath, though popularly esteemed one of the most innocent remedies yet discovered, is not however to be adopted indiscriminately. On the contrary, it is liable to do considerable mischief in all cases of diseased viscera, and ought not to be used too freely during costiveness. As a general bracer of the system, to persons of a relaxed fiber, especially females, it generally proves highly beneficial, and in most cases, when not carried to excess, is a good means of promoting a good state of health. When beneficial, a glow of heat succeeds the bathing; if chillness and headache are the result, it should immediately be abandoned, as being pernicious. Cold water is a powerful tonic, but, like all other valuable things, may be abused. Sea water, in general, is preferable to fresh, though when not attainable, the latter is a valuable substitute not to be despised.

HOT BATH

When we speak of the hot bath, we mean any degree of heat between 93 and 96 degrees. It has a peculiar tendency to bring on a state of repose, to remove local irritation, promotes personal cleanliness, and is excellent for those troubled with diseases of the skin, as well as children troubled with convulsions. It also restores suppressed perspiration, relieves rheumatic, and hectic patients, and is useful in complaints of the kidneys and liver. It is also especially useful in swellings of the legs, and in obstructions peculiar to females. It is often the means of throwing off the first attack of disease, by opening up the system. The shower bath is very similar in its effects. In insanity it is used with the greatest benefit, to allay mental excitement. When the patient appears overcome, it should be discontinued, and renewed when the violent symptoms recur. After four or five applications of this kind, the patient becomes entirely subdued, when they should be taken out of the bath, rapidly dried, warmly covered up, and put to bed. Calmness and sleep, as a rule, generally follow, with days of tranquility and ease. The daily use of the shower bath is often very beneficial. The Tepid Bath, is a bath at about 90 degrees. It is often very useful in fevers as well as diseases of the skin, and is quite sufficient to produce a salutary reaction, with a degree of perspirability on the surface of the skin. It is very useful in some stages of rheumatism, headaches, colds, and will often relieve suppressed menstruation arising from cold. The Vapor Bath, we have already spoken of its beneficial effects. The inhalation of the vapor of hot water proves highly serviceable as a soothing remedy in irritation or inflammation of the lining membrane of the throat, bronchial tubes and tonsils. Warm fomentations and poultices are employed to relieve inflammation, pain, tension, and spasms.

DROWNING

In the case of a drowning person being recovered, keep the head raised, dry the body, and as soon as possible rub with hot cloths, and let another person shove the belly up towards the chest with the flat hands, suddenly removing the hands, and in this way, by performing the action of respiration, endeavor to restore breathing. And as soon as possible, give a table-spoonful of the anti-spasmodic tincture, A hot bath is of great value, keeping up a constant friction by rubbing the body with the hands.. Clear the mucus from the mouth, hold the nose, and suck out the foul air with a tube, and blow in fresh air with a pair of common bellows, if no other and better machine is not at hand. Plenty of heat is what is needed, and if possible apply electricity. After restoration, purge or give such medicines as seem to be required.

SLEEP

A state in which the material body, and the senses, are voluntarily suspended. When nature demands that the system requires rest, and time to recuperate, the desire for sleep eventually overpowers us. Most animals sleep during the night, when the silence and darkness remove the ordinary impressions on the senses; the continuance of sleep varies much according to the age, constitution, and habit. New born children sleep a great deal, and thus their nutrition in the very early periods of life is favored, while the parent in her weakened state is not fatigued. It is impossible to specify a period for the duration of sleep, which may be adapted to all constitutions; but in an adult, healthy person, from six to eight hours may be considered sufficient. Too much sleep blunts the faculties, and makes loafers of young men, and shiftless women, causes corpulence, flabby and unwieldy habits. Some persons, like most animals are able to sleep on a full stomach on going to bed, while others, are unable to do so. It is by far the better idea, not to accustom yourself to eat much food upon retiring for the night, but if the stomach needs a little food, eat light food, and sparingly. In fact, eat to live, and that only.

FOOD

In infancy, the organs of digestion are naturally weak, but at the same time, there is necessity for much nourishment. And nourishment of that kind, that will assimilate readily with nature. By examining the properties of milk, will give us some idea of the nature of the food required. Milk is not a simple substance in its pure state; it is a mixture of coagulable matter, expressed oil, and sugar. Coagulable matter is that which will unite, and become solid, leaving the rest thinner and more fluid, viz. the curd, and expressed oil is such as can be procured from any substance by pressing, by expressed oil of milk, we understand the cream. The most simple food, then, does not appear the easiest of digestion: if it were, we should have expected that milk would have consisted of one substance only. That coagulable matter is capable of affording considerable nourishment. This coagulable matter in milk, is fluid when taken into the stomach; but combining with the juices of the stomach, renders it solid. We find a few drops of the juice taken from the stomach of the calf, will coagulate or curdle several quarts of milk. Milk, new drawn, is best and most wholesome for weakly persons and infants. It is of a costive nature, therefore it makes a healthy beverage for those of a lax fiber; boiled it is even more so, but it is less sour in the stomach, it is better for the robust and vigorous, particularly as it is in this state more cooling. As sugar prevents the spontaneous separation of the several parts of milk in the stomach, it is proper to give sugar along with it to convalescents.

Cheese: It has in general a costive quality; but it

differs, in proportion to the quality of oil in the coagulable part. The more rich and oily parts there are in cheese, the more nutritive it is, and soluble; that is, the readier it will digest. When cheese becomes rank and putrid, it looses its nutritive qualities, and can only be considered as an assistant to digestion. Cheese as a food is fit only for those having a good digestive apparatus.

Butter: A quantity of pure cream eaten, is undoubtedly unwholesome; being, from its disposition to get acid or rancid, very difficult of digestion; but, in the form of butter, it may be used with advantage. It is a strong nutriment, fit to accompany our vegetable diet, especially such vegetables as are naturally dry of themselves; in this case it gives them the properties of rich oily substances. But, to return, it appears then that milk, and, of course, all other food, must become solid in the stomach, and, after that, undergo a fresh change, that is, be redissolved, for digestion; for which purpose, it must remain some time there, before it be passed off as chime. Now, that the expressed oil, which is the cream, helps digestion, is evident from milks not digesting so well when it has been skimmed, the curd being harder, for the cream and sugar, being mixed with the curd, separate the different parts of it more from one another, so that the natural fluid of the stomach will penetrate the easier, it being from its nature more apt to ferment, will of course facilitate digestion. That expressed oil affords much nourishment, we find from men and animals being able to live a long time upon nuts, most of such containing a quantity of this oil. But expressed oil alone produces a sense of weight in the stomach, owing to a relaxation it brings on, preventing the stomach contracting and expelling its load; and, if taken in quantities, it will bring on sickness. That sugar affords great nourishment, is evident from animals thriving on the shoots of young plants, which contain a great deal of sugar; and from some of the inhabitants of southern countries, living almost entirely on sugar cane and other sugar producing vegetables. But sugar alone is viscid, and by adhering to the sides of the stomach, will stimulate it, disorder the system, and, if diluted with any watery fluid, would not stay sufficiently long in the stomach to be digested; but mixed with the coagulable part of milk, it is sufficiently retained. Either of these substances alone then, viz. coagulable matter, expressed oil of sugar, would be hard of digestion, but blended together, as in milk they are easy of digestion. At child birth, when the milk begins to flow in the mother's breasts, it contains a larger quantity of sugar and water, for there is always more or less water in proportion to the coagulable matter, but as the age of the infant increases, so it is with the coagulable matter in the mother's milk. For as the child grows stronger, its stomach can bear more of this coagulable matter, and digests it, if it be firmer. We learn from this, that weak stomachs require food of easy digestion; strong stomachs, food of harder digestion. Hence milk is equally fit at every period of life, being, in general, easy of digestion, and occasioning less heat to the system than any other animal or vegetable food, producing less feculent matter, and not offending the stomach, unless it form into two firm a coagulation, which occasions the fullness and weight I have mentioned. In such cases, if it be not corrected by sugar, it should be avoided. Boiled milk is found by experience, more costive than raw or new milk. A mixture of sugar with milk, prevents spontaneous separation of the milk into parts, as it unites with the fatty or oily parts of the milk, which therefore gives it the advantage of new milk. Whey carries with it a great part of all the ingredients of milk, though it may not seem so, and is more nourishing than the milk itself. Farmers fatten hogs solely on whey.

VEGETABLE FOOD

Taste and smell generally direct our choice in vegetables, and it may be said, with very few exceptions, that those esculents which are the most salutary, and vice versa.

But as the taste and smell in certain constitutions are often depraved and vitiated, we had best say, that those that sit easiest on the stomach are most wholesome. Vegetables tend to reduce a full habit, abate heat, and are of course, very proper for those that are corpulent, as well as those troubled with feverish heats and distensions of the blood vessels. That vegetables correct putrescence, is evident from their curing what is known as the sea-scurvy brought on by living on animal food, which without a mixture of vegetable food, is apt to continue long enough in the stomach to putrefy. Vegetables are particularly proper in hot climates, being less stimulant; and are more cooling than animal food; but as flatulence is seldom experienced by persons in a healthy state, it must be imputed to weakness of the stomach, rather than to the vegetables. All such vegetables as cabbage, cauliflower, lettuce, spinach, etc., of that class, may be greatly improved by the adding of some fatty matter, either in the boiling, or eaten as a salad with olive oil. Now these plants alone do not afford much nourishment; we use them to correct the putrescence of animal food, and particularly in the summer, as non-stimulating.

They are apt to ferment, and turn sour in a weak stomach, without the addition of some fatty matter; but when persons find, that such vegetables disagree with the stomach, by causing flatulence after eating, they must refrain from the use of such vegetables, until the stomach has been strengthened by the use of some of the many tonics, prescribed for weakness of that organ. Peas and beans are very difficult to digest, and are therefore very windy, and much more so than the green vegetable. Potatoes, carrots, and turnips are considered a very healthy food prepared in the proper manner. Potatoes are more easily digested than bread, and very rarely disagree with the most delicate stomach; but they afford less nourishment than either rice or bread, which proceed chiefly from the large quantity of water contained in their substance, yet many people in many parts of the world live almost wholly on potatoes and milk.

FRUITS

A proper use of fruits contribute to the preservation of health. Ripe fruit extinguishes thirst, moderates heat, and opens the body: Acids, particularly the native vegetable ones, moderately used in diet, are grateful to the stomach, assist the appetite, promote digestion, cool the body and correct a tendency to putrefaction; but the too free use of them will disorder both the stomach and bowels. Fruits containing the largest amount of sugar, and mucilage, naturally contain the greatest amount of nourishment. The sugar, acid and mucilage, are capable of fermentation; and of course, being converted into blood. Fruits containing a large amount of vegetable acids, afford so little nourishment, that they are only fit to quench the thirst, and if eaten in an unripe state, are well adapted to create disease, and even death. The fermentation of such fruit in the stomach, causes it to become distended to such an extent that it has often proved fatal; but we may correct this by adding sugar to them, or spices. Parents would do well to note the following, viz. That when a child has eaten, or taken a quantity of cherries, currants, or other fruit into the stomach, without first breaking the skin, or in other words swallowing them whole; and the stomach of the child had become so distended creating severe pain, and often death; immediately give the child to eat a piece of cheese about the size of a hickory nut, which will have the effect to dissolve the fruit in the stomach, and when the pain has subsided, allow them to partake of sugar, which will still further assist to carry off the offending matter.

We would say further, such as find certain kinds of fruit disagree with the stomach, if they value their health, should refrain from eating them. Some fruit act as a purge in the summer time, that would not act, or have the same effect at any other season of the year; showing conclusively that the state of the atmosphere has a great deal to do with conditions. And fruits, when eaten ripe, are in nowise dangerous; but often beneficial, for they act no further than as a mild purgative, and are of a cleansing nature as a rule. Cucumbers and melons, we have but little use for, except the water melon when perfectly ripe, in the hot summer weather, a small quantity eaten to relieve thirst is in nowise injurious, when the stomach is not overheated, some writers claim, that cucumbers and melons of all kinds, are cold and bad, and that a French physician, who had a large practice from such persons as ate much of them, built a country-seat, and whose sign, in gold letters, ran thus! "Cold cucumbers built this hall, and crude-musk-melons furnished it."

ANIMAL FOOD

Let us consider the difference between animal and vegetable food. Now as we said before, fermentation which takes place in food, within the stomach, is different from that which takes place out of it. If the stomach then be weak, so as not to bring on the fermentation which is natural to it, the fermentation that would take place out of the stomach, will take place in it, and bring on certain diseases. Thus the mischief of animal food putrefying, are greater and more dangerous than such as arise from undigested vegetable food, as this turns sour only. Another difference is this. Vegetable food, during digestion, stimulates less. When the stomach is distended with food, the whole system, during digestion, is more or less stimulated; but more so with animal food than with vegetable. Now the more our system is stimulated, the quicker is the circulation, and the more feverish we become. As animal food fills the vessels fuller, and with denser blood, than vegetable, it naturally increases muscular strength; but then it loads the brain, (every part being fuller of blood in proportion) and occasions heaviness and stupor; whereas, vegetable food, from not overloading the system with blood, is inclined to diminish the muscular, and build the mental strength, enabling the mind to act with greater force. Vegetable food, therefore, is more fit to give clearness of ideas, and strengthen the nerve centers, and gray pulp of the brain; whereas animal food is best adapted to physical labor, combined with such vegetable food, as the system has become accustomed to. The more vegetable food a person eats, the less drink he requires; and that drink should be pure water; the substance with which water is impregnated is of little consequence, as long so it agrees with the system; but those who eat much animal food may require fermented liquors; but it must be remembered, that, though fermented liquors contain an acid property to correct putrescence, they also contain an alcohol, which, though it stimulates, is hurtful to the stomach. The chief nourishment drawn from food, as I have observed, is the oil it contains; and there is more oil in animal food than in vegetable. A proof of this is evident, there being more corpulent persons among those in the habit of eating plentifully of animal food; by over 60 percent, more, than among those who eat of it sparingly, and those who live entirely on a vegetable diet. Nature in the structure of the body, has designed man to live on both kinds of food, and reason should dictate which to choose, and when. The more hard physical labor a man has to perform, the more animal food will be required to build muscular tissue, and the more animal he becomes, and the more a person labors with the mind, the more vegetable food is required, of such a quality that nature designed to build those particular tissues or organs of the brain, to withstand the greatest strain, and if we would but listen to the still small voice within us, which is nature; she will never lead us astray with regard to the requirements in our everyday life.

It is a question in our mind whether man requires this high degree of bodily strength, with all its inconveniences and dangers. Certainly those who lead a sedentary life, should avoid an excess of animal food. In hysteric and hypochondriac constitutions, animal food, mixed with a vegetable diet, is almost a necessity; but when a cure is performed, such persons should avoid animal food as much as possible. They should eat a great deal of bread, the safest of all vegetable food. Vegetable food is not only necessary to secure health, but long life. In infancy and in youth we should be confined to it mostly, in manhood and decay of life, animal food may be used sparingly, but in old age vegetable food should be used exclusively. Variety of food, seems to be necessary, and liquid and solid food should temper each other; the only danger of variety is eating too much. Heaviness in the stomach is seldom felt from the use of vegetable food, except tough pastry and the more viscid substances. It will continue longer in the stomach than animal, and gives little stimulus, and the system is affected in proportion of this stimulus.

THE WHY, AND THE WHEREFORE

There are not a few popular opinions, in regard to which it is useful at times to ask a question or two. For example, it is commonly thought that children must have what are commonly called "children's epidemics," "current contagious," etc.; in other words, that they are born to have measles, hooping-cough, or even scarlet fever, just as they are born to cut their teeth, if they live. Now, do tell us why a child must have measles- and it must take them- and it is safer that it should. But why must other children have measles? If you believe in and observe the laws for preserving the health of houses which inculcate cleanliness, ventilation, white-washing, and other means, and which, by the way, are laws as implicitly as you believe in popular opinion, for it is nothing more than an opinion, that your children must have children's epidemics, don't you think upon the whole your child would be more likely to escape altogether? Is it not living in a continual mistake to look upon disease, as we now do, as separate entities, and which must exist, like dogs or horses, instead of looking upon them as conditions, like a dirty and clean condition, and just as much under our own control; or rather as the reactions of kindly nature against the conditions in which we have placed ourselves. We were led to believe that small-pox for instance, was a something of which there was once a first specimen in the world, which went on propagating itself, in a perpetual chain of descent. What nonsense.

For you may both see and smell it, generally from first principals; in the low dirty dives, and slums of almost any large city, where it could not by any possible means have been "caught," but must have begun. Nay, more, you may see disease begin, grow up, and pass into one another. You may see for instance, with a little overcrowding, continued fever grow up; and with a little more, typhus, and all in the same ward or slum. Would it not be far better, truer, and more practical if we looked upon disease in this light? For diseases, as all experience shows, are adjectives, not noun substantives among people generally an extraordinary fallacy exists, which is a dread of night air. What air can we breathe at night, but night air? The choice is between pure night air without, and foul night air from within. Fully one half of the diseases we suffer from is occasioned by people sleeping with windows and doors closed. An open window at the top, most nights in the year, can hurt no one. I could better understand in towns and cities shutting their windows during the day than during the night, for the sake of the sick very often. The absence of smoke, the quiet, all tend to make night the best time for airing the patient. Often in fact the night air is the best and purest in the twenty four hours. Always air your room, then, from the outside air if possible; and with sufficient blankets beneath you to retain the heat of the body, with a well aired bed and dry sheets, you have nothing to fear from disease from that quarter. I was about to proceed and give a description and duty of the skin, but as I find Mr. Alfred Ford has put it in poetical form, I give it almost verbatim.

THE SKIN

> There's a skin without and a skin within,
> A covering skin and a lining skin;
> But the skin within is the skin without
> Doubled inward, and carried completely
> throughout.
> The palate, the nostrils, the windpipe, and throat,
> Are all of them lined with this inner coat;
> Which through every part is made to extend
> Lungs, liver, and bowels from end to end.
>
> The outside skin is a marvelous plan
> For exuding the dregs of the flesh of man;
> While the inner extracts from the food and air

THE OCCULT FAMILY PHYSICIAN

That is needed the waste in his flesh to repair.
If all goes well with the outside skin.
You may feel pretty sure all's right within.
But if anything puts the inner skin out
It is sure to trouble the skin without.

The doctor you know examines your tongue
To see if your stomach or bowels are wrong;
If he feels that your hand is hot and dry.
He will sometimes tell you the reason why.
Too much beer, whiskey or gin.
Will surely disorder the skin within;
While if dirty or chocked the skin without
Refuses to let the sweat come out.

Good people all! have a care of the skin,
Both that without and that within;
To the first you'll give plenty of water and soap,
To the last little else besides water, we'll hope.
But always be very particular where
You get your water, your food, and your air;
For if these be tainted or rendered impure
It will have its effect on your blood- be sure,

The food which will ever for you be the best
Is that you like most, and can soonest digest;
All unripe fruit and decaying flesh
Beware of, and fish that is not very fresh.
Your water, transparent and pure as you think it.
Had better be filter'd or boiled ere you drink it.
Unless you know surely that nothing unsound
Can have got to it, over or under the ground.

But of all things the most I would have you beware
Of breathing the poison of once breathed air;
When in bed, whether out or at home you may be.
Always open your window, and let it go free.
With clothing and exercise keep yourself warm,

And change your clothes quickly if drenched in a
storm
For a cold caught by chilling the outside skin
Flies at once to the delicate lining within.

All of you who thus take care of your skin,
And attend to its wants without and within.
Need never of cholera feel any fears,
And your skin may last you a hundred years.

HINTS IN EMERGENCIES

IF APPARENTLY DEAD FROM APOPLEXY

The patient should be placed in the cool air, and the
clothes loosened, about the neck and breast. A tablespoonful
of the anti-spasmodic tincture immediately administered,
with strong vinegar cloths applied to the head, which should
be shaved. All other stimulants should be avoided. In cases
of sun stroke, the same means must be applied. If
apparently dead from noxious vapors, remove the body into
a cool fresh air. Throw cold water repeatedly over the upper
parts of the body, and if the body be cold, apply warmth,
and friction with hot flannels. And if no other means can be
had, use a common bellows for inflating the lungs, also
apply electricity with an ordinary battery as soon as
possible.

ANTIDOTES TO POISONS

The treatment of cases of poisoning must, of course,
vary with the nature of the poison, the quantity taken, and
the temperament of the individual. In almost all cases,
copious vomiting should be excited as soon as possible by
tickling the throat, and by emetics, lobelia, ipecacuanha,
mustard, boneset, vervain, or even warm water and mustard,
if other means are not obtainable. Lobelia, however, we
mostly depend upon in such cases, as it is more effectual.

The vomiting should be kept up, and the stomach washed out with bland albuminous or mucilaginous fluids, such as milk, barley water, flour and water, or thin paste, etc. The quantity of mustard is two tablespoonfuls to the pint of warm water. Or warm milk, mixed with oil, or butter, is a very good emetic.

In Cases of Arsenic Poisoning: Administer freely of lime-water, chalk and water, and the hydrated sesqui-oxide of iron, all of which are strongly recommended; the last is decidedly the best.

For Mineral Acids, or Acetic and oxalic Acid: For this form of poison, give quickly large draughts of chalk, whiting, magnesia, soap and water, about as thick as cream; followed by albuminous dilutents, such as milk, and white of egg mixed with water. Or if these cannot be procured at once, warm water.

Alkalies, Soda, Potash, Ammonia, Etc: For this class of poisons, vinegar, or any mild acid and water, or even diluted mineral acids, such as water acidulated by them; olive oil, almond oil, etc.

Corrosive Sublimate: Take freely of white of egg and water; milk and cream, lobelia, decoction of cinchona, or an infusion of nut galls.

Sulfate of Copper: Sugar and water; white of egg and water.

Antimonial Poisons: Warm milk, gruel, or barley water, and infusion of nut galls.

Nitrate of Silver: A strong dose of lobelia and valerian, or draughts of salt water.

Sulfate of Zinc: Solution of carbonate of soda in

water, with milk, and mucilaginous or farinaceous liquids.

Acetate of Lead: Emetics of lobelia, solution of sulfate of soda in water; milk, white of egg and water.

Opium and its Preparations: Lobelia emetics, strong coffee, dashing cold water in the face, and preventing stupor by forced exercise.

Prussic Acid: Ammonical stimulants cautiously applied to the nose; ammonia, or sal-volatile in repeated small doses of solution of chlorine in water; small doses of chloride of lime and water.

Strychnine and Vegetable Alkaloids: Infusion of nut galls; decoction of cinchona; emetic of lobelia and vervain.

GENERAL OBSERVATIONS

On restoration to life, a tea-spoonful of warm water, should be given, and then if the power of swallowing be returned, small quantities of warm wine, or weak brandy and water, warm; the patient should be kept in bed, and a disposition to sleep encouraged, except in cases of apoplexy, intoxication or sun stroke. Care should be taken not to excite undue excitement. It is an absurd opinion that persons are irrecoverable, because life does not soon make its appearance, for while there is one spark of vitality left, there is hope, by following the directions laid down in this work. That one spark may be made the means whereby life may be saved, and the patient restored to health.

Before terminating this part of our work, we wish it to be distinctly understood, that the various remedies laid down for the guidance of suffering humanity here, being purely vegetable in its crude form, must necessarily depend upon the full virtue being retained in the herb, root, bark, seed, flower or gum; to ensure this, means must be adopted to procure such remedies fresh, that have been collected and stored in their proper season, so that the active principle or curative properties may be retained, and when prepared according to the directions laid down in this work, either alone or in compound, will deliver up or surrender said curative properties that nature has so benevolently provided for our use, many of the herbs, etc., that are sold by our drug stores, being valueless on account of their age and manner in which they have been kept; therefore we would advise those who are able to make collections for themselves, at the proper time and season, drying and storing them according the directions laid down in this work.

HERBS, ROOTS, BARKS, SEEDS, FLOWERS, ETC

THEIR PROPERTIES AND USES EXPLAINED

Angelica, Roots and Seeds Stim. Arom. Tonic.
For Colic, Colds, and for opening the pores of the skin. Also for incontinence of urine.

Agrimony Ast. Ton. Diu. Alt.
Useful in bowel complaints, diseases of liver and spleen.

Avens Root Styp. Ton. Ast. Stom.
For debility, and internal bleedings, relax, etc.

All-Heal, or Wound Wort. Vul.
Very useful for stopping and healing wounds.

Almonds, Bitter Ton.
Useful with other tonics for debility of stomach and bowels.

Aloes Stim. Cath. Ton.
Useful, combined with stimulants in costiveness, and a bad state of the stomach.

Angelica, Leaves and Seeds Stim. Car. Ton.
Excellent in Pleurisy, diseases of the chest and lungs, shortness of breath, etc.

Aniseeds Stim. Car.
Used in cough remedies, and for flatulence, colic, etc.

Asafoetida Anti-spas. Stim. Expec.

Used for nervous disorders, spasmodic cough, and disorders of the chest, flatulence, etc.

Ash, Flowering Ton. Ape. Diu.
Useful for stone in the bladder, and as a tonic, a good substitute for Cinchona. It also makes a good substitute for senna, as it is less griping.

Asparagus Roots Diu. Ape. Alt.
It has often cured jaundice and dropsy, when all else have failed.

Balm Stim. Car.
Useful to strengthen the stomach, and braces the nerves.

Barberry Bark Anti-scor. Deob.
Used for choleric humors, scabs, itch, ringworms, etc.

Bark, Peruvian Anti-bil. Feb. Ton.
Useful in fevers, ague, scrofula, etc.

Bay Tree, Leaves and Berries Ton. Ast. Diu. Dis.
The leaves are very useful for removing obstructions of the liver and spleen. The berries are effectual against the stings of wasps and bees; and against infectious diseases.

Beth Root Ast. Ton. Ant-sep.
Beneficial for bloody urine, excessive female evacuation, etc.

Bitter Root Ton. Cath.
For liver complaints, and to remove costiveness and correct digestion.

Black Bryony Diu.

Is one of the best diuretics known in medicine, and is useful in gravel, and other disorders of the kidneys.

Burdock Root Alt. Ape. Diu. Sudo.
Used in scurvy, rheumatism, and for provoking urine, etc.

Bitter Sweet Alt. Ton.
Used in syphilitic ulcers and scrofulous diseases.

Boneset Sud. Ton. Erne. Cath.
Used for colds, fevers, a good cleanser and useful in asthma.

Burdock Seeds Diu. Ton. Ner.
Good for inflammation of the kidneys, convulsions, etc.

Butter-Bur Root Sudo. Feb. Nev.
It is a great strengthener of the heart, and cheers the spirits. It is also good against pestilential fevers.

Bistort Root Ast.
Useful in hemorrhages or fluxes, externally or internally.

Balmony Anti-Bil. Ton. Ast
For dyspepsia, and affections of the liver, etc.

Benzoin, or Gum Benjamin Stim. Expect.
Used in connection with others, in old asthmatic cases and chronic catarrh, it is also applied outwardly to wounds, etc.

Blood Wort Ast.
For stopping bleeding internally, fluxes, and overflowing of the menses.

Green Broom Cath. Diu.
Used in dropsy and obstructions of the liver, and also useful in jaundice.

Cayenne Stim. Car. Ton.
Excellent in fevers, cholera, palsy, colds, etc.

Cinnamon Sti. Aro.
Used in sickness of the stomach, relax, etc.

Cranesbill Styp. Ast. Ton.
Used in diarrhoea, hemorrhage and whites.

Cloves Sti. Arom. Car.
Good in flatulence, gout, and dyspepsia.

Clivers Diu. Sud. Alt.
Used in eruptions gravel, dropsy and fevers.

Comfrey Root Pect. Dem. Bal.
Valuable in dysentery, cough, diseases of the bladder, kidneys and bowels.

Coltsfoot Exp. Pec, Dem.
Used in coughs, asthma and consumption.

Columba Root Ton.
Good in jaundice, liver complaint, and dyspepsia.

Cherry Bark, (wild) Ton. Diu.
Used to restore tone to the kidneys, gravel and stone in the bladder.

Cowhage Athel.
Used for destroying worms.

Capavia Bal. Stim.
Used in diseases of the urinary organs, and chronic

affections of the chest.

Cress, Water Alt. Diu.
Very useful in scurvy, female obstructions, and gravel. It is very cleansing.

Crowfoot, or Buttercup Caustic. Ceph.
Not to be used internally. Good as an ointment, to draw rheum from the eyes, applied to the nape of the neck.

Dandelion Root Deo. Diu.
A good remedy in diseases of the liver, gravel and constipation.

Dock Root, Yellow Alt. Hep. Anti-scor.
Used in combination with others of its class for skin diseases, and for strengthening the liver.

Dock, Seeds Sty. Hep.
Very useful for stopping all inward bleeding, etc.

Dock, Water Hep. Anti-scor.
Renowned for the cure of scurvy, and has good astringent properties. Powdered root makes an excellent dentrifice for the teeth.

Dropwort Root Diu. Ast.
Used in gravel and weak kidneys, a safe and gentle astringent.

Elder Flowers Alt. Sud.
Good in skin diseases and promoting perspiration.

Elecampane Exp. Ast. Ton.
Good in colic, cold, coughs, and dropsy, and cutaneous diseases.

Eye-Bright Deo. Nev. Stim.

Useful to restore weak eyes, by dropping the juice in the eyes for several days, or by drinking a decoction, or both.

Fern, Male Ver.
Used to expel worms, etc.

Fern, Water Ver.
Properties same as male fern, but more powerful. Makes a good ointment for wounds and bruises.

Feverfew Feb. Emoll.
Used in fevers, profuse menstruation, and a good fomentation for hardness of the womb, a strong decoction is good for over-doses of mercury.

Flag, Yellow Ast.
Excellent in all bleeding internally, and excessive menstruation.

Figwort Alt. Hep. Anti-scor.
Very useful in scrofula and skin diseases, and as an ointment for corroding ulcers.

Flax Mountain Car.
Useful as a purgative and cleansing medicine.

Fluellen Ast. Alt. Hep.
Used in the cure of foul ulcers, cankers, etc.

Fumitory Ton. Anti-scor.
Used in skin diseases, ulcers and leprosy.

Garlic Stim. Rub. Diu.
Used in colic, hysterical complaints and other diseases, proceeding from laxity of the solids.

Genetian Root Ton.

This is one of the best strengtheners of the human system.

Germander Sudo. Feb. Exp.
Useful in fevers, coughs, and hardness of the spleen, and difficulty of urine.

Ginger Stim. Stom. Rub.
Used in flatulence, gout, griping pains, indigestion, etc.

Goldenrod Diu. Dis. Vul.
Good in gravel and stone in the bladder, also profuse menstruation, and inferior to none as a wound herb, for wounds and bleeding internally.

Ground Pine Diu.
Is a powerful diuretic, promotes urine, and removes obstructions of the liver.

Ground Ivy Stim. Ton. Ape. Diu.
Useful in coughs, and pulmonary complaints, and urinary affections. Also to regulate weak kidneys.

Guaicum Alt. Anod.
Used as a cleanser and for the cure of rheumatism.

Harts Tongue Ton. Exp.
It is excellent to strengthen the liver.

Hyssop Exp. Ceph.
Used in humoral asthma, coughs, dropsy and sciatica.

Hemlock Spruce Fir, Bark Ast. Ton. Diu.
Good for diseases of the bladder and kidneys.

Hollyhock Muce. Diu.

Useful in gravel and to assist the urine.

Holly Ton. Car. Cath.
Used to expel wind, and good in colic; the berries
are a good purgative when ripe.

Horehound Exp. Stim. Ton.
Well known as a remedy for coughs, and diseases of
the respiratory organs.

Iceland Moss Dem. Ton. Ast.
Very useful in coughs, catarrhal consumption, and
in hectic fevers.

Ipecacuanha Sud. Eme. Exp. Anti-spas.
Used in chronic rheumatism, and as an emetic for
cleansing the stomach, etc.

Irish Moss Dem. Ton. Ast.
Same as Iceland moss.

Ivy Ast. Ver. Emm.
Good to restrain dysentery or bloody flux. The
white berries will destroy worms, taken in wine, good in
stone, provoke urine and menstruation.

Jalap Pur. Cath,
An excellent purgative for hot bilious
temperaments. It is best taken with a little cream of tartar
and a little ginger.

Kousso Anth.
Is almost a specific in tape worm.

Leadwort Dia. Stom.
Used in headache, and to excite saliva.

Lettuce, Garden Ape. Anod. Ton,

A gentle aperient, used to promote sleep, and relieve headache.

Lily of the Valley Diu. Stim.
Useful to remove obstructions in the urinary canal, serviceable in headache, earache, and strengthening the spine.

Lily, Water, White and Yellow Root Ast. Deo.
Useful in bleeding internally, severe purging, etc.

Licorice Root Exp. Pec.
Used in bronchial affections, coughs, etc.

Liverwort Deob. Pect.
Very useful in diseases of the liver and kidneys.

Lobelia Erne. Dia. Exp. Anti-spas.
There is no better herb in the *materia medica* for spasmodic asthma. Croup and diseases of the lungs, it has no equal.

Lungwort Muci. Emol. Pec.
Very useful in diseases of the lungs, cough, and shortness of breath.

Mallow, Common Dem. Emol. Pect.
Excellent to promote urine, and for the cure of stranguary and gravel.

Vervain Mallow Dem. Emol. Pec.
Has almost the same properties as the common mallow, but not as strong.

Mandrake Nar. Cath. Stim.
Makes a fine purge, cleanses the liver, and stimulates the kidneys and other organs.

Marjoram, Sweet Aro. Stom,
Useful in diseases of the head and stomach.

Marigold Bal. Stim. Disce.
Very useful to strengthen the heart, externally it has few equals as a liniment, or plasters of dried flowers, with lard, turpentine or resin.

Meadow Saffron Pur. Diu. Nar. Stim.
The tincture, or cholchicum as it is termed, is used for the cure of rheumatism, we find it useful as a medicine to purge the liver and pancreas, and in diseases of the heart.

Meadow Sweet Feb. Ast. Alt.
Used in skin diseases, fevers and scrofulous affections.

Mountain Flax Stim. Cath.
Good in constipation of the bowels. Makes a good medicine for children, it is very cleansing.

Misletoe Ner.
This is a good remedy in epilepsy, or falling sickness. And all nervous disorders.

Moss. Ast.
Moss partakes of the properties of the tree from whence it is taken. Taken from the oak it is astringent, therefore good in bleedings, dysentry, etc.

Motherwort Ner. Ton. Stim. Stom, Emo.
Very useful in hysteric complaints, and for the cure of palpitation of the heart, and female irregularities.

Mullen Emol Ast. Exp. Sud.
Useful in colds, catarrh, and chronic diarrhoea.

Myrrh Gum, Ton. Anti. Stim. Exp. Anti-Scep.

Very useful in dyspepsia, old coughs, green sickness, chronic asthma, ulcerated lungs, etc. The tincture with a little tea, will cure sore mouth, soft glands, ulcerated mouth, and bad breath.

Nettle Stim. Deob. Ver. Anti-Asthmatic.
This plant, although very common, is much neglected. The young shoots are a blood purifier, the juice will stop spitting of blood. Excessive corpulence may be reduced by using a few of the seeds, powdered, night and morning. It is also antiasthmatic. It is a good all round herb, for all parts of it are valuable as a medicine.

Nightshade Ref. Bal. Nar.
This herb must be used with caution as it is poisonous. It makes a superior wash for foul ulcers, ringworms, etc.

Oak Bark Ast.
Very useful in bloody flux, spitting of blood, and as injection, etc.

Onions Stim. Bal. Exp.
The medicinal properties, are stimulating, easing pain and promoting sleep, and will kill worms in children.

Orchis Root Mus. Emm.
This root makes a very nutritious and strengthening diet for sick and weakly persons.

Pennyroyal Car. Sud. Sti. Aro.
Excellent remedy for suppression of urine, gravel, and female irregularities.

Poly-body Root Pec. Dem. Exp.
Used in coughs, consumption and scrofulous diseases.

Poplar Bark, White Ton. Ast. Aro. Diu.
Very useful in diarrhea, debility, kidney difficulties and indigestion.

Parsley Pert Diu, Ton.
Excellent in obstructions of the urine passages, jaundice, and affections of the liver.

Quassia Ton. Feb.
Adapted to dyspeptic cases, and to allay fever.

Quince Tree Ast. Emm.
The green fruit is astringent, therefore good in fluxes, the seeds made into mucilage, will cure cracked lips, nipples, etc.

Raspberry Leaves Ton. Ast.
Used in canker and bowel complaints in children. It makes a good substitute for tea.

Rosemary Ast. Ton. Ner.
The flowers and leaves makes a good remedy in nervous affections and hysterical complaints.

Rhubarb Root Car. Ast. Ape.
Excellent in impurities of the blood, and to relieve costiveness.

Rue Ton. Diu. Stom.
Employed in hiccup, hysterics and epilepsy.

Spearmint Feb. Diu. Stim.
Excellent in gravel, flatulence, and suppression of urine.

Sage, Garden Anti-sep, Ast.
Good in colic, colds, and coughs.

Sarsaparilla Dem. Alt. Dia. Diu.
It possesses the power of improving a general state of the system. It is a good blood purifier combined with others of its class.

Sassafras Aro. Alt. Sud
It promotes sweat; and a good remedy for foulness of the blood, scurvy, etc.

Savine Catb. Emm. Stim.
This herb should not be taken in large doses, as it is dangerous, but should be used with caution. Its action is especially on the uterus of the female, small doses are useful for scrofulous runnings and sores.

Self-heal Ast. Bal.
Good for the cure of inward wounds, hemorrhage, and as a gargle in sore throat.

St. John's Wort Ast. Bal, Diu.
Beneficial in diarrhea, obstructions of urine and hysterical complaints.

Skullcap Ton. Sud. Ner.
Excellent in all nervous affections, convulsions, and lock jaw.

Sweet Flag Root Aro. Stom.
Used in flatulent colic, wind on the stomach, etc.

Summer Savory Sto. Aro.
Good in colds, slight fevers and to allay irritation.

Sumac Ast.
Very useful in relax of the bowels, and fluxes.

Skunk Cabbage Anti-spas. Ner. Dem.
Good for bleeding of the lungs, coughs, asthma, and

obstructed menses.

Tormentil Root Sti. Ast. Ton.
A splendid remedy in diarrhea and dysentery, hemorrhage, flour albus, or whites.

Tansy Diu. Emm. Ver. Ton.
Good to promote menstruation, to expel worms, and to remove obstructions.

Thistle, so called Blessed, Ton, Stom.
In small doses prevents vomiting, good for worms, in small doses.

Thistle, Woolen Thistle Anti-spas. Ner,
Good in spasms, convulsions, rickets in children, and other infirmities.

Trefoil Bal. Ast.
A very good remedy in bleeding piles, etc.

Vervain Sud. Ton. Ast.
It removes obstructions of the liver, and strengthens the nervous system

Valerian Ner. Anod. Sty.
Very useful in all nervous diseases, provokes urine, and relieves stranguary, or obstructed urine, pains in the side, and provokes the menses.

White Pond Lily Root Pect. Emo. Ast. Ton.
Used in scrofulous tumors, canker, gleet, and whites.
Wormwood Ton. Sti. Anti-bil.
Promotes the appetite and digestion, and very useful in intermittents.

Wall-Flower Alt. Emm.

It cleanses the blood, and the liver, removes hardness of the spleen, and reduces inflammations, swellings, etc.

Water Plantain, Seed Deo.
Good in excessive flow of the menses.

Winter Green Bal. Stim.
It is a good wound herb, a decoction of the herb relieves ulcers in the kidneys.

Worm Seed Plant Ver.
This is a good remedy for worms in children, the seed made into conserve.

Wood Betony Ner. Ton. Dis.
Good for head-aches, hysteria, and nervous affections.

Wild Mint Emm. Sti. Ast.
Used in debility of the stomach, cramps, and promotes the menses.

Yellow Dock Root Ton. Deo. Her.
Excellent in diseases of the skin, and scrofulous disorders.

Yarrow Ast. Sud. Dia.
Good for colds, bleeding piles, bloody flux, profuse menstruation, by washing the head with a decoction of the leaves and flowers, will prevent baldness, and thicken the hair. It is one of the most valuable herbs in nature.

ABBREVIATIONS AND PROPERTIES EXPLAINED

Alt: Alterative, changing the morbid actions of the secretions.

Ano: Anodyne, quieting, easing pain.

Anth: Anthelmintic, expelling or destroying worms.

A-bil: Anti-bilious, correcting the bile or bilious secretions.

A-Scor: Anti-scorbutic, useful in scurvy.

A-Sep: Anti-septic, preventing mortification.

A-Spas: Anti-spasmodic, relieving spasms.

Ape: Aperient, opening.

Arm: Aromatic, agreeable, spicy.

Ast: Astringent, contracting the fibers or solids,

Bal: Balsamic, mild, healing, stimulant.

Car: Carminative, expelling wind.

Cath: Cathartic, purgative, cleansing the bowels.

Ceph: Cephalic, remedy for diseases of the head.

Dem: Demulcent, softening and sheathing the parts from the action of acrid substances.

Deo: Deobstruent, correcting secretions, removing obstructions.

Dia: Diaphoretic, producing insensible perspiration.

Diu: Diuretic, increasing the discharge of urine.

Dis: Discutient, dissolving, discussing.

Eme: Emetic, causing vomiting.

Emo: Emollient, softening, causing warmth and moisture.

Emm: Emmenagogue, promoting menstruation.

Exp: Expectorant, producing discharge from the lungs.

Feb: Febrifuge, dispelling fever, allaying fever heat.

Her: Herpetic, curing diseases of the skin.

Lax: Laxative, mild purgative.

Mug: Mucilaginous, glutinous, lubricating.

Ner: Nervine, strengthening the nerves.

Pec: Pectoral, useful in diseases of the lungs and

chest.

Ref: Refrigerant, cooling, mitigating heat.

Rub: Rubefacient, producing heat and redness of the skin.

Sed: Sedative, depressing the vital powers.

Sial: Sialogogue, promoting a flow of saliva.

Stim: Stimulant, exciting action, giving strength.

Stom: Stomachic, to excite the action of and strengthen the stomach.

Styp: Styptic, stopping bleeding.

Sud: Sudorific, causing sweat.

Ton: Tonic, permanently strengthening.

Ver: Vermifuge, destroying worms.

Vul: Vulnerary, medicines which heal wounds.

OCCULT FAMILY PHYSICIAN

AN EXPLANATION OF SOME OF THE SECRET FORCES IN NATURE

The possibilities of the human mind are unfathomable. First know thyself, before attempting to define that belonging to another. For your possibilities cannot be seen, weighed, or measured.

THE OCCULT PHYSICIAN: OR, THE HIDDEN FORCES IN NATURE. THE HOME WHEREIN DWELLS HARMONY OP SOUL, CASTS A HEALING FRAGRANCE LIKE THE BALM OF A THOUSAND FLOWERS

The term Occult Physician. I would say has reference to the hidden forces and powers latent within us, powers that have manifested themselves in all ages, all countries, and among all classes of people, from the most highly educated, down to the most barbarous and uncivilized people of this earth plain. Let me give an illustration. Human thoughts flash quicker than with electric speed over the intended route, one phase of it may be known as public opinion, created and stimulated to move in one direction or another by various agencies; thus queer and improbable as it may sound, that our thoughts are not at liberty to roam in what direction they please, but are compelled to move, with the vast train of thought, stimulated by new discoveries and higher truths, which in turn influences trains of thought from the lower grades, to that of higher thought impulses or waves, hence all new discoveries be they ever so practical, are at first thought expelled, and only by degrees does the volume of thought accept them as matter of fact.

Mediumship then means, a new train of thought, which is pressing for admission, to the understanding of man, but having the barrier of over a thousand years of superstition, or trend of thought in an opposite direction, to overcome, it is with difficulty and the utmost exertion on the part of the propelling force, that new grooves may be made smooth and our thoughts by frequent use, run smoothly and easily along with comfort and ease. Realizing that we are in possession of certain well defined powers, that can neither be seen, weighed, or measured, and but little understood by the average scientist as yet. This vital energy or potent factor in the cure of disease, whose basic principle acting through mind, is the supreme absolute energy of nature, and the success that has attained in mental healing is attracting the attention of thoughtful, and unbiased minds. The many failures to effect a cure by the old school practice, have by the application of the truths of mental healing produced harmony and health. Whether man is ruled over by a Supreme Being or life outside himself, it is not our purpose to argue, but that there is something beyond the material which presents itself in what we call body seems a self-evident fact. But in the evolution of thought, and the lifting ourselves and others beyond the mortal limits, we can see in relation to the truth of mind, an issue by means of which it may be presented understandingly and demonstrated. Thought has no more to do with the body than we are aware. Our voice would cease to vibrate sound, or our blood would cease to circulate, and there would be no thinking power, except for the action of mind, of which body is but the representative. If matter cannot move itself, whence originates disease? Looking from the mental standpoint, which is, that mind is the basis of being, the conclusion is that no thought ever expressed itself, no hand ever moved, and no body ever walked,- in short, that nothing was ever created, from the least to the greatest; except through the action of mind. Where thought presents itself in discord, seemingly decay will follow. Perfect harmony, and the concentration of thought energy will destroy disease. It always follows that a change of thought, will bring about a change in the action of the body; the body being but the representative of mind, the expression of thought. "There is nothing good or bad, but thinking makes it so," other writers have said, "never a thing but was first thought," as a man thinketh so he is. All great minds have found in this one thought, oceans unfathomed, and skies studded with countless stars that lead us on only to find another countless number.

All laws, in the boundless and fathomless universe, are manifested in the single body of laws which operates upon us. The same laws which govern our earth and solar system, govern all systems, man's limited possibilities preclude him from gaining more than a glimpse beyond the veil of this life, his selfish and carnal desires, being the stumbling block to his advancement or development in things pertaining to his higher nature. The absolute spirit mind permeates all matter, whether it be the gaseous ether, inorganic rocks and nebula, or organic man and animal, expressed in all manifested objects, beings, powers and forces, which exist within absolute space and a part of the great mind of the universe. Controlling by a non-deviating, harmonious law, through the boundless ethereal elements, of, and through which, life is made manifest, by spirit, the fine ethereal elements, forming the connecting link with that of matter sustained by the great infinite and absolute unknown, which is, has no beginning, and therefore can have no end; which is both last and first. Evolution and involution. This is the inbreathing and outbreathing of the spirit of nature.

During the ages that intervene between man's first inception on this earth, and the present, man himself has undergone countless changes, until he has arrived at the present stage of evolution, when I say man, I refer to the ego or man proper, passing through countless conditions of matter, differing one from another, evolving from one stage of matter to a higher stage, each evolutionary round, until the present stage, and although far from perfect, still, the latent forces and capabilities which are at his command, if but conditions will be complied with, are at present, far beyond the capabilities of the average man to comprehend, much less to take advantage of. Matter, then, whether in its gaseous, inorganic, or organic form, matters but little, being the product of mind essence or spirit, and man in this sphere, being the highest, conceptive, organized body of matter, such body being the receptacle of soul, or material mind; and mind being the receptacle of spirit, which we call essence. This body being built up from without, as well as from within, by nature's, silent, workmen, yes! this mansion is built of atoms, by atoms, and through atoms, each atom guided by that life principal, viz. the affinity for that of its kind. For in nature's wonderful laboratory, are stored up elements and forces, little dreamed of by the college professor, in building, or re-building of this body, certain well established laws, are laid down by nature, for the government of her workmen in this building process, as well for the guidance and sustenance of the body when built. Disease then, is a transgression of one or more of these laws; and the duty of the modern physician, is to diagnose such cases with that mathematical precision, that it were not possible for mistakes to occur, having been brought face to face with that occult force for the last twenty years of my experience, I know whereof I speak, and during that time have experienced the pleasure of noting the foremost exponents of western science, gradually but surely relenting in their implacable hostility and skepticism, which at one time they assumed with regard to the existence of occult forces or phenomena running counter to the general experience of mankind. The trend of thought and utterances by the scientific men of this age, show conclusively, they have come to recognize that there are natural forces, of which our modern scientist know but little. Let us turn back a few pages of the history of the globe we are at present inhabiting, and see what wonderful phenomena has been developed by the most subtle of Aryan races in Asia, whose civilization and experience had developed an inner life even more strange and wonderful, than anything that has manifested itself so far among the western nations, "Let those who are imbued with the conceit of the modern western profession, and who assumes to have reached the highest pinnacle of intellectual culture, go to India." Let them go to that land of mystery, which was ancient centuries before the first great pyramid was built. Ancient ages before Abraham roamed the plains of Chaldea with his cattle, and if, after a careful study of Hindu life, religion, and philosophy. If, we say, the inquirer is still of the opinion that the palm of intellectual culture belongs to the western world- let him lose no time in having his cranium examined by some well developed medium. "By persistent effort the latent powers in man are susceptible of the highest culture." Look at the wonderful talent of the Italians for Art Painting, the Greeks for plastic Art; the Egyptians for stupendous buildings; and other nations for book learning. But the Hindu love for silent meditation, has been one of their pronounced characteristics from time immemorial, and as a race, had acquired mental faculties that the western world as a people are totally deficient.

For ages this characteristic seems to have been the rule, and not the exception, their philosophy was of a kind that does not depend upon an interchange of ideas for its development; for it is based entirely upon intuition, or upon the cultivation of certain innate faculties, which lie dormant within the gray pulp of every brain, waiting for conditions to enable it to manifest itself in solving the great riddle of life. We do not claim that eastern philosophy has been the means of solving the great problem beyond this sphere, we believe as a people they have approached nearer the truth, and discovered many strange and mysterious facts in which we are practically ignorant. One of the earliest triumphs in this direction, was the discovery and application of that strange psychic force, known to us as hypnotism. But a short time ago we began to realize that there is such a force, and are on the threshold, as it were, of a domain which is as boundless as it is marvelous; but the discoveries which we are making today, were made ages ago by the early Sanskritic Indians, who have the experience of over fifty centuries behind them. Volumes have already been written by western professors, attempting to solve the problem, and find a key to this occult force latent within man. Though the knowledge is confined to the few, it is only beginning to be seen in its various aspects and ramifications, and to assume the character of a science- a science of the deepest interest and importance- inasmuch as the phenomena of life transcend those of all inanimate matter, and the faculties of the brain- the mind- are the highest objects in the universe that man can study; and inasmuch as its power over the faculties of the body at large, and especially over the whole brain and nervous system, is immense, and therefore capable of application to prevent and remove suffering, and to cure disease far beyond the means hitherto possessed by the various arts of medicine. If we trace this wonderful phenomena through the ages, its footprints are discernible all through the literature, and sculptured monuments; not only as I said before, India, but Egypt, and in the traditions of Chaldea, Persia, Greece, Rome, and the early records of Christianity. It has ever been regarded by the semi-civilized and barbarous communities of men, as sacred, to possess the power to heal the sick, was to possess something magical and occult.

The unbroken stream of results in healing, has flowed down in obedience to law, that is equally perfect with the laws of light and heat, of gravitation and electricity. The experience of antiquity has been amply supplemented by the record of the last century, showing an unbroken advance slow but sure. The various schools of medicine fought hard to, and involved a bitter warfare against the practice of hypnotism as a curative agency. But as the medical schools, and intelligence spread, the fear of it being connected with what they were pleased to call, the black art, gradually died out, and cures by hypnotism increased and were acknowledged, until later on commission of learned men were appointed to investigate the phenomena, and after a series of dishonest and prejudiced reports upon side issues, finally with favor, in spite of the ravings of old fogies grounded in old beliefs. Attacks having ceased, physiologists commend the practice in the highest terms, (as they usually do with all well grounded facts.) The main objection being to find men properly qualified to pursue the practice, as no amount of technical knowledge will make a successful practitioner in the absence of natural endowment. Time will remedy all this, and a sufficient force of operators will be forthcoming to cope intelligently with a vast number of so-called incurable forms of disease, especially of a nervous character, to which hypnotism is wonderfully adapted. We do not claim that it is a universal remedy; no one but a charlatan would put forth such a claim; but that it possesses great remedial powers, when properly applied and where the conditions necessary to success are fully met, is unquestionable; and a greater number of maladies that cannot be relieved by medication will find their solution here. But of all the bones of contention that the old schools of medicine, professors of learning in our colleges, drug association, etc., have been compelled to admit, that the simple medicine of nature, hypnotism, can do what science and art cannot effect; and to give up many favorite theories- to lay aside old established doctrines- and to yield them before the simplicity of a curative agency which many have the power to impart, though each has not the skill to direct- and to revive the practice of the thousands of bygone years- years which are only dimly seen through the long vista, of pity for the ignorance and barbarism with which they were marked- and then to allow the practical value of these long forgotten processes as superior to the present results of science, by adopting them. These are difficulties that require no small degree of moral courage to surmount.

Now that the difficulty pending the introduction and use of hypnotism as a curative agency, have been surmounted and the battle fought and won. We will now turn our attention to other occult forces latent within the human organism. Many persons adapted to silent meditation, by sitting quietly and alone, concentrating the mind upon some given object, and endeavor to "visualize" it; that is, to bring it in all its detail before the minds eye, until the ego, propelled by spirit, becomes active, and develops ability to see on the astral plane, this and other methods which secures concentration, introspection, and lifts the individual out of self and away from the memory sphere and consciousness, through this law no knowledge which the race has once acquired in the past, can be regarded as hopelessly lost to the present, no man can know things of the spirit, but the spirit within man. They who as yet recognize only the body and natural life of mankind, know very little indeed, as compared with those who are so far unfolded in their interior natures, as to recognize the soul and its seven senses. For the soul with its astral body when once opened to the communion with the natural man with eyes and understanding, looks two ways, inward and outward. The knowledge of the law is with you, and you alone. Individual life is a world of itself, suspended within the realm of possibilities, while the soul is ever the center of gravitation. Here dwells the initiate of the mysteries that gradually unfold themselves, by lifting ones self, out of self, and living an unselfish, noble life, pure in thought and deed, thus preventing the interposition of any barrier between his exterior and interior self. And as we continue to develop or unfold the store of knowledge laid up in the great soul of the universe in which we are attuned and in perfect harmony, gradually unfolds itself until it may be truly said, all that is possible in the great mind of the universe, may be found within man. The world of thought say they can't believe, for they don't understand. True; if we strive to understand truthfully, and become acquainted with the capabilities of the soul, you will find that matter is only the covering or shield for spirit, overshadowed by a divine law of harmony, and that there could be no matter without mind essence or spirit; having a settled conviction upon that point, you have opened the first doorway. Now arise and continue your development in universal love and harmony, you will find the hidden mysteries open up to your enraptured gaze. The truth wears no mask, bows at no human shrine, seeks neither place nor applause. She only asks a hearing- look inward to self. Is it a selfish love you observe, barren of all that is noble and pure, if so, how do you dare to call yourself spiritual, when your very mirror in looking inward, causes you to hate the truth and stifle it on all occasions.

It is the mystery of the unknown that fascinates us; he who has cultivated psychrometric powers, may not only detect with unerring accuracy, the mental side of a given disease, but also the physical difficulty, at once, with the same unerring certainty. The most perfect telescope known to man is that interior, or minds eye. And those who wish to cultivate this gift of nature, and have the advantages of silent and oblivious composure will find a subtle natural gift of higher intuitional powers that few mortals dream of- a gift of the highest import, that may look into and report what has taken place hundreds, and even thousands of years ago, as well as able to report and notify what is to come, even to foretelling of approaching death. Attraction of mind with mind, combined with silent meditation, are the requisite conditions for the development of psychic power. We are able to possess ourselves of the knowledge of the power and permanency of being, which in the long ago ages of her past existence, the soul has made her own. All that is in us of love, and that which perceives and permanently remembers, is the soul, and all the soul has once learned is yours, by duly cultivating your relation with her. A person in a trance condition may be fully awake on a much higher plane of existence, and, be more wise and intelligent during that state; and when physical consciousness, and his attention is attracted to the lower plane, he or she will seldom remember what has been done or said during the entrancement, but is oblivious to the time and things as when he is asleep. Consciousness begins where sensation begins, but consciousness does not necessarily follow sensation. The more a person fully understands, all that concerns them, and makes self subservient to his inner man or spirit, the sooner will he or she develop to that of a medium of one faze or another, according to the temperament of the person to be developed.

To you that are seeking to obtain a mastery over the hidden forces in nature we would say, first prepare the conditions to receive them. Noble thoughts that are in perfect harmony with the universal mind or spirit, and a full command of your own thoughts, may become oblivious to such at once, and the ego or man proper are able to see and read thoughts that linger in the astral light which is the book of memory on whose pages all events are recorded; and the more deeply they engraved, the longer will they last, even when physical consciousness has faded and passed away. Thought then, is a vibration, composed of the finest magnetic ethereal atoms, and can only travel from one individual to another, when perfect harmony exists between the two bodies or minds to act as a medium or conductor.

Thus then, the mind may become a giver or receiver of thought vibrations, distance being no object according to the conditions of the operator; the positive giving and the passive receiving with the concentration of will power to govern the conditions, and impress the mind of the receiver. To attune oneself to those conditions, it is necessary to leave the sphere of self, and allow the universal love principal to sway and operate the mind, which is no changeable form, but is enduring. What is really known of the powers mind possesses, is not a circumstance in comparison to what is still unknown in the boundless universe of space. Those who have evil thoughts, and vulgar desires and and tastes, becomes the servant of them, to such we would say, "some men tread where angels fear to enter." The system of healing, by what is known as the magnetic, through spirit, by the laying on of hands, has been known for ages, even before Christ. When called upon to exercise the powder of this spiritual remedy, endeavor in silence to calm the patient that he may become receptive of the radiating magnetic influences. Then in your own mind silently form the true idea of the patient, as he really is in spirit; not the outer, but the true man within. And if he is in any degree receptive, you will inaugurate a change within him, and his whole inner being which sooner or later will work itself outward into a bodily expression. That the operator plants in his unconscious mind, a new and healthy germ, bearing the living seed of a higher and healthy condition of mind, which will work itself outward, dispelling all error and disease. For as all matter is the result of mind through spirit, and as disease cannot exist in spirit, so matter becomes subservient to mind from the same source, spirit, or the fountain head.

If the idea of the operator are through this same source, they will be transferred to the mind of the patient, and in harmony with the spirit, the patient becomes conscious of them, which ultimately becomes a physiological impulse in the direction of health and strength. Thus a cure must commence with the obliteration of a false conception, and the formation of correct ideas, both of our own inner being, and that of the patient. This is the economy of mind and spirit, over matter and its diseases.

> Spirit was, is, and ever will be
> The source of all, whether land or sea.
> Atmospheres, mists, or vapors dense
> Fill all space around this world of sense.

The Author.

THE OCCULT FAMILY PHYSICIAN

Spirit is distinct from matter, but not from energy; energy is the source of matter. It is therefore through energy and law, that matter is made manifest. The living thing, whether plant or animal, had in itself an element of life or spirit which was not matter, and that element, energy or vitality, can not be seen with the material eye, but is visible to the open vision of the clairvoyant who rises into possession of the spiritual senses, unencumbered by the material things of the earth. Spirit is the life, and soul the intelligence that guides that life. The very life force in our waters and flowers, sings a requiem in the forest pine, is a manifestation of an invisible life, volumes have been written by philosophers in all ages, attempting to define life. It is strange that at this period of the human race, how little we know concerning ourselves, and still more strange that the tendency of modern thought is to depreciate the little knowledge we do possess. To know is the birthright of man, all knowledge center there. So much has the unfoldment of mind apparently done for us within the past fifty, to one hundred years, that we look back with astonishment, and wonder what are the possibilities of the future; for as we have before stated, that man's possibilities are beyond his comprehension, and although physical science has been the means of relieving almost every want, requisite for man's comfort and physical progress; the great mass of mind in other directions, seemed to have remained anchored to old theories and supposed facts. For we view with sorrow the vast amount of degradation, crime, poverty and desperation existing within all our large cities, and with each succeeding year becomes more ominous. How then, has this great physical mind wave of so-called advanced civilization affected the great mass of humanity? We observe that in the city of New York alone, there were over twenty nine thousand evictions in one year; thirty-eight thousand paupers buried at the expense of the city; over two hundred suicides; and the hundreds of thousands huddled together in pestilence breeding quarters, and all this but a tithe of that which is of daily occurrence in every city in the union. With one class advocating moderation, love, and fear, continually instilling false ideas into the minds of those whose very hell is the fear of poverty, while yet another class, grasping and selfish in the extreme, taking advantage of this condition of the masses, extract for the smallest pittance, the last ounce of vitality from the already half starved and often over-worked individual.

All this, and a great deal mope, existing within our social system, will bear us out when we say, that the great mass of human thought, transplanted from various parts of this earth, concentrating its powers and forces in the particular direction, which appears to be the existing system which govern the actions and thoughts of the great mass of humanity on this continent. Selfish in the extreme in both body and mind, how is it possible we can reflect other than selfish ideas, from the lowest menial to that of the statesman. Governed by our thoughts and desires, which are selfish, and of that nature through education and long usage, that it becomes almost a physical impossibility to change the system under which we are governed, for it is as I said before, the volume of thought whose trend in any given direction, carries with it all the existing evils we here refer to; hence, our false system. The higher the range of thought towards that which is pure, emanating from the spirit, necessarily free from selfish taint, uplifting, and unfolding to the vision of the observer the profound secrets of nature: Thus is man permitted to look beneath the veil and view his own possibilities. Thus it is within man's own capabilities if he would, change the existing selfish system for that of a pure and unselfish. The dense volume of humanity dumped upon our shores annually, only add to the already existing evils. Man to act right, must first think right, and to think right, it must be made clear to his inner, or intuitive sense, it then becomes a positive fact, and a fact once established, may be crushed, but will never surrender.

When a sufficient volume of such thoughts,

naturally having an affinity for that of its kind; finds harmonious expression, then, and not till then, can we expect a change from the selfish to the unselfish, for "Within the charmed circle of matter there is no hope for redemption." This no doubt will be the ultimate decision arrived at by followers of science, who pause sufficiently to survey the result of their accumulated knowledge.

INTUITION, THE LANGUAGE OF THE SOUL

The trance condition, clairvoyance, clairaudience and all other phases and conditions of mediumship, including psychic, is yours, if you will but prepare the conditions necessary for the unfoldment of your inner self We are slaves to our selfish thoughts and desires. They dictate thus; and we yield submissively. If we would conquer ourselves we must first learn to know ourselves, and look for the good in mankind, finding it, we become our own master, we have conquered matter, life is no longer a mystery, we become possessed of the power to look beneath the veil of this life, and as the mind continues to unfold itself, new and grander opportunities are presented to our intuitive vision, we are made conversant with the laws governing matter; distance, time, and matter, are no barrier to the intuitive mind when fully developed. Intuition then is the operation of the soul through spirit, the power of the inner faculty absorbing the outer. To obtain mastery over this faculty of the mind, endeavor at all times to cultivate the inner voice, give heed to impressions of the soul, which will never lead you astray, because nothing ever came through the soul from spirit but that which is good. To further educate yourself into this condition, sit for a short time daily in quiet seclusion and concentration of thought in all that is noble and inspiring.

Endeavor to control your thoughts and desires until you are able to individualize yourself and lift yourself, out of self, you then cease to be the slave of your selfish thoughts and desires, you will then have accomplished the greatest feat of your life. It is the small things in this life, be they for good or evil, that make us what we are. We have spoken of the power of mind over matter; we wish to say further that the mind is the principle factor in all the various phases of mediumship; a certain condition of mind is just as necessary to develop the medium, as to produce a manifestation, be it spiritual or otherwise. We must not be led away by the common error that all we are apt to get through the average medium is of the spirit, for it is not. That we get through spirit, cannot be tainted with the impurities of a lower consciousness; governed by the same law, may be true in some things, but more apt to be mixed with the thoughts of those seeking some selfish information through the medium.

The great danger attending public mediums as a rule, is, that many of them being only partially developed in the particular phase of mediumship to which they are constituted, allow themselves to give utterance to impressions received through this lower consciousness, not being sufficiently conversant with the law to avoid it, and thereby are often led into error, and mistake, degrading not alone to themselves but the cause of spiritual progression.

All that is rank and immoral within you; let it die, it belongs to your animal desires, it is important that you do so, if you would succeed in developing the psychic powers from within, to enable you to remove the veil and look into the spheres beyond. Think not for one moment, that the psychic law can be disregarded, it is as fixed as the laws governing light, heat, or the movement of the planets. The train of thought which fills the mind when alone, molds the man. By unselfish ambition for the universal good, a better man is molded, his life becomes useful to his age and generation. Life then, will not be considered a huge joke, but a glowing reality, for as he looks beyond the veil, he discovers universal harmony and finds he cannot look upon human life as an accident, for in the wonders he beholds, the evidence of wondrous design. The road to success reminds you to be patient, persevering, silent, always aspiring and anxious to do some little good, for the love of doing it, and firm in your desire for some higher truth. The unseen world is destined to become like a newly discovered continent to those who are willing and able to prepare the mind to receive it. A fully developed medium endowed with power over space, mind, and matter, is a possibility just because he or she is so constituted to vibrate in perfect harmony with those beyond this earth plane. Every human being has the germ of all the powers and forces attributed to the greatest adepts or mediums that ever lived, the difference lying solely in the fact that we have in general not developed what we possess the germ of, while many mediums have gone through a system of training and experience which have caused the powers they display to have become developed, which to the casual observer is pronounced as something supernatural. As we have before stated that telepathy, mind reading, hypnotism and the trance condition, all long ago known to the ancients, and so thoroughly were these conditions known and recognized, that the mediums or adepts as they were termed where protected by law.

Mind-reading and the influencing of the mind by the hypnotized subject at a distance, prove the existence of a mind which is not wholly dependent upon a brain, and that a medium exists through which the influencing thought may be sent. It is through this psychic law that one person can communicate with another at no matter what distance, providing that the two minds are attuned and vibrate in perfect harmony, the one wishing to communicate a message, sitting in quiet seclusion free from other disturbing elements or vibrations, concentrating the mind upon that of the receiver, who immediately receives the impression; and if thoroughly developed or acquainted with the law, may as easily sit and write out the communication as a telegrapher would if sent by wire.

For these forces are natural although somewhat unusual, in consequence of the amount of superstition existing as to the pent up forces in man; for we are but beings in an undeveloped state. A medium when fully entranced in spiritual discernment, and governed by the intuitive law does not use the faculty of reason, because the law governing intuition does not depend on reason, it simply knows. This is one reason why so many of our great scholars depending on the intellectual side of their nature, have so far been unable to solve the problem of life and other secret forces in nature, depending entirely on their intellectual faculty which is cold and selfish. Accordingly as we depend on the intuitive side of our being, and the controlling moral influences by which we are surrounded, so we become possessed of that higher train of thought emanating from spirit, which cannot be otherwise than pure, and alike elevating to ourselves and useful to mankind.

CONCLUSION

Before closing our labor in this effort to do some little good, we desire to express our gratitude to those, who by thought, word, or deed, have in any way contributed to the success of this, our guide to health. The many acts of kindness displayed by some, can never be forgotten, as they leave an indelible impress on the spiritual mind, and are the expression of a true spirituality. Kind words and deeds are but small things in this life, and find their reward in the comfort and peace of mind they reflect in our silent moments. A generous act is a spiritual thought, descending through the lower or animal mind, and expressing itself by our actions; thus if we will but look inward, we may review the acts of the few years we have been capable of that which is good or bad; with perfect accuracy are we our own book keepers, constructing by our acts the garment we must inevitable wear in casting off this covering of matter.

So it is, that the kind words, acts, and deeds, constitute the true progression through this life. In the limited space allotted to the various subjects to which we herein refer, we recognize our inability to enter into any elaborate exposition of such subjects, but have endeavored as far as we have been able, to demonstrate those truths that are in harmony with nature. We have only to say we mean it to do good, and have a settled faith founded upon practical experience that it will do so.

"He that hath a mind to think let him think."

The Author.

TO THE AUTHOR

Dedicated by a friend on the 21st anniversary of control as
a
Healing Medium.

Silently as comes the evening,
Or descends the, falling dew,
So the loved ones round us linger.
So the spirit came to you.

Little knew you of the mission
Which this spirit had for you;
Or the work which lay outspreading
For your willing hands to do.

From the depths where spirit found you,
To the heights where now you stand.
Through its noble efforts bringing
Hosts of friends all o'er the land.

By and through that spirit power
Death and pain for thousands here;
By its soothing words has given
Many a sorrowing heart good cheer.

Surely they who count the treasures
In the spheres of life above.
Will know they are priceless jewels
In the coronet of love.

Day by day has spirit led you.
Giving strength for every hour
To give forth the balm of healing.
This has been the God-like power.

THE OCCULT FAMILY PHYSICIAN

Many times the bigot's dagger
Has been thrust into your heart,
When that subtle power commanding
Touched and healed its bitter smart.

Many times they've tried to bind you
With old errors galling chain,
When that spirit still commanding.
Turning what seemed loss to gain.

Thousands thank thee for thy wisdom,
Though you shut your eyes to-day
You have opened thousands wider
To the truth's all potent ray.

May that subtle power o'ershadow
You in future, as of yore
'Til love opens wide the portal
Leading to the fairer shore.

THE END

www.ingramcontent.com/pod-product-compliance
Lightning Source LLC
Chambersburg PA
CBHW051947150726

47999CB00004B/1289